RESOLVING ETHICAL DILEMMAS IN SOCIAL WORK PRACTICE

Norman Linzer
Yeshiva University

Allyn and Bacon
Boston • London • Toronto • Sydney • Tokyo • Singapore

Series Editor, Social Work and Family Therapy: Judy Fifer
Editor in Chief, Social Sciences: Karen Hanson
Editorial Assistant: Jennifer Muroff
Marketing Manager: Susan E. Ogar
Editorial–Production Administrator: Donna Simons
Editorial–Production Service: Matrix Productions Inc.
Composition and Prepress Buyer: Linda Cox
Manufacturing Buyer: Megan Cochran
Cover Administrator: Jenny Hart
Electronic Composition: Cabot Computer Services

Library of Congress Cataloging-in-Publication Data

Linzer, Norman.
    Resolving ethical dilemmas in social work practice / Norman
Linzer.
        p.   cm.
    Includes bibliographical references and index.
    ISBN 0-205-29041-8
    1. Social case work—Moral and ethical aspects.   2. Social
workers—Professional ethics.   I. Wurzweiler School of Social Work.
II. Title.
HV43.L53   1998
174'.9362—dc21
                                                        98-17573
                                                        CIP

Printed in the United States of America
10   9   8   7   6   5   4   03   02   01   00   99   98

To
Charles S. Levy—
teacher, colleague, and friend—
who taught me how to think about values and ethics

CONTENTS

CASES

TABLES

PREFACE

Ethics is in the air. Hardly a day goes by without a news story detailing breaches of ethical conduct in government, business, education, and the professions. Despite or perhaps because of violations, ethics is held up as a standard in the public sphere to which professionals are expected to conform. But even with the ubiquity of codes of ethics, the difference between right and wrong is becoming less clear. Traditional mores are challenged, contemporary values are changing, and conflicts among values seem to be on the rise.

Conflicts among values lead to ethical dilemmas. Value conflicts and ethical dilemmas confront social workers in various fields of practice. May one ethically avoid firing a close friend when budget cuts demand it? When an adult adoptee wants her adoption record unsealed, what is the moral responsibility of a family agency that promised confidentiality to the biological mother? What moral and ethical challenges do managed care and welfare reform pose for social workers? Is it ethical to circumvent a retirement home waiting list for the relative of a prominent lay leader? What is the social worker's ethical responsibility toward a battered wife whose husband threatens to kill her if she leaves him and might kill her if she stays, toward a nursing home patient who refuses to eat, toward elderly couples who refuse home care? These are only a few of the dilemmas discussed in this book.

Professional practice is characterized by the demand for immediate response and action. There is precious little time to deliberate the pros and cons of ethical dilemmas and their underlying rationales. Nevertheless, practitioners function with some ethical coherence, though it usually remains unformulated.

My aim in writing this book is to increase understanding of the nature and resolution of ethical dilemmas in social work practice. The text describes how some practitioners actually deal with their ethical concerns and offers social workers models of analysis to identify, evaluate, and resolve ethical dilemmas in a rational manner.

My interest in the resolution of ethical dilemmas stems from my teaching of the "Ideology" course in the doctoral program of the Wurzweiler School of Social Work of Yeshiva University. Course content focuses on the values and ethics of social work and social welfare and their impact on social work practice. Knowledge of values and ethics—as the major components of ideology—is an essential prerequisite for attaining practice skill. In their practice, students learn to trace conflict situations to value differences, which translate into ethical dilemmas. The ethical decision-making process follows.

MY ASSUMPTIONS

A number of assumptions about social workers have emerged from my teaching experience:

- Social workers desire to act ethically, but when they are caught on the horns of an ethical dilemma, they may not always do so because they lack time, knowledge, and analytical tools.
- The mind-set of social workers is toward "doing" rather than "thinking" about the theoretical underpinnings of a problem.
- The process of ethical decision making can be taught in a rational, systematic manner.

One of my doctoral students told me, "I don't want you to teach me what to do; I want you to teach me how to think. I will then know what to do." My ultimate aim is to provide practitioners with tools for analyzing and resolving ethical dilemmas; thus in this book particular decisions are *not* prescribed. My interest is not in telling practitioners what to do but in enabling them to make decisions for themselves. I believe that once a decision is made, the practitioner will "own" it and be able to explain the process that led to it. If we teach practitioners and students how to think about ethics, they will then know what to do.

CONTENT AND STRUCTURE

The text is divided into three parts: values, ethics, and autonomy and paternalism. These topics were chosen because they comprise the theoretical bedrock of social worker behavior. Values shape ethics—that is the hall-mark of the professional practitioner, and all social workers confront challenges inherent in the autonomy and paternalism dilemma. The text concludes with a chapter that integrates the major themes.

Part I. Values

Chapter 1 presents a theoretical framework of values in social work that includes the definition and function of values, differences between values and knowledge, classification of values, and conflicts between client values and professional values. Chapter 2 applies the values classification model to conflict situations in practice. Chapter 3 examines the relationship between personal and professional values.

Part II. Ethics

Chapter 4 defines ethics and explores the relationship between values and ethics, between morals and ethics, and between general ethics and professional ethics. It offers a model of ethical decision making, traces the philosophical roots of professional ethics, and relates professional ethics to social work ethics. The model of ethical decision making explained in Chapter 4 is applied to the cases in later chapters.

I deal with confidentiality first because of its pervasiveness on all levels of practice. The major issues in Chapter 5 are the parameters of confidentiality when there are threats to others, and the impact of technology on confidentiality. Domestic violence is the subject of Chapter 6. The husband's battering of his wife and his threats to her life create a difficult dilemma for the social worker. Child abuse, discussed in Chapter 7, is sometimes a function of domestic violence. In many instances, social workers are faced with the option of removing a child from the home of neglectful and abusive parents. Unsealing closed records and open and closed adoption also create dilemmas for social workers who have to weigh the interests of the child, the birth parents, and the adoptive parents. Child welfare is followed by welfare reform in Chapter 8. Welfare reform has exacerbated the conflicts between the political right and the social work community over the morality of welfare recipients and the morality of the welfare law itself. Moral dilemmas facing state legislators and administrators and practitioners in public welfare agencies are analyzed.

Managed care, an ubiquitous phenomenon in behavioral health care, is creating numerous dilemmas for social workers. Chapter 9 discusses its moral impact on social work, social workers' obligations to clients beyond the number of authorized sessions, and advocating for the client when doing so could jeopardize one's job. The economic power in managed care and the legal power in welfare reform parallel the social power of lay leaders in social agencies, discussed in Chapter 10. The power of lay leaders is expressed in policy formulation and program development.

Part III. Autonomy and Paternalism

Part III deals with the conflict between autonomy, beneficence, and paternalism. Chapter 11 defines the concepts and provides the theoretical framework for the conflict. The cases in Chapter 12 deal with elderly clients who express their autonomy by refusing agency-based and home care services, and the conflicts they engender for social workers. Assisted suicide, as an affirmation of autonomy, is discussed in Chapter 13 from legal, moral, religious, and practice perspectives. How should social workers respond to requests by AIDS patients for assisted suicide? The case of an elderly nursing home patient who refuses nutrition and hydration follows in Chapter 14, where the spiritual and ethical issues raised by the case are discussed by a panel of clergy and then from a social work perspective. The Epilogue reviews the major themes of value conflicts and ethical decision making. It concludes with the distinction between ethical and practice dilemmas, and the need for social workers to tolerate ambiguity and incorporate ethical behavior into their character.

The chapter topics represent major areas of value conflict for social workers. The cases are not limited to specific fields of service. Ethical dilemmas that arise in one field of service may also appear in others; the decision-making model is transferable. In several chapters, I use tables to highlight the conflicts among the parties.

Although ethical dilemmas transcend cultural differences, social workers should understand culture and its functions in human behavior, have a knowledge of their clients' cultures, and understand the nature of social diversity. Ethnicity, however, is not a significant factor in ethical decision making. In some of the cases in this book the client's ethnic identity is identified, but in others it is not.

A VISION OF AN ETHICAL SOCIETY

As society changes, so do its values. Values are variable; those that are prominent in one period may not be in another. As value priorities change, they affect ethics. New ethical dilemmas are constantly appearing, and a resolution that was appropriate at one time may be inappropriate at another because of changes in technology and in the facts of the situation. No book can encompass all the emerging ethical dilemmas in professional practice in an era of rapid social and technological change. My selection of subject areas and cases is but a sampling of the ethical dilemmas in social work practice. My expectation is that practitioners will be able to apply the analytical models to other subject areas as well.

Ethical decision making is a process. The application of models of value and ethical analysis to specific situations will facilitate this process. Resolving ethical dilemmas is ongoing and challenging.

Along with a revised code of ethics by the National Association of Social Workers and the emphasis in this text on ethical decision making, it is hoped that social workers will become more sensitive to the ethical dimension in their practice, thus contributing to a more humane and ethical society.

N.L.

ACKNOWLEDGMENTS

"From all my teachers I grew wise."
PSALMS 119:99

The 1996–1997 "Ideology" class in the doctoral program at the Wurzweiler School of Social Work of Yeshiva University was one of most intellectually stimulating in years. The atmosphere in the class was permeated with the mutual excitement of inquiry, learning, and creative thinking as we struggled together to understand, develop, and apply the concepts and models of values and ethics to social work practice. Class discussion and papers reflected students' serious efforts to integrate the subject matter and develop deeper and different ways of thinking about the conflicts that arose in their practice. Students in the second semester of the "Jewish Social Philosophy" course in the masters program were also challenged to acquire new ways of thinking about values and ethics in practice, reflected in class discussion and papers. The following students shared their cases/papers/ ideas with me in the preparation of this book: Eileen Ain, Joan Astrin, Michelle Farkas, Joseph M. Frisino, Marie-Elena Grosett, Lisa Jones, Ilana G. Keehn, David Kohl, Evelyn R. Laureano, Vicki Lens, Nancy Mamis-King, Matthew Null, Sonya Prystajko, Reuben Romirowsky, Jessica Rosenberg, Marilyn Sanders, Michelle Saracco, Ratzi Skovronsky, Deena Stubenhaus, Laurie Sullivan, Toby Tider, Simy Werbowsky, Marsha Wineburgh, and Dr. Frederick Streets.

I am deeply indebted to Margaret Gibelman, chair of the doctoral program, who gave unstintingly of her time, knowledge, and editing expertise to ensure textual clarity and technical accuracy. Louis Levitt added his expert knowledge. Other members of the faculty who read parts of the manuscript and made constructive suggestions include Dean Sheldon R. Gelman, Cheryl Kramer, Eli Levy, Joan Beder, Jerome Widroff, and Aaron Beckerman. Paulette Sansone, of the New York City Long-Term Care Ethics Network, was particularly helpful in clarifying the issues in work with the elderly.

Catherine Cassidy and Tessie Spivey were among the staff at Wurzweiler who assisted in the technical production. John Moryl, librarian at Yeshiva University, was especially helpful in locating and reproducing journal articles and references. Choice in Dying supplied many of the important court cases. Bernard Scharfstein of KTAV Publishing Co. gave me permission to use chapters from my book Ethical Dilemmas in Jewish Communal Service (1996). Rabbi Lowell Kronick, of the New York City Long-Term Care Ethics Network, gave me permission to reprint the proceedings of the clergy panel at the Spirituality and Ethics Conference, which he chaired, that was held in conjunction with the Wurzweiler School of Social Work. Part of the content of Chapters 1, 3, 4, 10, 11, and 12 is drawn from the earlier work. My mother-in-law, Miriam Hollander, was helpful in typing parts of the manuscript.

A special thanks is extended to Dean Sheldon Gelman, who made available the support services and resources of the school, read the manuscript, and continues to encourage the development of my scholarly interests.

Thanks also go to the reviewers who provided feedback on this proposal and the manuscript: Sally G. Goren, University of Illinois, Chicago; Michael Reisch, University of Pennsylvania; David A. Spruill, Louisiana State University; and Francisco A. Villarruel, Michigan State University.

My wife, Diane, has always supported my scholarly endeavors. She has had to endure the countless hours, days, and months that I spent at the computer, and I thank her for her love and belief in me.

N. L.

P A R T I

VALUES

1

THE NATURE AND FUNCTION OF VALUES

Part I offers a framework for critical thinking about values in the professional setting. This chapter initiates an exploration of values with the definition of values and discussions of the difference between values and knowledge, the function and classification of values, and the conflict between professional values and client values. A model for classifying value conflicts in social work is presented in Chapter 2. Chapter 3 discusses the conflicts between personal values and professional values.

DEFINITION

Values "imply a usual preference for certain means, ends, and conditions of life, often being accompanied by strong feeling" (Pumphrey, 1959, p. 23). Similar definitions have been made by others (Gordon, 1965; NASW, 1967; Levy, 1972; Rokeach, 1973; Siporin, 1975). Values carry emotional charges, with varying degrees of intensity. In this respect, they differ from casual preferences, which tend to be not as emotionally charged and more easily discarded. A preference for chocolate over other ice cream flavors can be readily changed when chocolate is not available, compared with a preference for a profession over a vocation as one's life work. People make greater personal investments in values in terms of effort, resources, time, and emotions, because values are felt more deeply. Values are more abiding than preferences because they tend to be inculcated during childhood and represent parents' dreams and ideals for their children.

VALUES AND KNOWLEDGE

As preferences of individuals and groups "toward which its members have an affective regard" (Levy, 1972, p. 489), values can be asserted without a need for defense or proof, for they are basically subjective in nature and feeling based. They differ from knowledge, which "refers to what, in fact, seems to be, established by the highest standards of objectivity and rationality of which man is capable" (Gordon, 1965, p. 34). Knowledge is objective and can be tested for empirical validity; values are subjective and need not be tested (Levy, 1973).[1]

Loewenberg (1988) has suggested that there is a reflexive relationship between values and knowledge. When the knowledge available is insufficient for the task at hand, social workers depend more heavily on values to guide their practice. He predicted that, as social work knowledge becomes more widely available, values will occupy a less prominent role in professional decision making (p. 61). But until then, values will continue to serve as the base of the social work profession and its code of ethics.

Gordon (1965) offers a rationale for distinguishing between values and knowledge. There are times when values should be used to support action, and there are times when knowledge should be used to support action. If one is substituted for the other, the outcome could be dysfunctional. "If a value is used as a guide in professional action when knowledge is called for, the resulting action is bound to be ineffective" (p. 35). If knowledge is required, and we substitute instead what we prefer (values), the facts necessary for a positive outcome may be ignored. "If knowledge is called on when a value is needed as a guide to action, the resulting action may be unpurposeful" (p. 35). If values should inform our decision, and we instead rely on knowledge, the outcome may contribute nothing to the solution of the problem. The dysfunctional outcomes greatly reduce the potential for successful practice. The two types of dysfunctional outcomes will be illustrated through several cases.

I. If a value is used as a guide in professional action when knowledge is called for, the resulting action is apt to be ineffective (Gordon, 1965).

CASE 1.1 Change the Locks

Mr. R, a frail, 84-year-old man, lives alone. He has been physically assaulted numerous times by a 27-year-old homeless woman whom he befriended. He gave her a set of keys, allows her to store her things in his apartment, and lets her sleep there occasionally. She steals his

[1]See Lewis (1982).

money and terrorizes him on a regular basis. After one of his beatings, a neighbor referred him to the social agency. The social worker, appalled by Mr. R's situation, immediately arranges for the locks to be changed. However, she later discovers that Mr. R has sought out the abuser and continues to allow her into his apartment. The worker is baffled and frustrated by the failure of the intervention.

Discussion
This case illustrates the ineffective outcome when a value is used as a guide in professional action but knowledge is called for. The value of protecting the aged from harm and preserving their safety guided the social worker's action to change the locks. This action, however, did not take into account knowledge of the complex psychodynamics of elder abuse in which the elderly victim's need for intimacy, companionship, and mutual dependency may take precedence over safety concerns. Had she applied this knowledge, the worker would not have precipitately changed the locks and would have explored the client's relationship with the homeless woman. Because she acted on a value—to protect the client from harm—the outcome was ineffective. Changing the locks did not prevent further abuse.

CASE 1.2 African Americans in Special Education

A second-grade teacher has been concerned about the behavior of a particular 7-year-old African American boy. She refers him to the school social worker for evaluation. The social worker, an African American male, contends that the educational system should work with students in the least restrictive environment. He also feels that too many students are in special education without just cause. The social worker does not support the teacher's recommendation, suggests alternative techniques to foster the child's learning, and develops a behavior modification plan. Unbeknownst to the social worker, this child was born with a positive toxicology for cocaine. The child remained in the class and continued to act out, which affected his learning ability negatively.

Discussion
Special education is an issue that draws controversy from a variety of individuals and groups. The concept of providing students with appropriate learning environments is appealing and logical. However, when a disproportionate number of African American males are referred for placement, the intent is questioned.

The social worker was guided by the values of keeping African American children out of special education and placing children in the least restricted environments. Operating on the basis of these values led to an ineffective outcome, for the child's learning did not improve. The social worker should have been guided by knowledge of biopsychosocial issues and knowledge of the child's history and behavior. This knowledge would have persuaded him that the child needs special attention to offset the deficits of the toxicology for cocaine.

CASE 1.3 Funding AIDS Prevention Agencies

The state HIV/AIDS Prevention Advisory Committee recommends funding to agencies for AIDS prevention activities. The committee is composed of individuals who are HIV positive and who have AIDS, as well as representatives from the many agencies that provide AIDS treatment and support services. Located largely in urban areas, these agencies are staffed mainly by black and Latino workers.

Current practice by the advisory group is to distribute funding to new, often small programs staffed by minority professionals, rather than to large agencies that have successful track records in serving this vulnerable population. The result has been that many of these small agencies collapsed during the grant year and were deemed not fundable in subsequent years.

Discussion

In establishing this framework for decision making, the advisory committee was essentially acting on the value of supporting small, ethnically based, community agencies that were not equipped to handle the task. It did not take into account the knowledge gained over the past few years that the large agencies have a greater success rate in their ability to provide AIDS prevention services. In substituting a value in place of knowledge in the decision-making process, the committee recommended funding that had a negative impact on prevention planning and services.

In sum, these three cases illustrate the ineffectiveness of acting on a value in situations that call for knowledge to influence action.

II. If knowledge is called on when a value is needed as a guide to action, the resulting action may be unpurposeful (Gordon, 1965).

CASE 1.4 Starting Where the Group Is At

The group at this community agency, consisting of African Americans and Latinos, represents what some may identify as "at-risk" adolescents. The social worker's goal for the group is the enhancement of members' self-determination. Through mutual aid and psychoeducation, members experience a self-actualization process, which results in their increased understanding of their full potential.

In preparation for this session, the social worker distributed to the members pamphlets covering substance abuse, sexuality, health, and education. At the session, he began to read from the materials. An observer noted that group members were conducting individual conversations and grimacing at the worker. Finally, one group member said, "I thought I just left school." The group began to laugh, and the worker lost control of the session.

Discussion

This case illustrates how the worker used the substantive knowledge of some issues affecting adolescents as the medium to educate the group members. His purpose—to impart the knowledge—was not achieved because they felt disconnected from him and the way he conveyed the material. If he had been guided by the values of cultural sensitivity and starting where the client is at, he would have related the ideas to the members' experiences and engaged members in discussion, rather than reading to them. If the worker had encouraged them to put in their own ideas and reactions to the material, they would have claimed ownership of the material, and his goal would have been achieved.

CASE 1.5 The Case Is Closed

A community-based organization has a contract with the city-run child welfare agency to provide intensive preventive and drug treatment services to women who have given birth to infants with positive toxicologies due to use/abuse of illegal substances. Clients must either attend this program, which requires five-day-a-week drug treatment and weekly home visits, as well as substantial individual counseling and intensive group work, or they must surrender their children to placement and foster care. All referrals are made through the child welfare agency; cases are managed by the assigned worker from the child welfare agency and the caseworker from the community-based agency.

Except for the initial intake and assessment, Ms. C did not show up for thirty days and was not at home at the time when home visits were scheduled. Ms. C rarely contacted her counselor; the one or two random urine samples taken when she was present at the program indicated continued use of crack cocaine. She gave little or no indication of cooperation with program requirements. Accordingly, and consistent with child welfare mandates, steps were taken to close the case, and the child welfare agency approved. Two days after the case was closed and a request for child placement made, Ms. C's infant died as a result of a fall from a piece of furniture in the home. One day later, Ms. C called the social worker asking for help (unspecified) and was told that the case was closed.

Discussion

The social worker, from observation and experience with the client, concluded that the client was still using drugs and would probably not enter the intensive preventive program; therefore, child placement was indicated. There was no prior history of child abuse or neglect. The social worker had rigorously followed child welfare and agency guidelines in the execution of her casework tasks. She had demonstrated her knowledge of child welfare protocols for the prevention of abuse and neglect by both closing the case and recommending placement of the infant. She had surpassed by far the number of attempted home visits expected by the agency and child welfare protocols. When questioned about why she did not respond to the call for help, she simply repeated that the case was closed and was in the hands of the child welfare agency.

The knowledge of child welfare protocols that she applied ended in a dysfunctional outcome. Values that should have accompanied the knowledge as a guide to action include the response to a call for help from a client, the primacy of a client's right to service, compassion, empathy, and concern for the emotional, spiritual, and material condition of the client during this tragic episode. If the social worker had employed these values instead of the knowledge, the child's life might have been saved.

CASE 1.6 Funding Maternity Stays in Hospitals

When health maintenance organizations (HMOs) established a policy of hospital maternity coverage for only twenty-four hours, a huge outcry went out from consumers and was picked up by the media, who pressured Congress to extend the coverage to forty-eight hours for normal pregnancies. As a result, Congress passed a bill toward that end. The HMOs were forced to retreat, and they complied with the new law.

Discussion

The HMOs' adoption of the twenty-four-hour maternity stay was based on solid professional research indicating that there was no adverse impact on the mother or child in the hospital as long as a postpartum home visit was made. The research was promulgated at conferences and published in professional journals. Unfortunately for the HMOs, public opinion and media attention crystallized against this policy, and they were forced to develop a substitute policy for forty-eight-hour maternity stays for normal pregnancies and a slightly longer stay for cesarean deliveries.

This case illustrates how knowledge, based on research, was used to develop policy. The knowledge clearly supported the new policy, but the outcome was dysfunctional because the HMOs disregarded the values in the maternity situation. If they had tuned in to the values of mothers who, in their vulnerable emotional state, desire another day to rest and bond with their newborns under the watchful eyes of medical personnel, they would not have altered the practice of the forty-eight-hour maternity stays and would not have lost face and respect from the population at large.

In sum, these cases confirm the need to be clear about the distinctions between values and knowledge and their application to practice. If one is inappropriately substituted for the other, the result can be dysfunctional outcomes. Inquiry as to causes begins with the dysfunctional outcome, such as the program did not work, the goal was not achieved, the client did not return, the group disbanded, the community groups grew more hostile toward each other. When any of these unintended outcomes occurs, one of the social worker's options is to trace the source of the dysfunction to the substitution of values for knowledge or knowledge for values. Therein may lie the solution to the problem.

FUNCTIONS OF VALUES

A "value-pattern . . . defines a direction of choice and consequent commitment to action" (Parsons, cited in Levy, 1973, p. 36). Values are not merely abstract preferences but are action oriented. When several choices of action are available, values lead the individual to choose one and to commit oneself to act on it. A person who asserts a deeply felt value may feel a special obligation to carry it out. For example, someone who values marriage will expend considerable efforts to become emotionally involved in a relationship that leads to marriage. Even if that person does not find a mate, the value still obtains as long as the search continues. Someone who values education will expend time, effort, and resources to obtain it. In both instances, the person feels duty-bound to act on a value.

Although the commitment to action is felt to be binding in personal life, it is more obligatory in professional life. Private individuals may or may not act on their values, and if they do not, sanctions may not ensue. Professionals *must* act on their values, and if they do not, sanctions may ensue. Professional values become a source of accountability and evaluation of professionals' actions (Levy, 1973). The "commitment to action" inherent in values creates an "ought" obligation that leads them to ethics. Ethics represents the action component of values; it is "values in action" (Levy, 1979).

Values are inherent in the goals of social agencies. Enabling individuals to negotiate their environments, building self-esteem, preserving the family, and strengthening the community can be construed as values because these goals are preferences invested with considerable resources, skill, and feelings by public and private agencies, the sanctioning community, the board of directors, and professional staff. Based on these values, agencies are expected to offer programs and services designed to achieve their goals. They can be held accountable by funding agencies and clientele if they fail to do so.

CLASSIFICATION OF VALUES

Values in social work may be classified along three dimensions: (1) as preferred conceptions of people, (2) as preferred outcomes for people, (3) as preferred instrumentalities for dealing with people (Levy, 1973). Social workers function on all three levels.

Preferred conceptions, the most abstract level, refers to the ways social workers want to view people. Social workers believe that human beings are inherently good, possess worth and dignity, and have the capacity to change. These preferred conceptions of people serve as the value base, the philosophical foundation of the profession. They conduce to what social workers want for people as preferred outcomes, such as self-actualization, meaningful social relationships, healthy family life, the satisfaction of basic human needs, the repair of person–environment ruptures. Preferred outcomes also include the short- and long-range goals articulated by agencies in their mission statements.

How social workers attain these ends is also determined by values. There are preferred ways of working with people, such as by respecting their privacy, showing empathy, being nonjudgmental, maintaining confidentiality, and offering support. The third level—preferred instrumentalities—refers not to programs and services but to how the social worker uses the professional self in relationship with the client system.

The three classifications are interrelated. When we prefer to view people as having dignity and the capacity for change, this value leads us to prefer certain outcomes for them that will enhance their dignity and social functioning. These outcomes are attained through preferred instrumentalities, which represent the tools—professional use of self, knowledge, skill, and methods—that social workers use in working with people. The following cases illustrate the application of the values classification model to clients.

CASE 1.7 *Discharging the Patient Home*

Mr. C, a 31-year-old quadriplegic, came to the hospital for plastic surgery on a nonhealing bedsore. Surgery would require a four- or five-day hospital stay, a three-to-six-week recovery period on an air bed, and ongoing medical attention. Mr. C's insurance company would pay for a hospital stay for only six days after surgery, after which he would have to be discharged. Mr. C's doctor would discharge him only to a nursing home, which Mr. C refused. There was a conflict between the patient's wishes for discharge to his home and the physician's orders for discharge to a nursing home.

Discussion

The social worker's preferred conception of Mr. C was that he possesses dignity and worth and has the capacity to decide where he would like to complete his recovery. The physician was not allowing Mr. C to be part of the decision-making process.

The social worker's immediate preferred outcome was that Mr. C exercise his rights to self-determination and have some type of choice in his discharge plan. The long-range preferred outcome was that Mr. C be able to function independently and improve his self-esteem.

The social worker's preferred instrumentalities were to show respect for Mr. C as an individual, to provide Mr. C with support and information that would enable him to make an informed decision about his posthospital placement, and to advocate on his behalf to the physician.

CASE 1.8 Overcoming Social Withdrawal

Ms. M, an extremely withdrawn 35-year-old woman, was diagnosed with paranoid schizophrenia. She would retreat into the bathroom just to avoid social contact. Ms. M recognized her problem and, along with her social worker, established the goal of overcoming social withdrawal.

Discussion

The social worker preferred to conceive of Ms. M as having the potential to make as much progress as she could, no matter how little, in social interactions. Her preferred outcome for Ms. M was to develop social skills so that she could derive fulfillment in her relationships with others. Her preferred instrumentalities included support, encouragement, and confidence building; praising her for the small steps taken; and empathy and acknowledging the difficulty of change.

CASE 1.9 Establishing an Agency
for African American Children

The Center for Child Development is a private children's mental health agency in an urban setting. It was founded on the premise that the emotional well-being of African American children is negatively impacted by racism and economic disenfranchisement. The cofounder of the agency conducted research on these issues, which led to the Board of Education's desegregation victory in the public schools.

The cofounder's preferred conception of African American children was that they were victims of racial discrimination and economic deprivation, which was manifested by poor academic achievement and low self-esteem. The act of creating this agency to respond to the needs of these "victimized" children and their families demonstrated the preferred outcome. The founders believed that with educational and mental health services, the children would be able to function at a higher level.

The agency's preferred instrumentalities were that services should be delivered in a culturally sensitive manner. It was also expected that staff treat clients with respect and hold confidentiality in high regard. These values, along with others, set the tone for the agency and guided clinicians in their practice.

Discussion

This model of values classification does not include the client's values; it includes only the social worker's values regarding the client. The model's application to these cases helps social workers to organize their perceptions of clients from a values perspective. Though the model can be used to understand the values underlying the individual client unit—individual, group, or community—the model's primary use is to analyze *conflicts between* social workers and agency or community constituents.

The further one moves away from the level of preferred conceptions toward specific people and conditions—the level of preferred instrumentalities—the more values become relativistic. "Certainly, as one moves toward the earthly levels of everyday life there occurs a loss of purity, an increase of relativism, and often an emergence of conflict between and among values themselves" (Perlman, 1976, p. 386).

The specialness of social work is manifested not in its abstract values, which are generally shared with other professions, but in its instrumental values—in the particular knowledge, skills, and resources that we have developed as a profession. The translation of abstract values into concrete instrumentalities creates uncertainty and confusion and differences in activities (Loewenberg, 1988). For example, we prefer to hold human life precious and are proud of the technological advances that have succeeded in prolonging the life span. At the same time, extended old age may become mere vegetation, and the senile person may want to die and not be a burden to the family and the community. In the course of serving elderly persons, social workers may enter into conflict with each other and with members of the health care team as to the action called for in a specific situation. The abstract value of human dignity may not fare so well when put into operation with a particular person in particular circumstances. "The unexamined value is not worth holding. . . . It must be scrutinized for its probable consequences as it is translated into action" (Perlman, 1976, p. 388).

PROFESSIONAL VALUES VERSUS CLIENT VALUES

Social workers believe in people's capacity to change, and they view themselves as change agents. Change is directed toward helping people improve their level of social functioning and their fit between person and environment (Germain, 1991). It is also directed against macro social systems that impact on mezzo and micro systems.

Clients, too, have values regarding change. They may resist entertaining different ways of coping with their situations and may dread the consequences of change. A battered wife may opt to remain with her husband because of her dependency needs and the fear of striking out on her own. A group may restrict membership because of the friendships that have already developed. A community may resist the establishment of a residence for the homeless because of concerns for safety and property values.

Though the resistance to change may be based on psychological, economic, or social factors, it also stems from the cultural values of an ethnic tradition. A Chinese American neighborhood may resent the introduction of low-income housing for fear that outsiders will upset the ethnic character of the neighborhood. A group of Latino youth may object to the presence of a white social worker. A West Indian father who, in beating his misbehaving child, reflects the traditions and values of his ethnic group will resist the traditions and values of American society that require desisting from this action.

The lines of the potential conflict between the social worker and client system can now be drawn. The social worker may be planning a strategy of change for the client, but the client may be more ethnic- and tradition-minded and resist any change that threatens old and cherished values. The social worker, guided by the profession's values and constrained by the client's values, must be ready "to relinquish his aspirations to effect planned change should his clients prefer not to have it" (Levy, 1972, p. 490).

In the course of rendering professional service, social workers may realize that their values are at odds with the client's values. Many ethical dilemmas derive from conflicts between professional values and client values. These conflicts challenge social workers to devise ways of working with clients whose values differ from theirs.

CONCLUSION

Values, as subjective preferences with affective regard, differ from knowledge, which is objective and empirical. Some situations in social work require the application of values, and some require the application of knowledge. When one is substituted for the other, the outcome may be dysfunctional.

In this chapter the classification of values into preferred conceptions of people, preferred outcomes for people, and preferred instrumentalities in working with people has been applied only to individual clients. The next chapter applies the model of values classification to conflicts between social workers and other parties.

2

VALUES CLASSIFICATION

The previous chapter delineated the nature, function, and classification of values. This chapter presents a series of cases that apply the values classification model to conflicts between the social worker and other parties.

ILLUSTRATIVE CASES AND ANALYSIS

CASE 2.1 Hospital Discharge

Ms. B, a 51-year-old vascular surgery patient, is frequently in and out of the hospital because of diabetes and severe peripheral vascular disease. This is her second admission since she suffered a stroke from not taking her insulin. She is not able to ambulate, has paralysis on her left side, and suffers from pronounced slurred speech. Her prognosis is not good. The doctors feel that if she suffers another stroke she will probably be left in a vegetative state. She has been living with her son, his wife, and her elderly mother and was receiving certified home health aide services. During the first admission, her daughter-in-law agreed to assume responsibility for making sure Ms. B took her insulin, because the home care worker was not allowed to assume this responsibility. Ms. B has returned to the hospital a second time with a stroke that has left her disabled. The social worker believes that the patient is being neglected.

The Conflict
The conflict (see Table 2.1) is among the patient's family, who wants the patient to be discharged home, the hospital administration, who wants her

TABLE 2.1   Values Classification Regarding Patient's Discharge Planning

Parties to the Conflict	Preferred Conceptions of People	Preferred Outcomes for People	Preferred Instrumentalities in Working with People
Social worker	Has dignity; is dependent on others; is in need of medical care	Ensure patient safety; take care of medical needs; discharge patient to long-term facility; ensure continuity of services	Respect; support; educating and enabling patient to exercise her rights
Hospital administration	Has dignity; is in need of inpatient care; has capacity to improve medical condition	Discharge patient in the fewest days possible; provide cost-effective quality-of-care services; ensure patient safety	Respect; social work services; acceptance of discharge-plan decision
Family	Is dependent on others; is in need of home environment to improve; has capacity to improve medical condition	Keep patient in hospital as long as possible; discharge patient home; ensure continuity of services; ensure patient safety	Respect; home care services; community supports

discharged in the fewest days possible, and the social worker, who wants her to be discharged to a long-term rehabilitative/nursing home because her home may be unsafe. The patient (Ms. B) is the subject of this model of analysis; therefore she does not appear in Table 2.1. Because the other parties differ over the disposition of her case, the values behind their respective positions require greater elucidation.

Social Worker

The social worker prefers to view Ms. B as a person who is dependent on her daughter-in-law. She sees Ms. B as a woman with dignity, despite her debilitating medical condition, who requires good medical care to preserve that dignity.

The social worker's goals for the patient are that she be independent of her daughter-in-law and be placed in a long-term-care facility that will provide for her safety and medical needs. As Gardner (1995) explains, long-term care is most often provided when friends and family are no longer able to provide needed services. The social worker supports Ms. B and treats her with respect and educates her about her rights even though these may be contrary to her preferences.

Hospital Administration

The hospital administration views patients such as Ms. B as people who are in need of inpatient medical care. Such persons have dignity and the capacity to improve their medical condition. The patients' bill of rights reflects the value of dignity by giving patients the right to make decisions about their medical care and to be treated respectfully by all staff.

The hospital administration wants the patient to receive good medical care, to be discharged as quickly as possible, to receive cost-effective quality-of-care services, and to be safe from further harm. Length of stay is a crucial variable for hospitals because hospitals lose money for inpatient stays that exceed the DRG (diagnosis related group) standard (Ross, 1995). Most managed-care companies will not pay for the extra days a patient stays because of "discharge problems." Currently, hospitals attempt to discharge patients in the fewest days possible once the patient is medically stable.

The hospital administration values treating the patient with respect, the provision of social work services, and accepting the discharge plan. The hospital expects patients to be discharged with appropriate referrals and services.

Patient's Family

The patient's family views Ms. B as having dignity, as being dependent but having a capacity to improve her medical condition, especially at home. The family wants her to be safe, to be kept in the hospital as long as possible, and then to be discharged with home care services. The family prefers that the patient be treated with respect and provided with community supports. At home she will thrive because she is in familiar surroundings and is part of her family and community.

In sum, the conflict between the social worker and the family is located in their preferred outcomes. The patient's family would like Ms. B to be discharged home with home care services; the social worker feels Ms. B would be better off in a long-term rehabilitative/nursing home because her own home is potentially unsafe. Abramson, Donnelly, King, and Mailick (1993) point out that often the needs and objectives of various involved parties (for example, organizational and family interests) are not congruent. The social worker and the family have opposing short-range objectives for the patient.

A conflict also exists between the hospital administration and the family. The hospital administration would like the patient to be discharged as soon as possible; the family would like the patient to remain in the hospital as long as possible.

CASE 2.2 Voter Registration

The clinical staff of the agency are members of the collective bargaining unit 1199 of the National Hospital and Health Care Employees Union. Historically, the agency has not participated in general union activities such as delegate assemblies, community mobilizations, and political action programs. But, unlike previous delegates, the current delegates are social workers who are politically aware and supporters of social action. They have attended 1199-sponsored activities in support of state budget cuts and Medicaid funding for mental health services, and they have been designated political action captains for the 1996 election.

As a result of a political action conference, the delegates, with the support of the agency administration and 1199, planned a political action forum for the agency's client population. The purpose of the forum was to educate clients about some of the critical issues of the election and the voting process and to conduct voter registration. All members of the clinical staff, who are also union members, were made aware of this forum and were asked to inform their clients of the importance of attending. No one expressed any discomfort with this issue at the initial staff meeting.

The agency, designated an official depression screening site, was sponsoring a National Depression Screening Day. The screening was expected to be a large event that would allow clients as well as community residents to be screened for depression and receive informational handouts and referrals for mental health services. The political action forum had to be scheduled in time to meet the deadline to register voters for the presidential election. As a result of this time constraint, both events were scheduled for the same week in October.

A week before the political action forum was to take place, the delegates attempted to make a general estimate of the number of participants they could expect. It became evident that the majority of the clinical staff had not informed their clients about the event. On the day of the forum, the only clients who attended were those of the social workers who were also union delegates. The delegates were disappointed by the lack of support from their fellow union members. The clinical staff believed that clients should not participate in voter education at the agency. The delegates felt that clients had a right to be informed about issues facing them in the election.

Discussion

Voter registration is an essential activity needed to increase participation in the political process. Historically, labor unions, professional organizations, colleges and universities, and civil rights organizations have mobilized voter registration drives. In 1983, Human SERVE (Human Service Employees Registration and Voter Education Campaign) was organized with the goal of implementing strategies to increase voter registration efforts (Piven & Cloward, 1988). More recently, government and non-profit agencies have been enlisted in the process of conducting voter registration. Piven and Cloward (1988) contend that "because of the growth of state functions, especially in the field of social welfare, and the resulting overlap between unregistered populations and the clientele of social welfare programs, government can readily reach and enlist nonvoters through an agency-based strategy" (p. 5). "Involvement in a registration drive is a healthy challenge to role definition, and stimulates social workers to rethink what constitutes therapeutic work" (Hanrahan, Matorin, & Borland, 1986, p. 142). Fawcett, Seekins, and Silber (1988) contend, "Registering voters at public agencies is believed to be an effective strategy for tapping the power of the poor and producing a political realignment more responsive to human needs" (p. 16). This case presents a conflict between two groups of social workers concerning voter registration within a community-based mental health clinic serving predominantly minority groups.

The conflict between both groups of social workers can be located in their differing preferred conceptions of clients. The clinical staff chose to view clients only as "clients" who come to the agency only for clinical services. They were not viewed as members of society concerned with social and political affairs. If an interest in political involvement emerged, the clinician would refer the client to a community resource and not discuss it in treatment. As such, voter registration and other public matters were considered off-limits in those social welfare agencies whose primary concern is with the mental health of their clients.

The union delegates preferred to view clients as capable of political involvement. Reeser (1992) supports social worker activism as part of the professional role: "One aspect of social worker activism is the means social workers will endorse to bring about change" (p. 81). The delegates' preferred conception views the clients as having the potential and capacity for political involvement. Their professional function seeks to enhance client empowerment and support political and social activism.

The conflict also exists on the level of preferred instrumentalities—that is, in the social workers' professional function. The clinical social work staff value the purity of the therapeutic process. The union delegates—social workers with an ecological/holistic perspective—value improving the relationship between the person and the environment.

The concept of agency-based voter registration has been successfully reinforced among public offices such as the Department of Motor Vehicles and income maintenance centers. Nonprofit agencies may not be as successful in their endeavors because of concerns that political activity may be perceived as unprofessional (Piven & Cloward, 1988). If the goals of social work include improving societal conditions and effecting change within individuals and communities, then an agenda that includes social goals is essential in social agencies. This case illustrates the need for agencies to develop policies on political organizing.

CASE 2.3 *Terminating a Group*

An ongoing women's psychotherapy group has been meeting weekly for a long time. The function of the group is to promote socialization skills and process feelings and concerns. Some members have a history of suicide attempts and psychotic breaks; others are more intact. All women present with symptoms of depression and anxiety. The majority speak Spanish monolingually and have experienced difficulties in acculturating to the host culture. All the women report that they benefit from the group.

The administration is concerned by the lack of revenue from the group and would like it to end, but if the cases are closed precipitously, there will be a negative impact on community relations. The cases will, therefore, be gradually closed. Practitioners have been instructed to tell their clients that their cases are being closed not because their insurance plan will no longer pay for treatment but because treatment is no longer necessary.

The social worker does not want to end treatment unless doing so is clinically justified. Furthermore, she is uncomfortable being asked to deceive clients. Her conflict with the agency concerns ending the group. She is in a bind between her loyalties to her clients and her loyalties to the agency.

Social Worker

The social worker prefers to view the group members as emotionally fragile women who need continued treatment to improve the quality of their lives. To that end (see Table 2.2), she prefers to respect their decision to remain in the group and to be honest with them about the administration's decision. Her raison d'être is the provision of services to those who need them. "Perhaps the paramount value of social work is the belief that human beings should have access to the resources they need to cope with life's stresses and the opportunities to develop their potentialities" (Hepworth & Larsen, 1993, p. 54).

Administration

The administration prefers to view the clients as emotionally fragile women who are expensive and a drain on agency resources. In the best of times,

TABLE 2.2   Values Classification Regarding Terminating a Group

Parties to the Conflict	Preferred Conceptions of People	Preferred Outcomes for People	Preferred Instrumentalities in Working with People
Social worker	Emotionally fragile; deserving of continued care	Emotional well-being; improved quality of life; maintaining agency's fiscal stability	Respect client self-determination; continue treatment; be honest with clients
Administration	Emotionally fragile; expensive; constituting a drain on resources	Decreased dependency on agency; termination of group; maintaining fiscal stability; maintaining good community relations	Restrict unreimbursed services as much as possible; be duplicitous with clients

when funding agencies fill the agency's coffers, the administration fulfills its community mandate by providing services to those in need. However, when these funds shrink, some clients are seen as depleting agency resources and needing to be terminated. The agency's preferred goal is to stay afloat and maintain its fiscal stability. Another goal—to maintain good community relations—requires that the clients not be told the real reason for termination. Duplicity is thus justified because it maintains the agency's benevolent image in the community.

The social worker is in conflict because she espouses two contradictory values: to continue serving her clients and to cooperate with the agency's policy to ensure its solvency. Even if she were to prefer cooperation with the agency, her professional values would prohibit her from being dishonest with clients.

CONCLUSION

The three cases presented in this chapter illustrate how a values classification model can provide social workers with a tool to analyze conflicts in policy making and service delivery. The analysis begins where the source of the conflict may lie—in the preferred conceptions of the client system. Discussion proceeds to preferred outcomes and ultimately focuses on instrumentalities—the values of direct practice, where creative alternatives can be found to resolve the conflict. Although this model does not purport to resolve the conflict, it enables practitioners to delineate the value stances of each party, so that the respective weights of each value may be considered.

In addition to experiencing value conflicts between themselves and other parties, practitioners may also be in conflict with themselves. The ubiquitous conflict between personal and professional values occupies the next chapter.

3

PERSONAL VALUES VERSUS PROFESSIONAL VALUES

Having classified value conflicts between social workers and client systems in Chapter 2, we now turn to conflicts between social workers' personal and professional values. These conflicts create internal strain, and if the social worker is also in conflict with the client's values, the strain is more pronounced. The conflict presupposes clarity about one's personal values, but people lack clarity as the number of available options increases. A professional needs to know what to believe in and what are deemed to be preferred ways of living and acting (Loewenberg & Dolgoff, 1992).

A major source of personal–professional value conflicts is religion. When personal values stem from religious sources, the professional must be more on guard against their intrusion on the performance of the professional function (Levy, 1976b). Personal values, whether of a religious or a secular nature, usually originate in childhood and tend to be deeply embedded in the individual's psyche. The individual feels committed to act on them and can brook little or no deviation.

WHAT TO DO WITH PERSONAL VALUES?

In the course of their work, practitioners may encounter ideas, values, and situations that are incompatible with their personal beliefs and practices. When conflicts between personal values and professional values arise, what are practitioners to do with their personal values?

Loewenberg and Dolgoff (1992) argue with Levy, who said that "To be a professional practitioner is to give up one's autonomy and to relinquish some of one's rights as a freely functioning being" (Levy, 1976b, p. 113). Loewenberg and Dolgoff understand this to mean that professionals must suspend or neutralize all personal values when serving clients. Rather, Levy intended it to mean that the professional may not give full expression to personal values just because they are important to the professional. Practitioners are not prevented by professional prescription from representing personal values. Indeed, there are times when personal values represent a practical and useful alternative for clients. But, Levy maintains,

> representing personal values as an alternative is different from insisting upon them as a preference, simply because they are a preference for the practitioner. The question the practitioner must ask of himself is whether he is offering his client an alternative to consider in light of his needs, or a bias to which his client must conform on pain of negative judgment or the deprivation of service. (Levy, 1976b, p. 119)

Practitioners must be true to themselves when engaging with clients. They come with their personal and professional values, knowledge, and skills. They are not value-free, nor must they leave their personal values at home. They represent their personal values in the kinds of questions they ask and the comments they make. When the client is asked to think about other options or the consequences of particular decisions that have not heretofore been considered, the practitioner is conforming with professional values. Only when the practitioner insists that the client conform to the practitioner's personal values are professional norms violated and the actions unethical.

STRATEGIES FOR CONFLICT RESOLUTION

Danzig (1986, p. 49) offers three strategies for the resolution of personal–professional value conflicts with religion, but they apply to secular values as well (see Table 3.1):

1. Identification with one's religious commitment;
2. Identification with, and accommodation to, both one's religious and social work commitments;
3. Identification with social work as the dominant culture.

In the first option, the practitioner prefers personal values over professional values, thereby acting unethically from a professional standpoint. At

TABLE 3.1   Three Options for the Resolution of Conflict between Personal and Professional Values

Personal values	Identification with one's religious/ secular commitment	Identification with one's religious/ secular commitment	
Professional values		Identification with, and accommodation to, one's religious/ secular and social work commitments	Identification with social work as the dominant culture

the opposite extreme, the practitioner does not permit personal values to intrude into the professional function; identification with the profession takes primacy over personal values. The middle option represents an attempt at synthesis. One is true to oneself; there is no denial of personal or professional values but an effort to accommodate both. This synthesis is accomplished when the practitioner represents, but does not impose, personal values as an alternative for the client's consideration.

The degree of conflict varies with the degree of personal commitment: the deeper the commitment to personal values, the greater is the possibility of conflict with social work values. A feminist-oriented social worker may be tempted to support a single woman's moving out of her parents' home to her own apartment even though strong cultural factors mitigate against it. An abortion rights social worker may try to persuade a pregnant teenager not to have her baby. Social workers who responded in a study that religion was an extremely important aspect of their lives scored high on measures of homophobia and heterosexism (Berkman & Zinberg, 1997), making it more difficult for them to treat gays and lesbians. A hospital social worker who believes in taking full advantage of modern medicine's resources may have difficulty respecting the right to self-determination of a patient who refuses a life-saving blood transfusion for religious reasons (Reamer, 1996). Professional values require the social worker to be guided by the client's self-determination. How the professional deals with this conflict indicates whether personal values, professional values, or their integration is the primary strategy of intervention.

The following three cases reflect different aspects of the personal–professional value conflict. The first involves a long-standing personal relationship that clashes with the professional function. The second involves personal relationships that prevent the fulfillment of an administrative responsibility. The third involves criticism of client actions based on personal values.

CASE 3.1 My Friend, the Executive Director

A committee that I staff at my agency has decided not to continue fund-ing a specific program at one of our constituent agencies. I may not share this information with my long-time friend, who is the executive director of the affected agency. The committee's policy is that decisions in the midst of the budgeting process may not be revealed because changes may still be made. This restriction weighs heavily on me be-cause my dearest friend, who was there for me then I went through cri-ses in my life, will be negatively impacted by the decision. When he finds out three months from now, there will be little time for everyone affected to make alternate plans. Early warning should be given to teachers who may have to be laid off and to working parents who will need to find alternate placements for their children. I know in my heart I should really share that information with him, yet I feel a responsibil-ity to the committee. It's frustrating.

There is an unwritten contract with my lay committee that what transpires at meetings will be kept confidential. My own ethical system also says I really should not be sharing that information. What creates the dilemma is not the withholding but the consequences of withhold-ing. I believe that the people being served should have the information so they can plan their lives. I could suggest to the executive director to prepare for some cuts in the programs. But if he asks me to provide more details, I will have to refuse. I made a decision not to do what I really want to do, and I agonize over it.

Discussion

The conflict between the professional's personal and professional relation-ship with the executive director is located in the tension between friendship and confidentiality. Maintaining the friend's trust necessitates the violation of confidentiality. Keeping confidentiality adversely affects the friend, the agency's staff, and the people served.

Although the professional could support his inclination to violate con-fidentiality by citing fidelity to the personal relationship, the fact is that this is not an ethical dilemma because it is not a conflict between two profes-sional values. Conflicts between personal and professional values are to be resolved in favor of professional values. There is no way that the personal friendship could override the obligation for professional confidentiality. The personal value could be used in service to the client, but it may not su-persede professional responsibility.

Even if one were to broaden the professional's responsibility beyond the friend to the community as a whole, which will be negatively affected by the cuts, thereby making the conflict a clash between two professional values, the fiduciary responsibility to the committee still takes precedence. The committee is known and is the professional's "client"; the community is more amorphous and is not the professional's client.

There are good reasons for not divulging the committee's decision. It may change, and change may bring other consequences in its wake. Previous experience confirms that leaks in budgetary decisions usually come back to haunt the decisionmakers and the staff. The reason for the committee's insistence on confidentiality is to avoid these negative consequences. The professional has opted to abide by the committee's policy on confidentiality but has found a way to warn his friend about forthcoming cuts that does not violate the policy. Some harm may ensue from not revealing the information at this time, but harm is inevitable when the cuts are announced. There is a net gain of promoting good over harm by preserving confidentiality. This decision was fraught with the moral anguish of an option not taken, of the hurt inflicted on a friend.

CASE 3.2 Retrenching Friends

There are two unproductive administrators who have been here for a very long time, are near retirement, and are ill. Neither of them needs the job for financial security. One is a close personal friend, and the other is someone of whom I am very fond. They have stood by me through personal and professional crises in this agency.

I have been asked to dismiss these people, because the agency is in a period of retrenchment. This could possibly save the jobs of four of the bright, newer workers whom we want to keep. We have a dossier of these administrators' wrongdoings that gives evidence of their incompetence and that has been shared with them. But I cannot dismiss them, even though I know that their retirement would benefit the agency. I have tried to get a postponement for several months, citing their progressive illnesses, the pending marriage of a daughter, their desire to retire on their own, and the presence of other inefficient staff on payroll.

Discussion

This case is similar to the previous case. The social worker is in a quandary over hurting friends while performing a professional duty. It is always difficult to fire staff, especially when one has had a close relationship with them. The professional is expected to place professional duty before friendship, an action that is facilitated here because of the staff's incompetence.

CASE 3.3 *Children Having Children*

A lot of young teenage girls in this ethnic community are having babies. I am a parent, and I would not want my 13-year-old to have a baby. That creates a personal conflict for me because 13-year-olds are not adults even though they want to act like them. They should abide by their parents' rules because the parents are still their guardians. If a girl wants an abortion, I personally would have a very hard time counseling her because, as a Christian, my religious beliefs are opposed to abortion. Professionally, I would send her for appropriate counseling around that issue.

Discussion

This social worker has two personal–professional conflicts. Personally, she is adamantly opposed to young teenagers acting out sexually and getting pregnant. Her preferred conception of them is that they are too young and immature to have babies and should develop their interests first. This value is not necessarily based on religion but on the psychodynamics of adolescence. She is also opposed to abortion because of her religious belief about the sanctity of life.

Although this social worker's personal feelings are critical of the behavior of these young girls, she places her professional values first, is not judgmental, and works with them or refers them to other services. She uses her personal values in the service of the clients, offering other alternatives to sexual acting-out behavior and abortion, but constrains herself from imposing her personal values on her clients.

CONCLUSION

The four brief illustrations—feminism, abortion, homosexuality, and blood transfusions, and the three detailed cases—breaching confidentiality, firing staff, and teenage sexuality—reflect different levels of conflict between personal and professional values. In the first four illustrations, the professional's personal value occupies a central place in the values hierarchy. There is a strong temptation to influence the clients' decision. In the three detailed cases, the value of friendship frustrates one practitioner and immobilizes the other. The first overcomes the personal frustration and abides by the professional value of confidentiality, whereas the second cannot perform her professional function. In the third case, the practitioner overcomes her personal disapproval of her clients' behavior in order to service them in a professional manner. This illustrates Danzig's (1986) middle option of identification with, and accommodation to, one's religious and social work commitments.

When social workers present personal values as alternatives to clients, it behooves them to be aware of the impact of their authority on vulnerable clients. Clients may feel induced to "go along" to please the social worker or may be too cowed to thwart the social worker, despite the worker's best efforts to remain neutral.

In the conflict between personal values and professional values, the professional is duty-bound to uphold professional values. Upholding professional values represents ethical action. The next chapter introduces Part II—the nature of social work ethics.

PART II

ETHICS

4

ETHICS IN SOCIAL WORK

In Chapter 1, we defined and classified values, distinguished between knowledge and values, and analyzed value conflicts between professionals and clients. Chapters 2 and 3 illustrated values classification and personal and professional value conflicts. The theme of Part II, social work ethics as "values in action" (Levy, 1979, p. 9), is introduced by a time line describing the changes in the National Association of Social Workers (NASW) Code of Ethics from its inception to the present (see Table 4.1). We then define ethics, distinguish between ethics and morals, provide the rationale for professional ethics, and trace the sources of social work ethics. This chapter serves as a theoretical base for the chapters that follow.

A TIME LINE OF SOCIAL WORK'S CODE OF ETHICS

Codes of ethics are established by professionals who seek common bonds, status, and respectability, and the assurance that individual members will uphold what the group considers good and honorable. The NASW Code of Ethics embodies the core values and principles of the social work profession.

1960. The NASW delegate assembly adopted a code of ethics on October 13, 1960. It was a one-page document that contained fourteen statements written in the first person. The preamble advised social workers to take responsibility for protecting the community against unethical practices by people or organizations engaged in social welfare activities.

TABLE 4.1   Time Line Summary of Formation of and Changes in the NASW Code of Ethics

1960	1967	1979	1990	1993	1996
First code	Amended	Rewritten	Amended	Amended	Rewritten

1967.   An amendment banning discrimination against any client due to race, religion, sex, or national ancestry was added to the one-page document.

1979.   The code was rewritten. The new code was a ten-page document that included six principles covering the social worker's conduct and responsibilities to clients, colleagues, employers, the social work profession, and society.

1990.   Two amendments were added to prevent social workers from exploiting relationships with clients for personal advantage and accepting anything of value for making a referral.

1993.   Five amendments were added. Social workers with personal problems such as substance abuse were directed to seek help for them and not permit them to interfere with their services to clients. Social workers were prohibited from engaging in dual relationships with current or former clients and from using their power position to exploit others. And social workers were directed to consult with an impaired colleague who has personal problems such as substance abuse and help that colleague to take remedial action.

1996.   The code was rewritten again. The latest revised code contains twenty-seven pages with a preamble, statement of purpose, ethical principles that include the profession's core values, and standards to guide practice. There are some significant changes in the current code compared to the previous code. The social worker's responsibility to society or to the law may take precedence over responsibility to clients. There is a requirement to report suspected child abuse and to intervene when clients threaten to harm themselves or others. Client confidentiality may be superseded to prevent serious and imminent harm to others. Areas addressed in great depth in the NASW Code of Ethics include informed consent, cultural competence, sexual harassment, conflicts of interest in family and group work, sexual and other dual relationships with clients and their relatives, and responsibility to impaired and incompetent colleagues (Congress, 1996).

Though more comprehensive than previous codes, the 1996 code of ethics cannot guarantee ethical behavior, resolve all ethical issues, or "capture the richness and complexity involved in striving to make responsible choices within a moral community" (National Association of Social Workers, 1996, p. 4; hereafter cited as NASW). It sets forth values, ethical principles, and standards to which professionals aspire and by which their conduct can be judged.

DEFINITION

An essential characteristic of values is that they commit the individual to action. The action, which is the ethics, is embedded in values. But not all values become ethics. Only those values that represent normative standards of behavior become ethics when they are converted into action. This is what Levy meant by "ethics is values in action" (Levy, 1979, p. 9). *The preference is the value; the action upon the preference is the ethics.* The action is ethical when it is based on the value. The "ought" component of the value is socially confirmed by the prevailing normative standards of behavior.

Examples of normative values include honesty, fidelity, care for children, fulfilling promises, respecting privacy. People are expected to act on these normative values in their interpersonal relationships. When properly performed, they become ethical behavior; when violated, the behavior is unethical.

Examples of non-normative values include dieting, owning a home, taking a vacation. These values do not pervade the society and are not ethical when performed or unethical when violated.

Values may or may not involve relationships, but ethics comes into play only in relationships. "The concept ethics is limited here to conduct arising from specific interpersonal relationships" (Levy, 1976a, p. 27). "Whatever its origins or impetus, ethics deals with standards or expectations of behavior and action (or inaction) in relation to others, and arises out of some definition of individual or collective responsibility to others or for others" (Levy, 1976a, p. 29). Epictetus said it long ago:

> Our duties are in general measured by our social relationships. He is a father. One is called upon to take care of him, to give way to him in all things, to submit when he reviles or strokes you. . . . In this way, therefore, you discover what duty to expect of your neighbor, your citizen, your community officer, if you acquire the habit of looking at your social relations with them. (Cited in Johnson, 1965, p. 96)

If one wants to know what one's duties are in a relationship, one can intuit them as inherent in the relationship itself. It is self-evident that children have obligations to their parents and parents have obligations to their children. These duties precede codes of ethics and law and apply even if not regulated. The process is as follows: value + relationship = ethics. When the relationship is valued, it imposes duties on the parties to act ethically toward each other. Ethical obligations inhere in social roles including friends, married couples, parents and children, teachers and students, professionals and clients, employers and employees. The mutual expectations in the roles constitute the ethics in the relationship.

Since duties are defined by interpersonal relationships, one cannot be ethical or unethical to oneself. Even if a behavior is self-destructive, such as drug addiction or alcoholism, it does not fall into the category of ethics. One cannot say that a drug addict is unethical to himself or herself. Behavior becomes ethical only if it affects others and is valued in a social context. When the focus of the behavior is the self, the behavior is not in the realm of ethics.

ETHICS AND MORALS

Though the words *ethics* and *morals* tend to be used interchangeably, they are not synonymous. Ethics is defined as a system or code of behavior, morals as standards of behavior that are codified in ethics. Ethics is the theoretical examination of the practice of morality (*Webster's*, 1964).

Our conception is that ethics differs from morals. *The assessment of conduct on the basis of general social norms is in the domain of morality. The assessment of conduct arising from specific interpersonal relationships is in the domain of ethics* (Levy, 1976a). Morality is the evaluation of conduct in general, without regard to specific people in interpersonal relationships. Ethics is the evaluation of conduct in specific interpersonal relationships.

As an illustration, infidelity in marriage is considered immoral according to the normative standards in society, because fidelity is the norm. Within a specific marital relationship, when one spouse cheats on the other, the action is immoral because it violates general societal norms, and it is unethical because it violates the couple's marital vows. Morals is the noun, ethics the verb. Child abuse is immoral; when parent X abuses his child, he is also being unethical. Here, the word *morals* will be used when reference is made to behavior that accords with general normative standards, and *ethics* will be used to describe professional actions in the social service relationship.

GENERAL ETHICS VERSUS PROFESSIONAL ETHICS

Professional codes of ethics seem to be superfluous when ethics already exist in the broader society. Everyday morality such as honesty, trustworthiness, and keeping promises should be a sufficient basis for prescribing the conduct of all people, including professionals. Why the need for professional ethics (Goldman, 1980)?

Ethical responses can take two forms: passive and active. One person ought not to take advantage of another, and one must also care for the other in a dependency relationship. In the family, along with the value of care, children's dependency obligates parents to care for them (Levy, 1982). Obligations to care for dependent persons can also be applied to adult children and elderly parents (Callahan, 1985). Children may not take undue advantage of their elderly parents and must also provide for their needs. Dependency at both ends of the developmental spectrum evokes ethical duties for those involved—parents to children, and adult children to elderly parents (Linzer & Lowenstein, 1987).

In social work, the dependency and vulnerability of clients obligate professionals to constrain their own behavior and to offer services to protect clients (Lewis, 1986). The first principle of ethics is to do no harm. When comparing parent–child and professional–client relationships, we observe that general ethics and professional ethics have two things in common. Values commit to ethical duties, and the dependency and vulnerability of one evoke ethical obligations in the other. A major difference between general ethics and professional ethics is the lack of sanctions in the former and the presence of sanctions in the latter.

Despite their similarities, a case can be made for professional ethics independent of general ethics because of the distinctive character of the professions (Levy, 1979; Loewenberg & Dolgoff, 1992). Caplan (1986) suggests that three factors support the need for professional ethics: moral uncertainty, autonomy, and special moral relationships.

Moral uncertainty exists when one system of morality cannot be applied to all ambiguous situations. General morality, for example, cannot guide medical practice in the case of euthanasia because decisions are idiosyncratic to the relationship of the physician, patient, and family. Society has apparently decided to transfer the painful decision of euthanasia and other moral ambiguities to the medical profession because of the moral uncertainty involved. In social work, too, moral ambiguity exists in the decision to remove a child from a home, to break confidentiality, and to override client autonomy. Social workers are entrusted by society to develop a code of ethics to monitor and regulate professional action in these and similar ambiguous situations.

Autonomy, a central theme in the literature of professional ethics (Autonomy, 1984), cannot be supported at all costs and in all situations. It is a most prominent but not an absolute value, and it should be respected whenever possible. Informed consent, for example, is an expression of respect for individual autonomy. But not all clients want to affirm their autonomy; many prefer to dump their autonomy into the professional's lap. "You know best" captures this mentality. They want the professional to make decisions for them. In addition, people who are incompetent cannot exercise autonomy. Professionals would seem to be justified in acting on what they deem to be in the client's best interests to prevent immediate harm and to restore autonomy (Caplan, 1986).

It is reasonable to believe that people who possess special knowledge and skill have ethical duties to those who seek their services. "Specialization and inequities in the distribution of knowledge and training are the moral foundations for professional ethics" (Caplan, 1986, p. 12). Greater knowledge and skill obligate professionals to behave in particular ways with clients—to provide services and to exercise constraints. The three factors—moral uncertainty, autonomy, and special moral relationships—serve to legitimate the rationale for distinctive codes of professional ethics.

A MODEL OF ETHICAL DECISION MAKING

Moral dilemmas may take one of two forms: (1) Act X may be morally right and morally wrong, but the evidence on both sides is inconclusive. Abortion is in this category and represents a terrible dilemma for some women. (2) An individual believes that he or she ought and ought not perform act X. The individual is obligated by a moral norm to perform act X and obligated by a moral norm to perform act Y but is precluded from performing both. The reasons for performing X and Y are equally weighty, but neither set of reasons is dominant. "If one acts on either set of reasons, one's actions will be morally acceptable in some respects but morally unacceptable in others" (Beauchamp & Childress, 1994, p. 10). In the *Tarasoff* case (Loewenberg & Dolgoff, 1992), discussed more fully in the next chapter, the moral dilemma facing the psychologist was whether to maintain the confidentiality of his client (X) or protect the life of the potential victim—the girlfriend (Y). X and Y are categorized as two actions because they affect two different people; in essence the dilemma is whether to perform act X—maintain confidentiality. Most of the ethical dilemmas in social work are choices between two actions because they involve more than one person and different actions are addressed to each.

Analysis and decision making are necessary when practitioners face ethical dilemmas. An ethical dilemma is defined as a choice between two actions that are based on conflicting values. Both values are morally correct and professionally grounded but cannot be acted on together in the situation. They are both "right" and "good," and that is what causes the dilemma for the practitioner. The decision on which course of action to take should be not instinctive but based on a logical, reasoned approach.

Theory alone does not suffice to justify ethical action because it is too abstract. Intermediate steps are needed. Beauchamp & Childress (1994) posit a deductive model of justification as follows:

4. **Ethical Theory**
3. **Principles**
2. **Rules**
1. **Particular Judgments**

Particular judgments are required in ethically ambiguous situations in order to act. The professional practitioner needs to justify the decision by resorting to a rule that is a specific guide to action. The rule needs to be justified by a principle that is a more general guide to action. All three need to be supported by ethical theory. The ethical justification of an act can be said to occur when the decision is framed within an umbrella of rules, principles, and theory. "Moral judgment is the application of a rule (principle, ideal, right, etc.) to a clear case falling under the rule" (Beauchamp & Childress, 1994, p. 14).

THE TYRANNY OF PRINCIPLES

Toulmin (1981) has argued forcefully that professionals should be more willing to use discretion in ethical decision making, instead of applying rules and principles. When one side in the abortion debate offers its absolute principle of the embryo's "right to life" and the other declares the woman's "right to choose," the only possible outcome is deadlock. There is no room for compromise.

The application of a rule or principle in decision making introduces objectivity; the use of discretion introduces subjectivity. Because of its objectivity, the rule/principle reduces the professional's creativity and insight and capacity to individualize the client. In the criminal justice system, when standardized sentencing is invoked for comparable crimes, the judge does not rely on professional judgments and experience. In the child welfare and public welfare systems, when paraprofessionals and caseworkers are hired to make critical decisions affecting the lives of children and families, they apply the rules because they do not have the knowledge and training to rely on discretion in individual cases. But not all client situations should be handled by objective rules. The rules of health maintenance organizations (HMOs) do not generally permit agencies to use discretion to extend coverage for clients. The threat of job loss deters professionals from using discretion in bending the rules of HMOs. In social work and social welfare, the areas open to professional discretion appear to be narrowing, and the areas subject to bureaucratic rules, principles, and accountability seem to be expanding.

In delineating distinct areas for principles and for discretion, Toulmin (1981) distinguishes between the ethics of strangers and the ethics of intimates:

> In dealing with our children, friends and immediate colleagues, we both expect to—and are expected to—make allowances for their individual personalities and tastes, and we do our best to time our actions according to our perception of their current moods and plans. In dealing with the bus driver, the sales clerk in a department store, the hotel barber, and other such casual contacts, there may be no basis for making these allowances, and no chance of doing so. In these transient encounters, our moral obligations are limited and chiefly negative—for example, to avoid acting offensively or violently. So, in the ethics of strangers, respect for rules is all, and the opportunities for discretion are few. In the ethics of intimacy, discretion is all, and the relevance of strict rules is minimal. (p. 35)

When people are waiting in line to see a movie, the rule is that one does not go to the front of the line but awaits one's turn. The ethics of strangers prohibits actions that would be offensive to others. When a husband forgets to celebrate his and his wife's wedding anniversary—a grievous error among intimates—the rules might be dispensed with, and he might be excused. An indiscretion among intimates might be handled with discretion and discarded as an insignificant breach of family norms.

In social work, clients are classified as intimates. A Latina social worker working with the Latina elderly considers herself and her clients to be one big family, for they share a deep rapport and common heritage. Thus, the social worker feels comfortable using discretion on their behalf and bending some rules. Clients, as well as colleagues, board members, and staff, are in the category of intimates. Strangers are those not served by the agency.

A model of ethical decision making has been presented that requires decisions to be justified by the application of rules, principles, and theory. Having discussed the role of rules and principles, we turn to the role of theory in ethical decision making.

SOURCES OF PROFESSIONAL ETHICS

The two main questions of ethics—What is right? and What is good?—evolved into two traditions: deontological, concerning duty, and teleological, concerning the ends of action.

The Deontological Tradition

In the deontological tradition, the categorical imperative (Kant, cited in Beauchamp & Childress, 1994), common sense (Ross, 1930), and intuition (Bradley, cited in Johnson 1984) denote some types of action as right and others as wrong. This approach does not exclude consequences from the determination of good conduct but adds that some actions are right and wrong regardless of their consequences. Kant's concept of the categorical imperative—the moral "ought," unconditional and binding—asserts that certain actions are right regardless of our desires. They require unconditional conformity by all rational beings.

When we make a promise, we ought to honor it not only because of the positive and negative consequences that might ensue but because we made it. When we borrow a book from the library, we ought to return it not only because we want to make it available to others and avoid being fined but because we borrowed it. The obligation to keep the promise is inherent in the act of promising. The obligation to return the book is inherent in the act of borrowing. It is common-sensical and self-evident to honor these commitments.

When we presuppose the self-evident nature of obligation as supportive of ethical duties, we discover that there are obligations that are not normative to the entire society. Some clients of social workers are not guided by the inherent nature of obligation because of the way they were brought up. Moreover, clients who come from diverse ethnic backgrounds may understand inherent obligations differently based on their cultural values and traditions. Social workers cannot assume that their clients will act from a normative self-evident sense of duty. Social workers may have to resort to utilitarian thinking—the consideration of possible consequences—when they engage clients in evaluating their behavior.

Deontological theory justifies action as right because of a past relationship that antedates the present action. The duty emanates from the established relationship. Utilitarian theory determines the present goodness of an act because of its future consequences.

In deontological theory, the concept of prima facie duties can assist in determining the right ethical action (Ross, 1930). Prima facie duty, which grows out of a relationship to others, refers to an act that is fitting or appropriate to a situation at the time. The duty is a self-evident part of community morality, always binding unless it is in conflict with another duty. The prima facie duty to keep a promise—fidelity—rests on a previous act: having made a promise to another person that requires no justification other than being the common-sensical thing to do in the situation. Other prima facie duties include those resting on

1. A previously wrongful act—reparation: We have a duty to repair a relationship that we wronged.

2. Previous acts that others did to the individual—gratitude: We have a duty to express gratitude to another for having benefited us in the past.
3. A distribution of pleasure or happiness—justice: We have a duty to see to it that goods and benefits are distributed equally and fairly.
4. Making the lot of other people better—beneficence: We have a duty to assist other people with their needs.
5. Improving our own condition—self-improvement: We have a duty to make our lot in life better.
6. Not injuring others—nonmaleficence: We have a duty not to cause harm to another person.

When there is a conflict between prima facie duties, one should study the situation as fully as one can before forming an opinion that one action is more incumbent than the other. "Then I am bound to think that to do this prima facie duty is my duty" (Ross, cited in Johnson, 1965, p. 401). Ross offers neither rules nor principles to guide the individual in establishing priorities. There are no objective guidelines for determining the right thing to do in a situation when two prima facie duties collide. Resorting to the concept of prima facie duties offers more leeway but also more ambiguity in the resolution of ethical dilemmas.

As an illustration, children's service to parents is a prima facie duty of gratitude, whereas parents' care of children is a prima facie duty of beneficence (Wurzburger, 1984). When these duties clash—for example, when an adult child is caught between the demands of elderly parents and dependent children—the individual needs to determine which duty is more incumbent in the situation and act accordingly. At times, the duty to parents will be stronger, and at times the duty to children will take priority (Linzer, 1986a). There is no infallible rule to guide individuals in all situations. Although we intuit moral principles, we do not intuit what is right in the situation. We have to find the greatest balance of right over wrong and give reasons for the decision.

In sum, deontological tradition posits the intrinsic awareness of the rightness of an act—the ethical imperative (Beauchamp & Childress, 1989). Both monistic deontologists such as Kant and pluralistic deontologists such as Ross have strengths and weaknesses in their theories. Kant's basic idea is that when an ethical judgment is supported by rational beings for good reasons, those reasons are good for any similar circumstances: actions must be universalizable if they are to be morally right and obligatory (Reamer 1993). However, the absolute nature of the categorical imperative, such as breaking a promise or lying, leaves little leeway for modification and makes it difficult to apply when there are conflicting considerations. When two obligations conflict, and it is impossible to do both, the actor becomes immobilized. When all moral rules are absolute, the ethical theory becomes incoherent, and the only possible practical outcome is deadlock (Toulmin, 1981). A similar objection was raised by Moody (1983) when he asked how one decides which rights have priority when rights conflict with one another or with another person.

Ross, through the concept of prima facie duties, introduces pluralism into deontological theory—that is, a variety of principles and rules with potential for flexibility and conflict. The need to weigh principles and duties in conflict situations offers practitioners some leeway in decision making. At the same time, because it does not provide objective guidelines or principles for ordering the prima facie duties, Ross's theory does not facilitate making hard moral and ethical decisions. Nevertheless, we will be using Ross's theory in analyzing ethical dilemmas because of its pluralistic nature and the opportunities it provides to use discretion in weighing priorities among prima facie duties.

The Teleological Tradition

The teleological tradition in ethics is primarily known as utilitarianism. The theory of utility, or the great happiness principle, affirms that "actions are right in proportion as they tend to promote happiness, wrong as they tend to produce the reverse of happiness" (Mill, cited in Johnson, 1984, p. 264). The teleological or utilitarian tradition determines an action is good if it leads to good results for a great number of people and if it produces more good than an alternative action. The ethics of an act can be determined only by its consequences.

A constructive evaluation of utilitarianism suggests that the principle of utility is highly functional for the development of public policy. Public policy is developed by an assessment of everyone's interests and a choice to maximize good outcomes. It is not only a consequence-based but also a beneficence-based theory. The theory sees morality primarily in terms of promoting social welfare.

There are several problems with utilitarian theory. The anticipation of consequences is difficult and uncertain. Accurate measures of outcomes can seldom be provided because of limited knowledge and time. To anticipate long-range consequences of a specific action is beyond expectation; short-range consequences are necessary in order to justify action (Reamer, 1980). The theory of unanticipated consequences of planned action (Popper, 1965) makes accurate prediction untenable and throws into question the rationale for justifying ethical action on the basis of utility.

A second serious problem with utilitarian theory is that it may permit subordination of the rights of a few individuals if a greater aggregation of good results. Suppose the only way to achieve the maximal utilitarian outcome is to perform an immoral act. Could utilitarians justify immoral actions to benefit a large number of people? "At least in principle, utilitarianism would justify trampling on the rights of oppressed groups and minorities (for example, by reducing welfare benefits or displacing low-income people for commercial development) if there would be some benefit to the majority. Clearly, such a framework runs counter to social work's deep-seated commitment to the least advantaged and oppressed" (Reamer, 1980, p. 536; 1993, pp. 73–74). In like manner, Beauchamp and Childress (1994) agree that ordinary morality demands that we not override the rights of people to maximize social consequences. However, they defend the utilitarian position: "If we can more widely and more effectively protect almost everyone's interests by overriding some property and autonomy rights, then it is far from clear that this course of action would be wrong merely because it contravenes ordinary morality and pursues the goal of social utility" (p. 55). This argument serves to justify Congress's welfare reform law of 1996—the Personal Responsibility and Work Opportunity Act—which assumes that it is not morally wrong for some people to suffer in the short run if the effects of welfare reductions, in the long run, will serve the public interest and lead to social benefit.

Act utilitarians could sanction the use of immoral means to achieve moral ends. Although an action violates certain rules, act utilitarians believe it is justified because a greater good ensues. Rules are expendable if they do not promote utility in a particular situation. The violation of rules in particular cases will not lead to the breakdown of moral law in society. It is therefore permissible to break a promise if doing so would produce an overall good.

Rule utilitarians, in contrast, do not sanction the violation of ordinary morality to achieve greater ends. They believe that an act's conformity to a justified rule makes the act right. The rule is not expendable in a particular situation, even if following the rule does not maximize utility. The social worker is not permitted to deceive the client even if doing so may redound to the client's benefit. The strong moral stance by rule utilitarians blunts the criticism leveled against utilitarianism that the ends justify the means. They do not, especially when conformity to the means represents a violation of moral norms.

Moody (1983) cites a major problem with utilitarianism in the field of aging. The theory seems to hold out little reason for investing any resources for the care of the very old or the very sick. Limited resources dictate giving to those who can benefit from them. Why do coronary bypass operations for 80-year-old patients? Moody concludes that utilitarianism, when advocated on a rigorous and consistent basis, "seems to do violence to some of our most fundamental ethical ideals of justice, fair treatment, truth-telling, and so on. . . . Judged on such a harsh criterion, the elderly in long-term care settings might fare poorly indeed" (p. 107).

We resort to both utilitarian theory and deontological theory to guide practitioners in ethical decision making even if they sometimes lead to the same results. Both deontologists and utilitarians contend that promises should be kept, but there are situations in which their decisions may differ. For example, laws in most states require that suspected child abuse be reported to Child Protective Services. A deontological social worker would report because abiding by the law is the right thing to do. A utilitarian social worker might not report because of possible negative consequences such as retarding the client's therapeutic progress or the client's decision to leave the agency (Reamer, 1982b). But the same social worker might report because doing so could lead to a greater good—saving the child's life. Operationalizing both theories is complex because plausible arguments can be offered to justify taking opposite stances in ethically ambiguous situations.

The deontological position reflects moral imperatives that are inherently correct. The utilitarian position offers more leeway for ethical exploration because of the indeterminacy of anticipating consequences and defining the greater good.

There are serious drawbacks to each theory. Neither is infallible in justifying action nor without criticism in applying its reasoning to particular cases. Arguments can be mustered against each theory's claims, and both theories can be evoked to support opposing judgments. Nevertheless, they are the most developed, widely used, and easily applicable theories available. Efforts by Reamer (1979) to invoke Gewirth's principle of generic consistency and by Imre (1989) to apply the feminist theory of caring to social work have not borne fruit, the former because of its abstract philosophical bent, the latter because of its lack of external standards to guide moral decisions.

Freedberg (1993) has attempted to bridge the gap between the feminist ethic of care and the scientific and theoretical frameworks of social work. She examines the tension that exists between intellectual rigor and emotional commitment, and she suggests that more work needs to be done to find a balance between them. In our view, the underdeveloped nature of feminist theory precludes its application to the resolution of ethical dilemmas in social work at this time.

SOCIAL WORK ETHICS

Despite their drawbacks, both deontological and utilitarian theories can serve as the bases for social work ethics. Levy adopts the deontological approach. "Ethics, in effect, is a function of the relationship between parties to any transaction, and the responsibilities which inhere in that relationship"

(Levy, 1982, p. 1). The functional relationship between the social worker and the client forms the basis of ethical activity (Nulman, 1984). It is the context, not the consequences, of the professional relationship that determines the ethical imperative of the social worker (Levy, 1974). Lewis (1984) supports both theories in making ethical assessments. Utilitarianism is likely to yield a tentative choice of action that could be revised when new information changes the service situation. The deontological approach requires the social worker to reason from general ethical imperatives to guide the specific instance. The social worker may choose either approach but needs to be consistent.

In sum, professional ethics can be traced to two philosophical traditions—the deontological and the utilitarian. There are situations in which both theories lead to the same action and situations in which they lead to different actions. The practitioner has a choice of theory to support ethical principles, rules, and actions.

CONCLUSION

The theoretical framework for professional ethics encompasses its definition, its relationship to values and morals, and the distinction between general ethics and professional ethics. A model of ethical decision making offers social workers an approach to resolving ethical dilemmas. This model justifies the ethical decision through values, rules, principles, and theory. It offers a systematic way of thinking about ethics to help social workers control instinctive responses to complex conflict situations. This model of ethical decision making will now be applied to diverse cases, beginning with confidentiality.

5

CONFIDENTIALITY

Three related concepts encompass social workers' obligation to maintain confidentiality: client privacy, privileged communication, and informed consent. The cases in this chapter concentrate on dilemmas of client privacy because it pervades social work practice.

CONFIDENTIALITY

Confidentiality is based on the individual's right to privacy. It requires that disclosures by the client to the professional are not to be revealed to others except under certain circumstances, and then only for the purpose of helping the client. Confidentiality is worthless unless clients feel assured from the outset that whatever they say may be kept confidential (Reynolds, 1976).

The justification for confidentiality is based on four premises, three supporting confidentiality in general and the fourth supporting professional secrecy in particular (Bok, 1983). The first premise is that of individual autonomy. Individuals should be respected as being capable of having secrets. Without some control over secrecy about themselves and their thoughts and plans, people could not maintain privacy. The second premise legitimates not only having secrets but also sharing them with others. It assumes respect for relationships and intimacy among human beings.

The third premise maintains that a pledge of silence creates an obligation beyond the respect due to persons and to existing relationships. Once we promise secrecy to someone, we no longer start from scratch in weighing the moral factors of a situation. We relinquish some portion of our freedom of action.

The fourth premise assigns weight to professional confidentiality because of its utility to people and to society. Professionals grant secrecy even when they would otherwise have reason to speak out. Thus, lawyers feel justified to conceal past crimes of clients; priests, the sins they hear in confession. "According to this premise, individuals benefit from such confidentiality because it allows them to seek help they might otherwise fear to ask for; those most vulnerable or at risk might otherwise not go for help to doctors or lawyers or others trained to provide it" (Bok, 1983, p. 25).

Limits to Confidentiality

Confidentiality is limited when clients pose a danger to others or to themselves. At the outset, social workers should inform clients that what they reveal in session will generally be kept confidential, but they also should warn them that there are limits to confidentiality. Concerning limits to confidentiality, the NASW Code of Ethics (Section 1.07c) declares: "The general expectation that social workers will keep information confidential does not apply when disclosure is necessary to prevent serious, foreseeable, and imminent harm to a client or other identifiable person" (NASW, 1996). Some social workers consider the duty to warn someone of a danger a compelling justification for overriding the principle of confidentiality; others are concerned that disclosure will prevent those infected or ill from seeking early treatment and erode the trust between the health care community and clients.

Setting limits does not necessarily inhibit successful therapy (Corey, 1996). Although keeping secrets may be beneficial in small doses, concealment has an overall potential for causing harm. It is for this reason that most social workers attempt to help clients share their secrets within the therapeutic relationship.

> Confidentiality may be a protection for the individual against fear of discrimination, but secrets can impede understanding, foster isolation, prevent access to services, increase stigma, and interfere with a sense of community, keeping society separated into "us" and "them." The energies that should be invested in finding a cure, changing behaviors, and fighting discrimination are drained by the demands of secrecy by patients, families, and health providers. (Abramson, 1990, p. 172)

Duty to Protect

Social workers have a double duty: to protect other people from potentially dangerous clients and to protect clients from themselves. The *Tarasoff* case (*Tarasoff* v. *Regents of the University of California*, 1976) pointed to the need to protect others from potentially dangerous clients. The psychologist in this case failed to warn his client's girlfriend that the client was threatening to kill her. Eventually he did kill her, and her parents sued on the failure to warn of a dangerous patient and won. The majority of the judges concluded that "public policy favoring protection of the confidential character of the patient–psychotherapist relationship must yield in instances in which the disclosure is essential to avert danger to others. The protective privilege ends where the public peril begins" (Loewenberg & Dolgoff, 1992, p. 88). Therapists cannot claim protective privilege when their clients intend to harm others.

In a minority opinion, one judge argued that doctors violate patients' rights if they fail to observe standard rules of confidentiality. If it were common practice to break these rules, the fiduciary nature of the professional relationship would begin to erode. The mentally ill would refrain from seeking aid or divulging critical information because of the lack of trust that is essential for effective treatment. The other four judges, in overriding this opinion, felt that the therapist has a duty to warn the potential victim when life is in danger.

Following the principles set forth in *Tarasoff*, Reamer (1991) asks what happens when the conflict pits ethical responsibilities for keeping clients' communication confidential against legal and dangerous consequences. Who decides whether and how much information should be divulged? In effect, he is asking under what circumstance *Tarasoff* applies. The moral dilemma creates inner turmoil for the social worker and can damage the therapeutic relationship. The burden of guilt falls on the social worker, not the third party.

Reamer and Gelman (1992) debate the relevance of the *Tarasoff* decision to AIDS-related cases in which the client with AIDS refuses to inform his partner and insists that the social worker refrain from doing so too. Reamer opts for relevance because "it comes close enough to what we generally mean by a serious threat of harm to satisfy the criteria ordinarily applied to 'duty to protect' cases" (Reamer & Gelman, p. 355). Reamer is well aware of the threat to the privacy of the client and the possible consequences of betraying confidentiality, but he believes that the social worker has a responsibility to report the condition to the public health authorities even where state laws forbid social service personnel from revealing confidences in HIV- and AIDS-related cases. Reamer insists that the duty to save a human life takes precedence over the duty to keep information shared by clients confidential.

Gelman urges more caution in violating confidentiality. The reasons behind the increasing number of states banning such disclosures except by physicians under extensive restrictions are to encourage individuals to ask for help. In addition, "whereas the social worker may have a moral responsibility to alert the person at risk, she may have no professional or legal obligation to do so" (Reamer & Gelman, p. 350). The social worker is faced with a choice between competing social values since there are not necessarily clear legal guidelines. The variability among states regarding the application of the *Tarasoff* case to cases of possible harm suggests that room for discretion still exists. For these and other factors, Gelman supports the social worker's responsibility to maintain the confidence.

Health officials and advocates for people with AIDS have pierced the cloak of privacy by pushing for more testing and the mandatory reporting of those infected with HIV. They claim that the strong legal protections against discrimination have eased some of the pressure for confidentiality (Richardson, 1997). There is still no unanimity in this proposed change of direction, as the rights of those affected must be balanced against the right of all people to protect themselves (Stolberg, 1997). The issue of protecting the privacy of individuals' medical records gained prominence when the government proposed broadening police access to medical records in order to prevent excessive abuse and fraud in the health care industry (Pear, 1997a).

At issue in this debate is the definition of "compelling professional reasons" (NASW, 1996, 1.07c) for which confidentiality may be violated. Unfortunately, "there is no consensus in the profession about all of the conditions that warrant such disclosure, although there is general agreement that it is appropriate only under extreme circumstances" (Reamer, 1996, p. 897).

PRIVILEGED COMMUNICATION

Moral dilemmas can also arise with reference to privileged communication. As a legal exemption granted to professional groups, privileged communication permits any member of the group functioning in a professional capacity to be released from the obligation to disclose in a court of law certain client confidences (Promislo, 1979). The right to refuse to disclose information is governed by law. Clients of social workers have been granted the right of privileged communication only in some states. In states where clients do not have this right, social workers must choose between a court order to disclose information shared by a client in confidence and a client's right to confidentiality (Reamer, 1996). If the right to confidentiality is upheld, the social worker may risk court sanction.

In applying the law of privilege, a distinction must be made between privilege and confidentiality. Confidentiality is a professional duty to refrain from speaking about certain matters; it is an ethic that protects a client from unauthorized disclosures of information. Privilege is an exception to the general rule that the public has a right to every person's evidence; it is a relief from the duty to speak in court proceedings (Slaughter, 1996).

The Supreme Court, in *Jaffee* v. *Redmond* (1996), ruled that federal courts must allow psychotherapists and other mental health professionals to refuse to disclose patient records in judicial proceedings. "The decision brings the federal courts into line with the 50 states, all of which now recognize some type of psychotherapist–patient privilege" (Greenhouse, 1996). In discussing the implications of the Supreme Court decision for social workers, Alexander (1997) contends that *Jaffee* v. *Redmond* applies only to cases heard in federal courts, not in state courts.

Most states do not provide absolute confidentiality for social workers. Various states provide that social workers and their clients have the right to privileged communication unless the information involves homicide, criminal acts, or "harmful acts." Thus, Alexander concludes, "social work agencies should provide in-service training on the conditions of privileged communication in their state" (p. 390).

Confidentiality and privileged communication are two related concepts concerning client privacy. A third is informed consent.

INFORMED CONSENT

Informed consent refers to the use of clear and understandable language to tell clients about the purpose, risks, and limits of the service, relevant costs, reasonable alternatives, their right to ask questions and to refuse or withdraw consent to the service or treatment, and the time frame covered by the consent (NASW, 1996, 1.03). Special provisions have to be made to elicit consent from clients who are not literate, lack capacity, are receiving services involuntarily, or are being videotaped, or when electronic media are being used.

Individuals who agree to the release of confidential information must know (1) who wants the information; (2) why the information is desired; (3) how the receiving party wants to use the information; (4) whether the receiving party may pass the information on to a third party without the client's consent; (5) exactly what information is to be disclosed; (6) the repercussions of giving or refusing consent; (7) the expiration date of the consent; and (8) how to revoke the consent (Wilson, 1983). These stipulations place the client in charge of the information to be released to others.

The concept of informed consent originated in the medical field, where its purpose is to enable patients to make intelligent, rational decisions about treatment procedures. Physicians, health administrators, and nurses, however, tended to resist providing clients with sufficient information to assist them in making rational decisions. Thus, there was a disparity between the idea of informed consent and the reality—going along with whatever the doctor prescribed (Parry, 1981). Perhaps this indictment of informed consent is overly harsh. We would like to believe that health care professionals have become more respectful of patients and inform them of their options in unbiased ways.

For social workers, too, the process of informing can be problematic. Social workers may not want to overburden clients with too much information, yet they want to provide sufficient information for a meaningful choice. Should the social worker proceed when the client gives permission (says, "Do whatever is best for me," or nods "yes"), even though the client's consent is less than informed? Or should the social worker delay help in order to give the client additional information (which the client may not even want)?

Assisted consent is a concept that refers to the health care professional's involvement of other people to help clients, especially the elderly, make decisions. This is usually done through sustained conversation and allowing the client to process the information, to formulate and ask questions, and to process the responses with the assistance of family members and professionals (Kapp, 1990b).

Involving the client in providing informed consent is an ongoing process, not a one-time activity. The power gap and inequality between the client and the social worker require constant vigilance and monitoring of the meaning of the client's consent. The client's consent for disclosure of confidential information should in all feasible circumstances be in writing. Oral consent may be obtained without significant reprisals but at times may backfire. In *Doe* v. *Roe* (1977), a psychiatrist, while treating a married couple, expressed her desire to publish a book about their therapeutic experiences and allegedly obtained oral permission to proceed. Years later, after the termination of treatment, the book was published and gave an extensive account of details shared by the couple in therapy. The wife sued for violation of privacy. The court ordered the book removed from circulation and awarded damages. Had the psychiatrist obtained a specific written consent (and disguised the patients' identity more thoroughly), the court might not have ruled against her (Wilson, 1983).

A Florida court (*Sullivan* v. *State of Florida*, 1977) used the concept of informed consent to mandate clients' access to their records. This decision was based on the request of a patient in a state mental hospital to receive a copy of the summary of his mental condition. Thus, client access to records may be required when concepts of informed consent are fully implemented (Wilson, 1983).

The cases in this chapter reflect a number of ethical dilemmas involving confidentiality in an age of technology, the reporting of an alcoholic's misbehavior in a group home, and informing the partner of an HIV client.

CASE 5.1 *Transmitting Information Technologically*

Debbie, a social worker in an outpatient mental health agency, is updating an intake summary on a computer terminal. The agency computers are networked to a file server in the agency's administrative office. All the computers are maintained by the network administrator, who is also in charge of billing for client services. While Debbie is working on this document, she inadvertently "signs" the note and exits the program. In order for Debbie to return to the document to complete her work, she must ask the network administrator to "unsign" the document.

While Debbie is at lunch, she misses a telephone call from another social worker from a different agency. The social worker reaches Debbie's voice mail, on which he leaves a detailed message about a client who has been expelled from a day treatment program. The social worker also informs Debbie that the client's expulsion papers will be faxed over immediately.

Discussion

The case of Debbie and her use of technology raises a number of evolving issues regarding confidentiality. Security and privacy are two of the major concerns for social agencies. Security refers to the protection of hardware, software, file tapes, and so on. Privacy refers to the protection of information in the system (Schoech, 1982). There are two major security concerns for users of computer networks: whether the network is safe from unauthorized people and whether the information is protected against loss in the event of a computer failure. In the case of Debbie, the issue is the social agency's transmission of sensitive information between itself and other agencies where it is accessible to many people.

Because faxed data and computer files are generally available to many different employees of social agencies, extra care must be exercised to prevent access to unauthorized persons. Clients' personal data can become public knowledge even with precautions and careful storing of data. The NASW Code of Ethics pays special attention to electronic records:

> Social workers should take precautions to ensure and maintain the confidentiality of information transmitted to other parties through the use of computers, electronic mail, facsimile machines, telephones and telephone answering machines, and other electronic or computer technol-

ogy. Disclosure of identifying information should be avoided wherever possible. (NASW, 1996, 1m).

Computerization of personal information threatens privacy and leaves all parties vulnerable. Those who exchange information on the Internet should realize that all communications are public:

> 2000 patient records from a pharmacy in Arizona were still on a computer purchased at an Internet auction. All the software the pharmacy had used for record keeping was still on the computer's hard drive including patient names, addresses, social security numbers, and a chronological list of all prescriptions filled at the pharmacy. (Markoff, 1997, p. A14)

Social workers' use of e-mail also raises concerns about client privacy. Clients who may be communicating with social work agency personnel regarding day care, health care, substance abuse treatment, and reports of domestic violence may find that their employer has knowledge of this personal information. Individuals have limited guarantees of privacy in electronic communication (Gelman, Pollack, & Weiner, 1997).

The growing power of computers and the expansion of commercial databases have made it quicker, cheaper, and easier than ever for private investigators to collect individualized information. Governments are also sharing more confidential data with companies that manage child support enforcement, prisons, and welfare benefits. The buying and selling of information has become a huge business (Bernstein, 1997). There appear to be few ways an individual can prevent the dissemination of private information since so much knowledge has become readily accessible to the public. But, at the very least, social workers' knowledge of clients should be protected as much as possible.

The latest emerging practice area in which social workers are providing services to individuals and groups is on-line counseling (Levenson, 1997). Social workers are using different ways of counseling over the Internet, which raises the issue of confidentiality among other "ethical gray" issues. Because clients are not seen, the issue of verification of client identity poses a critical challenge. The client may be a minor. Chat-room conversations are especially insecure because passwords can be freely cracked by hackers. E-mail messages are becoming part of court evidence submitted by divorce lawyers. By engaging social workers over the Internet, clients risk losing confidentiality. Social workers functioning on-line have far less knowledge of and control over their clients' information and cannot guarantee adherence to confidentiality agreements.

Social workers who study the Internet predict online practice will remain controversial until many ethical, legal, and practical questions are answered. In addition to concerns about protecting confidentiality, lack of nonverbal cues and problems with informed consent and continuity of service, these questions relate to interstate licensing, knowledge of distant communities, verification of providers' credentials, and lack of definition of professional relationships. (Levenson, 1997, p. 3)

The rapid growth of technology in human services will continue to pose ethical questions about the confidentiality of social worker–client relationships.

CASE 5.2 Alcoholic in an Adult Home

B is a 45-year-old single male who came to the adult home from the men's shelter. From an early age his alcoholism led him to become clinically depressed, a condition for which he was briefly hospitalized. He could not hold a job, and for twelve years he lived in and out of shelters. When he came to the adult home, he had been sober for five months and had regularly been attending Alcoholics Anonymous meetings. Since living at the home, he has obtained a job at the library.

One day B told the social worker in confidence that, after hearing that his last existing relative had passed away, he felt all alone in the world and drank until he passed out. He understood the no-drinking policy of the home, which meant expulsion, and promised not to drink again. He spoke about the losses in his life and difficulties in forming trusting relationships. As he was about to leave, he asked the social worker, "Are you going to tell management?"

Discussion

The social worker is faced with an ethical dilemma because she has a conflict between two values: keeping the client's secret confidential or reporting it to management. Since both values cannot be acted on, she must choose the one that she deems to be more ethical in this situation. The ethical decision-making model described in Chapter 4 requires actions to be justified by rules and principles and supported by theory.

The social worker's decision to maintain confidentiality could be justified by the rule that professionals are obligated to preserve client secrets when they do not cause harm to others. This rule is justified by the principle of respect for autonomy (Bok, 1983). Both the rule and the principle can be supported by the prima facie duty of fidelity, which requires the social worker to keep her promise of confidentiality to the client.

The decision to violate confidentiality and report the client to management can also be justified by rules and principles and supported by theory. The rule of the agency stipulates that violations of policy are to be reported to management. The principle of utility requires actions that will redound to the greater benefit of all residents. The rule and principle are supported by utilitarian theory, which deems as ethical that which results in the greater good for the greater number. The no-drinking policy redounds to the good of all residents because it maintains a standard of sobriety in the home and offers a chance for recovering alcoholics to work on their problems. The threat of expulsion serves as a deterrent to potential violators of the policy. Adherence to agency policy would appear to be the ethical thing for the social worker to do because of the benefits that would accrue to all residents.

Resolution

After weighing both sets of rules, principles, and theories, the social worker decided not to tell management. She reasoned that, despite the client's violation of agency policy, he did not become a danger to himself or to others or cause a disturbance in the home. No one knew he was drinking until *he* reported doing so to the social worker. The social worker opted to adhere strictly to the value of confidentiality, believing that the prima facie duty of fidelity outweighed the principle of utility. The outcome proved to be most beneficial, as the client continued to maintain his job and to show improvement in his functioning.

CASE 5.3 Informing the Partner of an HIV Client

In family and couples therapy, perhaps the most widely encountered ethical dilemma concerns confidentiality (Goldenberg & Goldenberg, 1991; Corey, 1996).

> A social worker at a community mental health center was counseling an unmarried couple: S, a 31-year-old man with a history of substance abuse and mental health problems, and T, a 30-year-old woman with a history of alcohol abuse. They were in therapy to reduce the tension between them and to help them sustain the relationship. At times the social worker saw them together, at times separately. During one session alone with S, S began to sob and told the social worker that he was feeling very depressed because a physician told him that he had tested positive for HIV.
>
> After considerable discussion with S about the implications of this troubling diagnosis, including the need to practice safe sex, which S promised to do, and the consequences of not doing so, the social

worker asked whether S planned to inform T about the diagnosis. He said that he did not think he would be able to. He talked about how much he needed T's support, how much he loved her, his past difficulty maintaining intimate relationships, and his fear that T would leave him if she knew about his HIV diagnosis and bisexual experiences.

The social worker did her best to persuade S of the need to share this sensitive information with T, but S refused. The social worker was torn between one partner's right to confidentiality and the other partner's right to know and the potential risk to the other partner's well-being. How should the social worker balance S's presumptive right to confidentiality with her duty to protect T, a potential victim (Reamer, 1991)?

Discussion

The social worker's ethical discomfort arises from the need to balance the competing principles and to systematically analyze the justifications for choosing one principle over another (see Table 5.1). In analyzing Case 5.2, we utilized the Beauchamp and Childress model of ethical decision making

TABLE 5.1   Model of Ethical Decision Making in Couples Therapy with an HIV Client

Parties to the Conflict	Values	Rules	Principles	Theories	Ethics
Client	Keep secrets confidential; preserve intimacy; maintain trust and professional relationship	Secrets are to be protected in the therapeutic relationship.	Respect for autonomy	*Deontological:* Fidelity to the professional relationship	Do not inform partner.
Social worker	Maintain confidentiality; protect third parties from harm; preserve client's mental health	Secrets are to be protected in the therapeutic relationship. Third parties are to be protected from harm. Confidentiality is not inviolable.	Respect for autonomy; nonmalefi- cence	*Deontological:* Fidelity to the client *Utilitarian:* Negative conse- quences for couple and for client–therapist relationship	Persuade client to inform partner. Inform partner if client refuses.

(1994); here we use a more detailed, slightly modified version. The original model and this variation are interchangeable in decision making.

The Client

Although the couple is essentially the client, S is the focus of the discussion because he is being seen individually around his HIV diagnosis. S has become very depressed as a result of his HIV diagnosis. He clings to the relationship with his female partner to satisfy his need for intimacy and acceptance. Were he to reveal his diagnosis to her, he claims that she would leave him, which would be a devastating blow to his self-confidence. The client expects the social worker to be guided by the rule of keeping secrets confidential. For the client, this secret is of utmost importance, for it is his only expression of power in the therapeutic relationship.

> Most of these people have nothing to offer but their privacy . . . to have some control over giving information about themselves is one of their only ways of exercising power in the relationship. If they have no security that this is not going to be used on their behalf, or it is going to be spread around, or it is going to be ignored or taken without any real intention of maintaining privacy—they have lost almost any dignity whatsoever in the human helping relationship. (Lewis, 1986, p. 16)

The rule protecting confidentiality is justified by the principle of respecting autonomy and supported by the prima facie duty of fidelity to maintain the client's secret.

The Social Worker

Table 5.1 reflects the painful conflict for the social worker in all categories. Confidentiality is constrained by the harm that may be caused to others, as attested to by the *Tarasoff* case (Reamer & Gelman, 1992). Most of the states with confidentiality laws in HIV cases permit disclosure of the information in response to a court order based on "compelling need" (Rothstein, 1996).

A chronic problem in social work, however, is that threats to third parties are often ambiguous. "It is not unusual for a client to make a vague threat toward an estranged spouse or partner. In these instances, social workers often have difficulty deciding whether confidentiality should be breached to protect a third party" (Reamer, 1991, p. 56). These conflicting values are reflected in conflicting rules guiding the social worker's informing or not informing the partner. The rule to preserve the client's secret is justified by the principle of respect for autonomy. The rule for overriding confidentiality is justified by the principle of nonmaleficence, which takes precedence over the respect for autonomy (Ross, 1930).

Deontological theory posits the social worker's self-evident respect for the client's secrets based on their fiduciary relationship. From a utilitarian perspective, there are a host of possible consequences, both positive and negative. Not revealing S's HIV-positive diagnosis to T can lead to positive ends for S. It can prevent the possible dissolution of the relationship, preserve S's need for intimacy, and enable him to maintain the facade he so desperately needs for his sagging self-image. The negative consequences of not revealing the diagnosis include a breach of trust in the relationship with T, delaying a lessening of tension between them, and not coming to terms with the illness. In addition, T takes no steps to protect herself because she does not know of S's condition, nor can she help him get the proper medications to prolong his life.

Resolution
The social worker could go either way. She could preserve the client's secret or decide to override it—in states where this action does not violate the law. New York State Public Health Law #2782 (February 1, 1989) forbids social service professionals from disclosing any confidential information about people with HIV or AIDS. Only physicians may do so under special circumstances. In New York, the social worker has no option but to maintain confidentiality. Elsewhere, where no statutes exist, the social worker has the option of revealing the diagnosis to the partner. Nineteen states have laws that protect the confidentiality of HIV records. Their purpose is to control the spread of the HIV virus by encouraging the public to submit to voluntary testing (Rothstein, 1996).

The fatal consequences of AIDS have caused a great deal of panic and fear among Americans. As a result, individuals infected with HIV are increasingly facing criminal charges such as attempted murder and assault under traditional criminal statutes for knowingly exposing other people to HIV. While an increasing number of states are adding laws to protect the confidentiality of HIV records, they are also prosecuting individuals with HIV for knowingly transmitting the virus to unsuspecting partners (David, 1995).

If the social worker were to maintain S's confidentiality, the decision would come after much agony and soul searching. Not revealing the diagnosis creates a situation that puts T in danger of contracting HIV, if she has not done so already. T cannot protect herself or leave the relationship because she lacks knowledge of her partner's condition. The social worker is privy to information that could possibly save T's life yet is duty-bound to withhold it. The "moral traces" (Nozick, cited in Beauchamp and Childress, 1994) accompanying the social worker's constraint would be deeply troubling. The action taken, however, would be ethical because it can be supported by values, rules, principles, and theory. The concept "moral traces" refers to the consequences of having chosen one path, as opposed to the other path in an ethical dilemma. Since both choices are ethical, the decision to act on one creates the feeling of having violated the other. There is no winner in ethical decision making.

If the social worker were to reveal the HIV-positive diagnosis to T, this decision would also come after much agony and soul searching. The social worker knows the importance of confidentiality and believes that its violation might deter S and other clients from seeking the desperate help they need. But she would be guided by the need to protect an innocent victim from contracting a terminal illness. The "moral traces" that would ensue would wrench the social worker because she overrode an abiding professional value. However, this action also would be ethical because it can be supported by values, rules, principles, and theory.

Reamer offers several steps for social workers to take to balance their obligation to protect the rights of clients who have HIV or AIDS and pose a genuine threat to third parties, with their obligation to protect clients' sexual partners from possible harm. First, social workers need to become familiar with state and local laws and statutes regarding mandatory reporting procedures that pertain to HIV and AIDS and other sexually transmitted diseases. Second, social workers should inform their clients early in the relationship that there are limits to confidentiality. They should help clients to understand that although confidentiality is an important professional value, it is limited by law and professional ethics. Third, social workers should become familiar with the guidelines concerning informed consent. They should maintain thorough case notes that document any discussion of confidentiality, the need to protect third parties, and informed consent.

Judgments about the limits of confidentiality in HIV- and AIDS-related cases are among the most complex judgments social workers are called on to make. They require social workers to choose among the most sacred values of the profession. No professional looks forward to being forced to choose among such principles as client confidentiality, client welfare, and protection of third parties (Reamer, 1991).

CONCLUSION

Confidentiality, privileged communication, and informed consent are interrelated concepts that derive from the right of privacy and respect for autonomy. As fundamental values in social work, they are given prominent discussion in the NASW Code of Ethics (NASW, 1996). The perplexing issue in maintaining confidentiality is how serious the threat is to another person.

Additional time and patience are required of social workers to make certain that clients understand the information offered and the options available for making decisions. Some clients may be illiterate, incompetent, unfamiliar with the language, culturally dependent on people of authority, or wanting to "dump their autonomy" (Caplan, 1986) onto social workers. Under these conditions, it behooves social workers to be more sensitive and empathic, to wait, and to be certain that the client's consent is authentic.

As social workers gain legal credibility through state licensing, their clients are given rights of privileged communication. These rights are to be highly encouraged and respected, for they represent another victory for clients' rights to privacy.

As computer technology expands and information is stored and transmitted electronically, more personal information is available to multitudes of people and institutions, the inalienable rights to privacy are impugned, and individuals lose control over the dissemination of personal information. It behooves social workers to make extra efforts to exercise careful control over clients' records so that they remain confidential. Preserving the confidentiality of these records is the least social workers can do to maintain clients' dignity and autonomy by protecting their privacy. Confidentiality is one among many knotty ethical issues that arise in cases of domestic violence—the subject of the next chapter.

6

DOMESTIC VIOLENCE

Domestic abuse[1] is a systematic use of force or other means of coercion to control one's partner. It encompasses physical and sexual abuse, isolation, economic, psychological, and emotional abuse, using children, threats, and intimidation (Jacobs & Dimarsky, 1991). It is commonly assumed that domestic violence is an involuntary response to anger provoked by the victim's improper behavior. This belief allows abusers to escape responsibility for their behavior. Far from being an uncontrollable reaction to rage, the decision to abuse one's spouse is a conscious choice made by the batterer for a particular purpose. The batterer's goal is domination and control (Enos, 1996).

PATTERNS AND SCOPE OF THE PROBLEM

Domestic abuse usually occurs in a three-phase cycle: a tension-building phase, conflict, and a calm respite, often called the "honeymoon phase" (Walker, 1979). These phases last varying amounts of time, from hours to weeks and months. The cycle adds to the confusion the victim feels. When she is abused, she is conflicted and feels unloved. During the honeymoon phase, in which the abuser promises to be good and not mistreat her again because he loves her, her confidence is restored and she believes him. But her confidence is shattered again when he explodes at what he deems to be another provocation. As time wears on, the honeymoon phase wears thin, and the woman anticipates and fears the repetition of the cycle.

[1]The terms *abuse* and *violence* will be used interchangeably.

Although there is no typology for a batterer or a victim, there are six variables that are attributed to domestic abuse: socioeconomic factors, relationship status, age, childhood experience with violence, race, and alcohol use (Davis, 1995). Wife abuse is present in all socioeconomic environments, but three specific factors are associated with the highest rates of wife abuse: poverty, unemployment and underemployment, and employment in a blue-collar job. Legally married couples have lower rates of domestic abuse than cohabiting couples because of the personal investment in marriage, connections with one's social networks, and a clearer balance of control and autonomy.

Battering is the single largest cause of injury to women in the United States, resulting in more injuries than auto accidents, muggings, and rapes combined (Stark & Flitcraft, cited in Spitzer, 1995). Violence against women occurs regardless of race, class, age, religion, abilities, and sexual orientation (Weinsberg, 1994). In general, women stay in abusive relationships for three to five years (Siegel, 1994).

The issue of wife abuse has been slow to rise to the forefront of social consciousness because the dominant attitudes toward women in America have been maintained by strong male forces. In addition, violence within the family was perceived as a normal part of its functioning, and violence between spouses was perceived as a private matter in which police and government should not intervene (Kramer, 1990).

Wife abuse gained national attention during the 1970s due to the newly espoused belief in equality for all groups and sympathy for the plight of all victims, including battered women. The stage was set for family violence to be a major social issue. Following the civil rights movement, interest in all types of abuse grew, and the women's movement and its cry for equality for all women became a powerful force that awakened society to the gravity of wife abuse. There was public acknowledgment that beneath the orderly surface of many families lay a substratum of domestic violence that permeated all layers of society. Books on the subject served to educate the American public and to raise consciousness about its pervasiveness (Kramer, 1995). The O. J. Simpson trial spotlighted the issue of domestic violence on the national scene and riveted the public to its possible tragic consequences.

PUBLIC POLICY DEVELOPMENT

In 1975, the National Organization for Women identified domestic violence as a focal point for change and created a national task force on battered women and household violence. The following year, the International Tribunal on Crimes Against Women stressed the need for worldwide education on the victimization of women. In 1977, the International Woman Year's Conference formulated resolutions recommending increased services for battered women. These had the effect of raising awareness through the media and resulted in action on federal and local levels.

Federal policy provides support for the emergency and short-term needs of victims and their dependents. In 1984, the Family Violence Prevention and Services Act provided funds for states to make allocations, primarily for temporary shelters for abuse victims. In the same year, the Victims of Crime Act gave battered spouses priority for crime-act compensation (Davis, 1995). The Violence Against Women Act (VAWA) of 1991 provided substantial funding to construct battered women's shelters (Violence Against Women Program Funding, n.d.). There are no mandatory reporting laws at the federal or state level, apparently because of the continuing conception of domestic violence as a private matter between the couple.

At the state level, coalitions of women have formed to provide services, raise awareness, and lobby for government funding. Many states have been proactive in creating resources and accessing federal funding opportunities. States have become responsible for providing approximately one third of all domestic violence services directly. States are serving as a resource for another third from the federal government and are establishing standards for quality maintenance (Davis, 1995).

PROFESSIONAL VALUES

Domestic violence cases often challenge or are in direct conflict with professional values. Such values include being nonjudgmental, self-determination, confidentiality, and client agenda versus social worker agenda. The conflict occurs in the translation of each value into practice.

Nonjudgmental Attitude

Social work values require practitioners to maintain a nonjudgmental attitude toward clients. How does the social worker maintain a nonjudgmental stance toward a court-ordered batterer? The reason why the individual has been ordered into treatment by the courts is a violent action perpetrated by the client toward the spouse or partner. The social worker may be privy to police or client reports that attest to harm or injury inflicted. With this information in hand, the social worker may find it very difficult not to react to the client in a judgmental manner.

Can we honestly say that we approve of the behavior that brought many of our clients to us? Are we not repulsed by, or even indignant about, the sexual or physical abuse of a helpless child or the rapes and beatings some women receive from strangers or their husbands? Do we really approve of irresponsible sexual activity that results in the birth of children into impoverished, fatherless homes, in the spread of herpes and other venereal diseases, or in emotional trauma to one of the partners? Can we remain neutral—*nonjudgmental*—[italics added] when faced with such clients? My guess is that, for most of us, the answer is no. But have we faced our own moral values squarely and been honest with our clients about them? (Glasser, 1984, p. 9)

Since being nonjudgmental is not a value conflict—all social workers subscribe to it—but a practice challenge, the most effective way of dealing with this situation is for social workers to consciously separate the individual's actions from the individual's self. By judging the action as unacceptable while accepting the person as capable of changing, social workers are able to maintain (in most cases) a nonjudgmental stance. Although distinguishing the abuser from the act is the most feasible approach, it is not easy to do, for it requires significant emotional self-control.

By the same token, it is often difficult to sustain a nonjudgmental attitude when working with a victim of abuse. The social worker may want to condemn the abuser for what he has done. But if the social worker assumes this judgmental stance against the abuser, it makes it extremely difficult for the victim to express her caring/love for the abuser. In the case of a victim who declares that she will never return to the batterer, if the social worker supports her in this direction without any options or reality testing that she may change her mind, the therapy is doomed to failure. The social worker must walk a fine line between supporting the current wishes of the client and recognizing that she may not follow through with them. The social worker must also maintain a neutral stance toward the batterer. If the social worker becomes judgmental about the batterer, the victim may become reactive. It is one thing for the victim to curse the batterer, but it is another for the social worker to do the same.

The social worker may find it difficult to remain nonjudgmental when faced with a client who shows physical signs of injury from one session to the next. The social worker may act out this frustration by becoming very distant with the client or by feeling overly responsible for the client's safety and well-being. Neither scenario is productive for working with victims of domestic violence. Here, too, the social worker cannot ignore the injuries but must address them without making a judgment. The issue should be framed in terms of the social worker's concern for the safety of the client. If the social worker is distant, the client will view this reserve as rejection and may move toward the batterer. If the social worker is overly responsive to the client, the client will not take responsibility for her own safety but will ultimately and falsely believe that the social worker will keep her safe. This delicate balancing act avoids either distancing from or closeness with the client and requires a disciplined emotional stance.

Self-Determination

Can the social worker sit with an injured client week after week and wait for the client to make her own decisions? If the social worker believes, given the available evidence, that the client's life is in danger, can the social worker allow the client to be self-determining? If the client has an injury, the social worker must raise the issue and express appropriate concern for the client's welfare. Unfortunately, social workers often attempt to convince clients that their situations are life threatening or, at the very least, that staying with the batterer is wrong. This generally occurs when the social worker is genuinely afraid and will feel relief only when the client is out of immediate danger.

The client will not opt for any change until she is ready to do so, no matter how dangerous the social worker thinks the situation is. If the situation is life threatening, the social worker must articulate that fear to the client and process the client's view of the situation. It must still be left to the client to make any change. Though the client ultimately decides whether to stay in this relationship, the social worker alerts her to the implications and consequences of each option, including the dangers involved.

Can the social worker allow the batterer to make the decision on whether to stop his abusive/violent actions? As an agent of social control, the social worker must not condemn the person but clearly state that his behavior is unacceptable. It is up to the social worker to hold that individual accountable for his actions.

Here, too, reality testing is important. The batterer may repeat the old behavior even as he learns new techniques for dealing with anger, stress, and frustration. He must report to the social worker any outbursts so that the social worker can work on helping him change his pattern of reaction. There should also be built-in consequences for noncompliance, but they should not include dismissing the person from treatment. Batterers can be seen in more than one modality—that is, individual and group sessions—if they need to be seen more than once a week as a consequence of noncompliance. There could even be a recommendation to separate from one's partner. Thus, these are not ethical dilemmas on *whether* the social worker should support self-determination but practice issues on *how.*

Confidentiality

The parameters of reporting threats to another person's life are outlined in the *Tarasoff* case discussed in Chapter 5. The impact of reporting on the client–social worker relationship is similar to reporting child abuse. In both instances, reporting could interfere with the client–social worker relationship, and the client may terminate. The major area of difficulty in domestic violence cases, however, is the social worker's ability to predict or determine when the batterer presents a danger of violence in the course of treatment. Prediction is always ambiguous, though the threats may be real, making it difficult to invoke the majority opinion in the *Tarasoff* case.

Client Agenda versus Social Worker Agenda

The social worker's dilemma is whether to allow the batterer to control the session by skirting the issue of the violence or for the social worker to control the session by raising the issue. Batterers will come to sessions prepared to talk about everything but the abuse/violence that they are perpetrating. Should the social worker collude with the client and avoid the issue or begin a dialogue about the abuse/violence? How does the social worker create a balance between taking over the session and allowing the client to control what is being discussed?

The same issue arises when working with the victim. There is a fine line between setting the agenda for sessions and avoiding the unpleasant issues of violence/abuse. This is not an ethical issue but a practice issue.

CASE 6.1 What Should Mrs. R Do?

Mrs. R, married to Mr. R for eighteen years, has three children ranging in age from 12 to 16. The abuse began in the second year of their marriage when Mrs. R became pregnant with her first child. Initially, Mr. R was verbally abusive and on occasion became physically abusive by pushing, slapping, and shoving his wife. Mrs. R reported that the abuse has been steadily escalating in frequency and severity. The most recent incident left Mrs. R with broken ribs, a black eye, and many bruises. She then came into treatment and was encouraged by her social worker to file for a restraining order against her husband. Mr. R was ordered by the court to stay away from his wife and the family residence. He was permitted to see his children on a regular basis. When he picked them up for visitation, he repeatedly attempted to cajole Mrs. R into dropping the restraining order.

Mrs. R was encouraged by her social worker to maintain the restraining order lest she endanger herself by allowing Mr. R back into their home. In light of the last incident of abuse, she was advised that Mr. R's out-of-control behavior could only lead to further injury and harm to herself.

After four months, Mrs. R became increasingly depressed. Her children blamed her for the breakup of the marriage, the loss of their father, and the lack of money in the family. Mrs. R expressed her ambivalence to her social worker, who was extremely concerned about the danger to Mrs. R if she acceded to Mr. R's wishes and returned to the status quo ante. Mrs. R's social worker had difficulty understanding her client's desire to have her husband return to the home. She could not understand why the children blamed her client for all of the family problems because she clearly held Mr. R accountable for the difficulty. When Mr. R threatened to kill Mrs. R if she did not drop the restraining order, the social worker saw this threat as an indication of how dangerous Mr. R was. Mrs. R perceived the threat to be real and felt that Mr. R was capable of acting on it.

Although this appears to be a no-win situation, both Mrs. R and the social worker must review their positions in order to gain clarity, evaluate the situation jointly, and organize a plan of action.

Discussion

The conflicts in values (except for confidentiality) discussed earlier are clearly evident in practice dilemmas for the social worker—how one acts in a nonjudgmental manner in the face of violence, gives priority to the client's agenda, and encourages self-determination when another person is being threatened. Nevertheless, there is a pervasive and unnerving ethical dilemma for practitioners who work with battered women. Because many wives are ambivalent about staying with their husbands, the social worker is unsure whether to support the wife's inclination to leave him to start a new life or support the wife's inclination to stay because she loves him and both will provide a home for their children. He has threatened to kill her if she leaves, but he may kill her if she stays because the battering could worsen. This appears to be a no-win situation. No matter which way Mrs. R leans and the social worker supports, Mrs. R's life is threatened.

This is an instance in which, to resolve the dilemma, one needs to seek the least harm rather than the most good. The least harm could result from the decision to remain with the batterer on the condition that he agrees to enter therapy, permits closer monitoring of the violent incidents, and agrees to strategies to protect the children from his outbursts. The least harm could also result from the decision to leave the batterer, move to another state and assume a different identity, and take a chance of not being discovered. Mrs. R and the children might live with a cloud over their heads for many years, but at least they would be rid of the abuse. Neither option offers a perfect, lasting solution. Each one calls for the social worker and Mrs. R to enter into intensive exploration of its possible consequences.

The children's reactions are noteworthy. They are angry at their mother and blame her for causing the family to disintegrate. Children suffer profound psychological injury as a result of witnessing domestic violence. Studies have shown that children who are exposed to abuses against their mothers become traumatized and exhibit a wide range of somatic symptoms. Domestic violence also may affect the way they interact with intimate partners in future relationships (Enos, 1996).

CONCLUSION

Domestic violence is a social problem that has become more prominent since the widely publicized O. J. Simpson case. Legislation has increased on the federal and state levels to support battered women, but no mandatory reporting laws exist. The dilemma for the woman is serious and life threatening. The dilemma for the social worker working with either party is difficult and painful. The choice is between options resulting in least harm, not most good. The social worker needs to walk a fine line and be extremely careful of taking sides. Working with this population poses a difficult challenge.

Domestic violence can occur not only between a husband and wife but also between a parent and a child. Child welfare, the topic of the next chapter, embraces a variety of social and ethical issues that include child abuse and adoption.

7

CHILD WELFARE

In the field of child welfare, ethical issues arise in dealing with child abuse and neglect, and adoption.

CHILD ABUSE AND NEGLECT

The Child Abuse Prevention, Adoption, and Family Services Act of 1992 (42 Sec. 5106g) defines child abuse and neglect as

> the physical or mental injury, sexual abuse or exploitation, negligent treatment, or maltreatment of a child by a person who is responsible for the child's welfare, under circumstances which indicate that the child's health or welfare is harmed or threatened thereby. . . ; the term "person who is responsible for the child's welfare" includes (A) any employee of a residential facility and (B) any staff person providing out-of-home care. (quoted in Wells, 1996, p.1)

States vary in specifying the basis on which the protective service agency should intervene. Some states emphasize serious injury. Others include positive drug toxicology in a newborn, truancy or educational neglect, children being left alone, head lice, and parents' behavior that does not result in specific observable harm to the child (Wells, 1996).

The U.S. Department of Health and Human Services has provided a dismaying picture of the scope of child abuse and neglect: "1,012,000 children in 48 states were victims of substantiated child abuse and neglect. Forty-three states reported that 1,111 children died as a result of abuse in 1994" (Health and Human Services, 1996). Reports of neglect far outweigh reports of abuse, though alleged sexual abuse is increasing. Most reported incidents of child abuse do not involve immediately life-threatening injury or death.

The causes of child abuse and neglect include violence between family members or other members of the household, lack of extended family support, loneliness and social isolation, inadequate housing, unemployment, limited education, and serious marital problems including separation and divorce. In addition, there may be high expectations of the child's achievements, lack of knowledge about bringing up children, depression, abuse of alcohol and other drugs, mental or physical ill health, low self-esteem, work pressures, and parents' own experience of being abused as children. Some community attitudes such as the cultural acceptance of physical punishment of children may downplay the seriousness of child maltreatment (Government of Western Australia, 1996).

In all fifty states, parents have a legal duty to protect and provide for their minor children (Enos, 1996). A state becomes involved with a family after it receives a report of possible abuse. States and localities have established child protective service (CPS) agencies to investigate reports of child abuse and neglect, assess the degree of harm to the child, determine whether the child can remain safely in the home or needs to be placed in the custody of the state, and work closely with the court system to ensure the child's safety and well-being. The courts decide whether children need special protection in order to remain at home or whether to remove them from their parents' custody and place them in the custody of foster care agencies. Foster care consists of different structural arrangements, such as family foster care, kinship care, or residential group care (Liederman, 1996).

Family Preservation

Family preservation services help parents support and care for their children through (1) family resource, support, and educational services that enhance family functioning, (2) family-focused casework services that address problems as they arise, and (3) intensive family-centered crisis services that seek to stabilize families when there is an imminent risk of separating children from their parents because of abuse or neglect. All three forms of family preservation promote functioning of the family as an interdependent unit by facilitating the development and social functioning of children, supporting parents in their child-rearing role, and improving family and community life (Liederman, 1996).

The family preservation social worker functions as a family counselor and as an educator, teaching parenting skills, how to provide appropriate discipline, and how to deal with the problems posed by the changing developmental stages and expectations of children. The social worker teaches the parents nonviolent ways of influencing child behavior and insists that the family work out its own approaches for nonviolent behavior.

The philosophy of family preservation rests on the assumption that abusive parents do not intend to harm their children and, with the right combination of interventions and services, can meet criteria for adequate parenting. Family preservation approaches can be applied even in cases of serious physical and sexual abuse perpetrated by boyfriends and stepparents. Maltreating parents are viewed not as sick but as needy and under stress. Supporters claim that family preservation programs are in the best interests of children because children do better when they live with their natural or biological parents (Berliner, 1993).

Critics of family preservation cite the paucity of empirical research to bolster effectiveness claims. Not all parents can be rehabilitated, they say, and those who inflict severe harm on their children or kill them are categorically different from those parents whose maltreatment does not involve life-threatening harm to children (Gelles, 1993). In addition, critics maintain, because family preservation services are characteristically short-term, they cannot reverse long-term behavior patterns.

The parents in the following case were not physically abusing their children but were emotionally harming them through neglect. At the end of an eight-week intensive family preservation service, the social worker was required to tell Child Protective Services (CPS) whether additional services were required and, if they were, what form those services should take.

CASE 7.1 Should the Children Be Removed from the Home?

Family A consisted of Mom (25), Dad/Stepdad (38), T (16), J (7), A (5), T (3), and M (2). The referral was made to our family agency because M had been left alone and unsupervised at a pet store for over three hours. M was placed in protective custody for three days. During a home visit by Child Protective Services, the house was found to be infested by cockroaches. Feces were found on the children's beds. The children were dirty, and there was no food in the refrigerator. Dad was employed doing odd jobs. Mom was unemployed. J had been diagnosed with attention deficit hyperactivity disorder (ADHD) and was receiving weekly home-based counseling. The family accepted family preservation services as the condition for retaining custody of M.

The family participated in discussions with the agency's staff and received other services for eight weeks, from two to four times weekly. Although the services were voluntary, the family felt "forced" into treatment. The team's goal was to increase the quality of parent–child relationships and to enhance the ability of the parents to meet the needs of the children, particularly M. At the end of the services, a recommendation had to be made to CPS about whether to permit the children to remain in the home or place them in protective custody to protect them from further emotional or physical harm.

Discussion

One of the categories of social work values is preferred conceptions of people (Levy, 1973). How does the social worker prefer to view this family? It appears to be dysfunctional (a negative value), as reflected in the condition of the apartment and the children, as well as the lack of food. It is poor: not enough income is available, and the parents demonstrate marked irregularities in raising their children. But does it have the capacity to change and improve its living conditions and child-rearing practices (a positive value)? The parents do not want their family broken up through outplacement of their children. This goal is attested to by the family's acceptance of the family preservation team's efforts, though not without ambivalence. Thus, the social worker's preferred conceptions of this family are mixed. This mixed view of the family is reflected in the social worker's mixed preferred outcomes.

An ethical dilemma confronts the social worker, who is torn between two preferred outcomes: the preservation of the family unit and the safety of the children. One goal is to preserve the family intact, leaving the parents and children together despite the parents' neglect. The other goal is to ensure the safety of the children, which precludes their remaining in the family. The situation is a dilemma because both values cannot be actualized at the same time.

The social worker is clear about preferred instrumentalities—values that guide the work with the parents and children. To achieve family preservation, the social worker offers support for the parents' efforts, respects them as people who are struggling to make ends meet and care for their children, refers them to community supports, and educates them about nonphysical discipline and patterns of parenting. The decision to keep the family intact in order to preserve it is justified by the principle of utility— children's well-being, mental health, and growth into mature adulthood are best achieved through remaining in their family of origin.

To achieve the goal of safety, the social worker might attempt instrumentalities similar to the ones used for family preservation, but removing the children from the home in order to protect them is always a strong option. The choice of this option would stem from a judgment that the parents are basically incapable of caring for their children at this point in their lives. The decision to remove the children could be justified by the prima facie duty of nonmaleficence, which takes primacy over other prima facie duties (Ross, 1930).

Resolution

The social worker's decision was to recommend the children's removal from the home on a temporary basis. The weight of the evidence—the children's malnourishment, the condition of the home, and parental incapacity—pointed the social worker in that direction. The family preservation services had not made a sufficient difference in parenting. The social worker also recommended that the parents receive intensive counseling and supervised visitations and that the children be returned to them in the future if the evidence indicated that they would not be neglected.

CASE 7.2 Reporting Suspected Child Abuse

Most states have mandatory reporting laws for suspected child abuse or neglect. The responsibility for reporting falls on community members as well as professionals. Because laws exist, it may appear that social workers face no ethical dilemmas because they are obligated to uphold the laws. Such is not the case. "The ethical concerns focus on ways to assure the safety of the abused child. Nowadays the question whether reporting will enhance or endanger the child's safety is *the* critical ethical and factual issue" (Loewenberg & Dolgoff, 1992, p. 76). This was the social worker's dilemma in the case of ND.

> ND is a 10-year-old boy who was referred by his school to the family agency because of suspected child abuse. He had come into school with bruises on his arms and legs throughout the school year, but he denied parental abuse. When the principal met with the father, the father denied any abuse, claiming that the family was happy and loving and did not need any help.
>
> One month later, ND arrived at school with bruises on his arms and legs and admitted to his teacher that his father had beaten him with a wire hanger. This was the first time that he admitted abuse, though it had been going on for years. He added that the abuse had escalated ever since his father was called in to meet with the principal.
>
> The principal then contacted Child Protective Services. In the meantime, ND was sent to a physician to determine the extent of the abuse. The physician found that the bruises were not absolutely indicative of physical abuse ("not founded"), though he conceded that there was reasonable cause to suspect and therefore to report the case to CPS.

Discussion

It is mandatory for social workers and educators to report child abuse to Child Protective Services. It is also mandatory to report suspected child abuse, but there is more leeway for the social worker to decide *when* to report a case that is ambiguous. The dilemma for the social worker is whether to report *suspected* abuse. The fundamental value is preservation of the child's health and safety, but it is unclear which action will lead to the fulfillment of this value. Should the social worker follow a literal interpretation of the law and report the suspected abuse as being in the best interests of the child? Or should the social worker take advantage of the discretion permitted in the law and not report it, for doing so may arouse the father's ire and increase the abuse, thereby endangering the child even more? In some situations in which suspected abuse was reported, the parent has threatened the social worker with bodily harm. In other situations, lawsuits attacking the competence of the reporting professionals have been filed.

In a study of ethical dilemmas faced by family therapists, Green and Hansen (1989) found that 68 percent of family therapists would report parental child abuse to the authorities and 78 percent disagreed with the statement: "Don't report it, but ask the parents to have the children stay with friends or relatives until you have done some significant work with the parents" (p. 153). Apparently a significant minority of family therapists would hesitate to report suspected child abuse. To understand the social worker's ethical dilemma, we apply the model of ethical decision making that examines the values leading to the action, which is then justified by rules, principles, and theory.

The social worker's fundamental value is the preservation of the child's health and safety. Instead of one action that would lead to this outcome, two actions are possibilities: (1) The social worker could report the suspected abuse to the city agency as the law requires, thus leading to greater protection. The rule and principle require obedience to the law to prevent harm. Both deontological and utilitarian theories support the least-harm principle, which buttresses the social worker's inclination to report. (2) The social worker could opt not to report because of the painful consequences that would likely ensue for the child when the father finds out. As an alternative to notifying the authorities, preserving the child's quality of life could be achieved through involving the family in therapy. Not reporting is justified by the rule that children should be protected from enraged parents and by the principle of nonmaleficence. In this instance, too, both theories could be enlisted to equally support not reporting.

Resolution

The social worker chose to report the suspected abuse to the child welfare authorities. She arrived at this decision after weighing the relative strengths of each side of the dilemma. She felt certain that the child was being beaten at home, regardless of whether he was reporting the abuse to the school authorities. She believed that her responsibilities to preserve the child's health and safety made it imperative for the authorities to step in. For her, the rule to abide by the law outweighed any other consideration because it was designed to protect children.

CASE 7.3 Should Joe Be Returned to His Biological Mother?

Joe is a 14-year-old African American male who has been in the custody of his great-aunt, Mrs. H, since he was 3. She assumed custody of Joe through the kinship foster care system as a result of her niece's (Joe's biological mother) history of addiction and incarceration. Scannapieco and Jackson (1996) point out that "Extended families are taking over the care of children who would otherwise be placed in out-of-home care. The African American family is overcoming incredible odds to maintain the stability of the family"(p. 192). Mrs. H clearly holds family preservation in high regard; this value has guided her assumption of custody.

In 1995, Joe's biological mother was released from prison and became inconsistently involved with Joe. Her erratic involvement stimulated a series of negative behaviors by Joe. Since then, Mrs. H has been complaining that Joe has been oppositional and frequently disrespectful of her authority by continually breaking his curfew, using disrespectful language, not completing his tasks and chores, and staying outside the home overnight without permission. These behaviors led Mrs. H to seek individual and family therapy for herself and Joe.

Joe's biological mother petitioned family court for custody since she has been drug free. Mrs. H contends that she can no longer provide care for Joe and has inquired about the possibility of granting custody to Joe's mother. If the mother does not receive custody, Mrs. H wants Joe removed from her guardianship. She feels he is acting out because he is not in the care of his mother. The social worker has made several attempts to engage Joe's mother in his therapy, but she has not been responsive to the outreach efforts. Joe became less active in therapy and missed a considerable number of appointments. Mrs. H became increasingly despondent about her role as caretaker and began telling Joe that he wasn't going to be in her care much longer.

At a recent court hearing, the judge asked the social worker to provide a recommendation to the court. The social worker feels conflicted in making a recommendation because of Mrs. H's plan to surrender custody, Joe's acting-out behaviors and lack of progress in therapy, and the biological mother's lack of participation in Joe's therapy and her erratic involvement in his life.

Discussion

The conflict for the social worker is whether to recommend that the court grant custody of Joe to his biological mother or to recommend placement in a residential care facility because his great-aunt is no longer willing to provide care.

Table 7.1 reflects the respective parties' values, actions, rules, principles, and ethical theories. The entries on the child, mother, and guardian are internally consistent and do not present any conflict. The entries for the social worker highlight the ethical dilemma.

The social worker has conflicting values. As she does with every client, she believes that, with additional assistance, mother and son have the capacity to change. She would like to preserve family unity by reuniting them, because this is the ideal arrangement for growth. But she is also concerned about the child's safety because the mother has not yet proven her ability to parent.

TABLE 7.1   Model of Justification for the Ethical Decision

Parties to the Conflict	Values	Actions	Rules	Principles	Theories
Child	Self-determination; family unity	Return to mother's custody	Children should live with their parents	Fidelity Autonomy	*Deontological:* Prima facie duty to mother
Social worker	Mother's and child's capacity to change; child's safety	Recommend residential care facility	Parents who cannot provide a stable home should not be given custody of their children	Beneficence	*Utilitarian:* least harm includes institutional care
	Family unity	Recommend custody to the mother	Parents should be afforded every opportunity to keep their children	Respect for autonomy	Supporting autonomy
			Mental health services should be provided when parenting is ineffective		
Biological mother	Self-determination; family unity	Obtain custody	Parents should be held responsible for the care of their children	Autonomy Fidelity	*Deontological:* Fidelity to child
Guardian	Self-determination	Surrender custody	Children should respect adults' authority	Autonomy	*Deontological:* Do what is right

Conflicting values lead to conflicting actions. The social worker would like to recommend that the mother receive custody, and she would like to recommend that the child be placed in residential care. Literature suggests that residential care facilities provide a specialized treatment milieu and a more structured environment than would be available through foster care. Findings from a 1984 study on the effectiveness of residential care facilities for adolescent boys (Gilliland-Mallo & Judd, 1986) indicate that a higher rate of runaway behavior by black youths than by white youths was the major barrier to program success. The social worker is concerned about locating the most appropriate setting for Joe to become more functional. She anticipates that Joe will act out in placement in negative ways, for he is oppositional and disrespectful of authority.

The social worker is also confronted by conflicting rules. Parents who are ineffective and incapable of parenting should not be entrusted with raising their children. But some parents could benefit from mental health services and parenting education to assist them to be more effective parents. These services should, therefore, be provided to enable them to keep their children. Conflicting principles justify the conflicting rules. The social worker would like to support the mother's autonomy by granting her custody, and the child expresses a wish to be reunited with his mother. But the social worker is also concerned with the client's safety. The principle of beneficence guides her to place the client in residential treatment, where he will be protected and his needs met.

Deontological theory could support the respect for autonomy because reuniting a mother and a son is only right. Utilitarian theory could support the opposite point of view—that the child be placed in residential treatment as the least-harm alternative and the greater possibility of safety.

Resolution

After weighing the variables on both sides, the social worker came down on the side of family unity. She recommended that the mother be awarded custody on the condition that both mother and child participate in individual and family therapy as a mandate of family court. The social worker considered the option of placement in a residential care facility and anticipated negative consequences such as the child running away and not functioning at his optimal capacity. Placement would not achieve the value of family unity because the relationship between the child, mother, and guardian would probably deteriorate.

ADOPTION

Adoption is a universal practice, sanctioned and recognized by law, whereby a child born into one family subsequently grows up in another family

(Watson, 1979). The implicit question often raised in adoption cases is "Who is the primary client?" Brieland (cited in Curtis, 1986) contends that the adoptee, not the adoptive or biological parents, should be viewed as the primary client because the adoptee is potentially the primary victim in the situation. Brieland believes that laws, policies, and procedures that disregard the rights of the adoptee in favor of the rights of the adoptive parents and biological parents are unfair and discriminatory. However, given children's status as minors, seldom are they viewed as fully occupying the client role. In some instances, a law guardian is appointed to protect their rights, and for the law guardian they are, in fact, clients. Generally, though, given the age of child clients, the dynamics and interactions typical of client–worker relationships are not present. In most instances, children are the bystanders of adoption proceedings, and the real drama is acted out between the biological parents and the adoptive parents. The status of bystander only obtains when the adoptee is an infant or child. When adoptees become adults, the designation of the client changes. The adult adoptee takes center stage.

Adoption is sometimes conceived as a triangle constructed of the biological parents, the child, and the adoptive parents. The interests of one party are not always aligned with the interests of one or both of the others—hence, the need to set priorities in the best interests of the child. Some of the ambiguities in adoption stem from the historical fact that adoption was a way to provide heirs for childless families and only many years later became an altruistic institution for providing permanent homes for children. The most important societal value in adoption is the availability of permanent families for children whose biological parents cannot keep them. The secondary gain is the availability of children for families who cannot bear children or wish to expand their families.

Each of the parties to an adoption faces a central conflict. The conflict for biological parents: "My wish to have you versus my need to delegate your care to others so that I can go on with my life." The conflict for adoptive parents: "Making you part of our family versus the need for a place in your birth family as well, even if only knowing about them." The conflict for adult adoptees who have achieved independence from their adoptive parents: "I love you both but I have to find my biological parents" (Dukette, 1984, p. 235).

Open versus Closed Adoption

Open adoption has been defined as an institution in which "the birth parents meet the adoptive parents, participate in the separation and placement process, relinquish all legal, moral, and nurturing rights to the child, but retain the right to continuing contact and to knowledge of the child's whereabouts and welfare" (Baran, Pannor, & Sorosky, 1976, p. 97). In closed adoption, "all actual contact, as well as legal relationships between the child and biological family are severed completely and permanently, with the expectation that the child will develop primary emotional attachments exclusively with the adoptive family" (Borgman, 1982, pp. 217–218).

Historically, closed adoption was the norm. Adoption records were sealed by courts and agencies. Adoption legislation was designed to achieve a legal fiction—namely, an attempt to extinguish all ties to birth families in order to create the illusion that the child was a child of the adoptive family as if by birth. An additional rationale for closed adoption was based on concern for the social and psychological welfare of the adopted child. Professionals believed that adoptees would bond more effectively with adoptive parents if they ceased to have contact with their biological family. It was presumed that if adopted children made a formal break from their biological family, adopting parents would more readily accept the children as their own.

Sealed versus Unsealed Records

In the last decades of the twentieth century, a new trend has developed that militates against sealed records. The argument was advanced that all people should have access to their birth records. "This drive to reestablish family ties has an intensity and compulsiveness that command attention. It seems to be one more effort to overcome a sense of dislocation in a world whose future seems extremely uncertain" (Dukette, 1984, p. 238). The latest thinking among professionals places major importance on the child's need to maintain original ties in order to foster completeness and identity. According to this point of view, it is not sufficient for identity to be based only on the relationship with the adoptive family. The adoptee is a product of two families and, as an adult, should have the opportunity to incorporate membership in both the biological and the adoptive family into a unique sense of self.

Presently, society at large seems to favor open adoption. Rompf (1993), in a cross-sectional sample of adults, found that 86 percent of his respondents believed that adoptees are justified in searching for biological parents. More than three-fourths believed that adoptive parents should assist adoptees in their search. "Clearly, social attitudes have been transformed from those of the 1970s when closed adoption was still the norm" (Bleich, 1997). These changed attitudes are reflected in a bill passed on December 5, 1994, by the New Jersey state legislature that granted adoptees access to their original birth certificates (Sullivan, 1994).

The controversy over open versus closed adoption applies primarily to the adoption of infants and young children. The controversy over sealed versus unsealed records applies to adult adoptees whose adoption in infancy was closed and who now want to know their biological parents. The following case presents the dilemma of unsealing the closed records of an adult adoptee.

CASE 7.4 Should Sealed Records Be Unsealed?

Judy is an 18-year-old white female who was raised in a loving adoptive home and is socially well adjusted and scholastically successful. However, since she was 5 years old, when she was told that she was adopted, she has pictured herself as "having a hole inside myself, as if a piece of the puzzle is missing." She wants to know, "who am I?" Judy also wants genetic information about her biological parents so that she can watch out for various illnesses to which she may be predisposed.

Judy has been suffering from what has been called "genealogical bewilderment" (Pannor & Baran, 1984). She set out to find out more about her biological roots. Her adoptive mother was very understanding and supportive and helped Judy contact the agency that had arranged her adoption.

Lilly is a 34-year-old white female, happily married for ten years, with three children. She and her husband have good jobs. Lilly has never told her husband about her past and the birth of a daughter when she was 16. She feared that the marriage would break up if he knew. She signed an agreement with the agency, which assured her that privacy and confidentiality would be respected forever. She fully expects this agreement to be honored, for she does not want to disturb the status quo in her life.

Discussion

When an adult adoptee decides to undertake a search, the adoption agency faces an ethical dilemma. The agency contracted with the biological mother (Lilly) to maintain confidentiality by not revealing her identity; the adult adoptee (Judy) wants to ascertain the identity of her biological mother, thus requiring the breaking of confidentiality. What is the ethical thing to do?

This dilemma results from conflicting agency and professional values: the promise of confidentiality to one client, the biological mother, versus the commitment to the emotional welfare of another client, the adult adoptee. Breaching confidentiality may be harmful to one, and refusing to breach confidentiality may be harmful to the other. To whom does the agency have primary allegiance?

Two prima facie duties are in conflict. The duty of fidelity reinforces the promise of confidentiality, and the duty of beneficence affirms the needs of the adoptee. The principle of utility supports both options: Confidentiality should be maintained; otherwise, birth mothers would refuse to seek the agency's services. And the sealed record should be opened in order to secure the wholeness of the adult adoptee's identity.

Resolution

In this case as in many ethical dilemmas in which there is no possibility of compromise, only one decision can be made. The social worker eventually decided on behalf of the adult adoptee because of the mental anguish she otherwise would suffer. The social worker offered counseling services to the birth mother to help her deal with the stress of being found by her birth child. Although the birth mother will suffer repercussions from the violation of her confidentiality—a major breach of fidelity to a client—the greater concern of the agency was the physical and emotional health of the adult adoptee. Thus, the prima facie duty of beneficence prevailed. The social worker suffered moral traces over the breach of confidentiality.

Either way, there are negative consequences. When confidentiality is broken, biological families feel betrayed. When confidentiality is maintained, adoptees feel discriminated against. Adoptive parents are divided on this issue. Some agree to the opening of agency records because their adoptees desire it. Others may see it as a betrayal of their relationship.

The decision to unseal adoption records is supported by recent court decisions. In *Doe* v. *Sunquist* (1997) the U.S. Court of Appeals upheld a Tennessee court's decision to allow disclosure of previously confidential adoption records to young adults. The appeals court maintained that the Tennessee statute does not violate federal constitutional rights of familial privacy and does not unduly burden the adoption process, and that the right to avoid disclosure of such confidential information does not exist. The appeals court's decision appeared to be favored by a majority of Americans in a survey on adoption practices: 68 percent said that adopted children finding their birth parents was good for the adopted person, 56 percent said that it was good for the birth parents, and 44 percent said that it was good for the adoptive parents (Lewin, 1997).

CASE 7.5 *Closed Adoption versus Foster Care*

This case concerns a foster mother who wants to adopt two of three siblings in a "closed" adoption, defined as prevention of the oldest sibling's social contact with his younger siblings. The alternative is the three siblings' living together in a foster home.

The Lopez children are currently in the foster care system. Santiago, age 13, has severe emotional and behavioral difficulties, which caused him to be placed in a residential treatment center for the past two years.

Before being admitted, he and his two younger sisters (Maria, age 8, and Elena, age 7) lived together in the same foster home for two years. The foster mother, Mrs. Sanchez, was progressively unable to manage Santiago's behavioral problems and requested his removal from the home. Once his removal had taken place, the Lopez children were scheduled for sibling visits twice monthly, in keeping with foster care regulations.

Clearly, the girls are fond of their big brother and bring drawings they have made for him to hang in his room. He, too, is quite fond of them and always has candy for them, which he buys with money he earns from doing chores. He also reads stories to them when they visit, which they seem to love. When the visiting hour ends, it is always difficult to get the children to part company. Inevitably the girls begin to cry, and Santiago withdraws and remains quiet for an hour or two after the visit.

The Sanchez home was the third foster home for these three children. They were removed from their mother's care on an abuse/neglect petition at the respective ages of 8, 3, and 2. Santiago has always considered himself the protector of his younger sisters. Their separation has caused him much anguish. He is an angry young man with many physical scars from abuse. About the only time the child care workers see him smile is on visiting day when his sisters arrive in the cottage.

The Lopez mother never named a father for any of the three children. The last contact with her was three years ago, despite several diligent searches. No one is sure whether she is alive or dead. Her parental rights have recently been terminated, and the Lopez children have been freed for adoption.

Mrs. Sanchez, a single woman, has made known her desire to adopt the girls but not Santiago. She admits that she is intimidated by his size and says that his aggressive outbursts are more than she can handle. Separating the siblings became necessary when Santiago's behavior became unmanageable. However, the permanency plan has always been to reunite the three siblings in a single adoptive home. Not only is this out of the question as far as Mrs. Sanchez is concerned, but she is against future contact between the girls and their brother. She has refused to consider or participate in an open adoption arrangement. Her adoption of the Lopez girls is conditional on maintaining a closed adoption.

Mrs. Sanchez feels strongly that Santiago's influence on the girls is a negative one. She is suspicious of his relationship with them and is not comfortable with the way they rough-house at times. She has witnessed his violent temper outbursts, and she fears for the girls when they are in his presence and things begin to escalate. The girls, however, care for their brother but also have become very attached to Mrs. Sanchez. They have resided with her for the last four years and appear to thrive in her care. The girls have often said how unhappy they would be if they ever had to move to another foster home.

Dilemma

The waiting lists for adoptive homes are long. The waiting time for sibling groups of two or more is even longer. There is no way to tell when Santiago will be able to be discharged to a lower level of care. As long as he is in a residential treatment center, he is not able to be adopted. Therefore, the likelihood that all three Lopez children will be adopted into the same home is small.

The social worker on the case must make a recommendation about Mrs. Sanchez's expressed desire to adopt the girls if their contact with their brother is discontinued. If the social worker decides that the condition is unreasonable and recommends against the adoption, the girls will have to be removed from the Sanchez home and placed in a fourth foster home. There is no guarantee that a new adoptive home will be found anytime soon, if at all. The older they get, the less likely they are to be adopted. But these three siblings are the only family each one has, and it seems wrong to sever one set of family ties in order to create new ones.

The social worker inclines toward an open adoption as the only permanency plan that is right for this situation. Minimally, she would like to encourage Mrs. Sanchez to reconsider the possibility of an open adoption with the understanding that Mrs. Sanchez can regulate the frequency and duration of future visits and contacts among the children. If Mrs. Sanchez refuses, the social worker must decide whether the girls should be adopted by Mrs. Sanchez and sever contact with Santiago or be removed from Mrs. Sanchez's care and maintain contact with their brother. The social worker is particularly disturbed by these two alternatives, for she views this situation as yet another form of abuse perpetrated against these children. She feels trapped between two bad decisions. She must find something to guide her through this decision-making process.

Discussion

This form of open versus closed adoption is atypical because there is no relationship and no agreement between the adoptive and biological parents. Instead, the agreement concerns the permissibility of visitation by the older brother to his younger sisters. If the adoptive parent consents to an open adoption, the older sibling would be able to visit. If she insists on a closed adoption, visitations would be eliminated.

The issue for the social worker is complex. She must recommend to the courts a course of action in which one of the parties to the conflict will inevitably be harmed. The social worker's ethical dilemma is whether to support the foster mother's request to adopt only the girls, or remove the girls from her home and attempt to reunite them in another foster home.

There are positive and negative values on both sides of the dilemma. A value supporting the closed adoption is the provision of a permanent home and stability for the sisters after years of drifting from one foster home to another. They would have the family that has eluded them since early childhood. The relationship between the girls and their foster mother appears to be warm and satisfying, conducive to a plan for greater permanency. The negative value is their brother's prevention from joining them in this new family and from social contact in the future. It is precisely the absence of a permanent family all his life, which is now again being denied, that may have precipitated Santiago's acting-out behavior and emotional difficulties.

A value supporting the three siblings' return to foster care is their potential reunification and preservation as a family—the only family they know. They show affection and care for each other and like to be in each other's presence. The negative value in the foster care arrangement is its impermanence and the denial of permanency for the sisters by means of adoption. Table 7.2 portrays the social worker's dilemma in relation to the foster mother.

The table reflects the client's unequivocal position in the case. Mrs. Sanchez wants to be a mother to these two girls but not to their brother, who is prone to violence and could disrupt the stability of the home that she is attempting to secure. She claims that she has the right to decide which children to adopt. The principle of utility could be invoked to support her claim. In her view, greater benefits will accrue to the two sisters from a permanent home with her than from impermanent foster care for all three siblings.

The social worker confronts an ethical dilemma, and because the options are not objectively weighted in any one direction, she must balance values, rules, and principles in arriving at a decision (Beauchamp & Childress, 1994). From a value standpoint, which is preferable: breaking up a family of siblings in a foster home in order to provide adoption for some or postponing adoption for all in favor of eventually reuniting them in some other foster home in the future? Given these values, the social worker has the choice of two actions: holding out for an open adoption to protect permanency and maintain family contacts or, if this outcome is not possible because of Mrs. Sanchez's intransigence, removing the sisters from Mrs. Sanchez's home and seeking a foster placement that would maintain the sibling ties.

TABLE 7.2   Ethical Decision Making in Open versus Closed Adoption

Parties to the Conflict	Values	Actions	Rules	Principles	Theories
Social worker	Permanent home for the girls	Recommend open adoption to preserve sibling ties	Children should grow up in permanent families	Utility	Utilitarian
	Preservation and reunification of the family	Recommend removal of girls from foster home to avoid closed adoption	Contact between siblings should not be deliberately severed	Nonmaleficence	Deontological
Foster mother	Love of non-disruptive children	Closed adoption	Adoptive parents have a right to decide which children to adopt	Utility	Utilitarian
	Motherhood				

The rules that justify each decision have societal supports. There is general consensus that, ideally, children should be raised and nurtured in permanent families and, short of that arrangement, they should maintain contact even under impermanent conditions until such time as permanency for some or living together for all is feasible.

The ethical principles of utility and nonmaleficence justify the conflicting rules. The principle of utility guides decisions toward the maximization of benefits for the greater number of people. In the choice between permanency for some or impermanence for all, the greater benefit may accrue to permanency for some. However, the principle of nonmaleficence—doing no harm—might suggest a preference for impermanence for all so as not to inflict harm on even one member by severing family contact.

The principle of utility is supported by utilitarian theory, which claims as ethical that which benefits the maximum number of people. The greater benefit in this case is the permanence of a home for the sisters. The principle of nonmaleficence is supported by deontological theory, which claims as ethical that which is self-evident and intuitive (Beauchamp & Childress, 1994). It is self-evident that family unity is a desired goal for children. Therefore, it is more harmful to break up the family through the closed adoption than to maintain it in an impermanent arrangement toward the end of eventually reuniting it in another foster home.

In the course of balancing the relative weights of each side of this dilemma, the social worker will be engaging the client, Mrs. Sanchez, with the options available to her and their possible consequences. The social worker will focus on the client's insistence on closed adoption and the benefits and deficits of open versus closed adoption. Ultimately, the social worker will abide by the client's preference in her recommendation to the court.

CONCLUSION

Children are among the most vulnerable groups in society, and the social work profession has always been concerned with their welfare. Social workers have fought to prevent child abuse, to rectify the foster care system, to improve health care benefits, to strengthen families so they can keep their children, and to support adoption when maintaining the family is no longer possible.

Situations arise in which parents neglect or abuse children and are unfit to be parents yet removing children from the home is not clearly mandated. In these situations social workers face ethical dilemmas about the right and good thing to do for the children. In the first case, the social worker recommended that the children be temporarily removed from the home until the parents' parenting abilities improve and the parents take responsibility for caring for their children. In the second case, the social worker opted to report the suspected abuse with the goal of preventing more abuse by the father. In the third case, the social worker recommended that the child be returned to his biological mother to preserve the family unit. There was no consistency among the cases. Each case was evaluated on its own terms, and the social worker made the decision after weighing all the available evidence.

Two adoption cases were presented that typify value and ethical dilemmas for social workers. In one the social worker faced an ethical dilemma when an adult adoptee desired to know her biological parents, who did not want to be known. In the other, the social worker faced the dilemma of supporting a closed adoption that would exclude the oldest sibling from contact with his younger siblings or recommending a foster home arrangement in which all the siblings would be reunified as a family.

There are no absolute guidelines in these ambiguous situations; consequently, each social worker made what she thought to be the ethical decision at the time, using a process of ethical reasoning. Given the absence of absolute guidelines, there appears to be a need to develop some objective criteria with which to make decisions, such as a scale that rates healths and strengths, as well as limits and pathology, of family functioning. There needs to be a way to score families and use the scores as the basis on which to make decisions. And when a decision is at odds with the score, the reason for the discrepancy needs to be clear, to ensure that social worker bias is not affecting decision making. In situations requiring inexperienced caseworkers and untrained supervisors to decide whether to remove children from their parents, the need for greater objectivity is especially strong (Siskind, 1997).

In the absence of objective criteria for decision making, the resolution of dilemmas can be facilitated by the weighing of the values, rules, principles, and theories informing each side. In preparing to make the decision, social workers will be sensitive to the struggles and anguish of the parties involved in the child abuse and neglect situations and in the adoption triad. The ultimate decision will inevitably leave moral traces for social workers.

The welfare of many children who are neglected by their parents and are placed in foster homes or adopted by new families is closely intertwined with the welfare system itself. It is to the moral issues involved in this system, with its complexities and changes, that we turn in the next chapter.

8

WELFARE REFORM

The political right and the social work community have different ideas about the morality of welfare clients and the morality of the new welfare law. This chapter presents their moral perspectives on recent welfare reform efforts and describes the moral dilemmas faced by state legislators and by administrators and practitioners working in the welfare system or with clients served by that system. We begin with a general discussion of the scope of welfare, the impetus for the new welfare law, and the provisions of the law pertaining to public assistance, which have changed the social and economic landscape of financial services to the poor.

THE SCOPE OF WELFARE

Although welfare and the need for welfare reform have become synonymous with problems in Aid to Families with Dependent Children (AFDC), welfare as a concept actually encompasses a much more comprehensive system of benefits and entitlements, beyond AFDC, that cover almost all members of society. Welfare includes every benefit that government provides for its citizens. A broad definition of welfare could include tax shelters, public transportation, health care, public education, and Social Security. Titmuss (1965) described three systems of welfare: social welfare provides limited financial and in-kind benefits; fiscal welfare increases the income of individuals and businesses by taking less in taxes or fees; occupational welfare results from one's employment status and may be in the form of cash or in-kind benefits. In effect, we are all on welfare, but social welfare is the system that is most targeted, vilified, and exposed to tinkering. Within social welfare, financial assistance to the nonworking poor is most disfavored by politicians, the media, and citizens.

When the discussion centers on the magnitude of welfare spending, it usually focuses on a range of programs including Social Security and medical care. When the policy debate centers on economic self-sufficiency, it usually focuses on the smaller income maintenance programs (Segal, 1997). Once a term referring to human well-being, *welfare* is now universally held to be a pejorative term for public largesse for undeserving people (Lynn, 1996). This distortion has crept into everyday political discourse despite the assertion in the U.S. Constitution that the very purpose of government includes providing for the "general welfare."

Every human society faces the dilemma of coping with people who cannot support themselves. In modern societies, there are groups of needy citizens whom the government must assist to ensure their survival and, at the same time, to prevent the effects of poverty from creating broader harm in the society at large. For this reason, most Western nations have instituted systems of income, health, and education benefits that maintain the poor at varying levels at or above subsistence. Throughout history, however, the acceptance of such a social obligation has been consistently and passionately disputed (Withorn, 1996). Welfare has never been popular, and its recipients have been the persistent targets of legislative efforts attempting to control behavior and reduce costs. Welfare unpopularity climaxed in the 1990s.

In 1988, Congress passed the Family Support Act, which sought to balance providing support with fostering personal responsibility. This law marked the emergence of a bipartisan consensus among federal legislators that welfare programs had helped to create dependency and had failed to move recipients from welfare to work. The Family Support Act created the Job Opportunities and Basic Skills (JOBS) program. JOBS required participants to find work or be subject to sanctions, and it required states to move designated percentages of recipients off welfare and into work. Congress provided support for recipients' work efforts by funding education and training, child care, transportation, and health care. But neither Congress nor the states allocated adequate funds to support the work requirements. Consequently, in 1992, only 6 percent of adult AFDC recipients nationwide participated in more than twenty hours of work activities per week (Nice & Trubek, 1997).

As both the poverty rate and the number of people living below the poverty line climbed during the early 1990s, frustration with the welfare system increased. After some difficult negotiations with Congress, President Bill Clinton signed the Personal Responsibility and Work Opportunity Act (PRWOA) in August 1996. The new law dismantled AFDC and gives states unprecedented flexibility in designing their own welfare programs. The result constitutes a major shift in welfare policy.

The political groups that were largely responsible for passage of PRWOA were pleased at the overhaul of the welfare system and the opportunity to implement their ideology of personal responsibility. Social workers, critical of the harmful effects of the existing welfare system, feared that the new law could lead to the progressive deterioration of the weakest and most vulnerable members of society—children, elderly, handicapped, and mentally ill. Nevertheless, there was grudging political support from the Democrats and many of their supporters, and this law was seen as the best compromise that could be attained in a Republican-dominated Congress.

PROVISIONS OF THE PERSONAL RESPONSIBILITY AND WORK OPPORTUNITY ACT

PRWOA ends the federal guarantee of cash assistance. Each state receives a lump sum of federal money to run its own welfare and work programs. The social services block grant from the federal government is reduced by 15 percent. States must maintain their own spending on welfare at 75 percent of the 1994 level—or 80 percent if they fail to put sufficient numbers of welfare recipients to work. States that do not meet goals for the employment of welfare recipients lose part of their welfare block grants. The penalty rises from 5 percent in the first year to 21 percent in the ninth year. States may not penalize a woman on welfare who does not work because she cannot find day care for a child under 6 years old. They may pay additional benefits to cover children born to women already on welfare. They must provide Medicaid for anyone who would qualify for welfare under the current law.

A number of controversial provisions in the law have created moral dilemmas for public welfare officials and practitioners:

- The head of every family on welfare must work within two years; otherwise, the family will lose benefits. Some states have a shorter time period. After receiving welfare for two months, adults must perform community service unless they have found regular jobs. States may choose not to have a community service requirement.
- Lifetime welfare benefits are limited to five years. Twenty percent of families may be exempted because of hardship.
- States may provide payments to unmarried teenage parents only if a mother under 18 stays in school and lives with an adult or in other appropriate living arrangements.
- Future legal immigrants who do not become citizens will be ineligible for most federal benefits and social services during their first five years

in the United States. Supplemental Security Income (SSI) and food stamps will end for noncitizens now receiving benefits. States have the option of providing or denying Medicaid for noncitizens already in this country.

- Stricter eligibility standards will exclude many disabled children in low-income families seeking Supplemental Security Income.
- A woman who refuses to cooperate in identifying the father of her child will lose at least 25 percent of her benefits (Proposals for Welfare, 1996).

Welfare is no longer an entitlement, a right; instead, recipients must give something in exchange for benefits. Actually, this exchange relationship was always manifest in public assistance programs: in return for benefits, recipients gave a loss of privacy and were stigmatized. The major shift in welfare policy is the obligation to work in exchange for benefits, an obligation more or less blind to the individual problems or life situations of welfare recipients.

Earlier welfare programs' focus on helping individuals and families through income supports to stabilize their lives and on facilitating their participation in the labor market has been narrowed to a punitive preoccupation with their work habits and family life. PRWOA requires recipients to work, and if they fail to become self-sufficient within a specified period of time, they will be denied assistance. In addition, at least nineteen states have implemented family caps, which deny additional benefits to welfare mothers who bear additional children. The fundamental policy change is the transfer of many federal welfare responsibilities to states in the form of block grants, even as the federal government still retains control over eligibility requirements through work requirements. As a result, much of the burden of welfare falls to states and communities (Poole, 1996). Concomitantly, states have the right to impose their own brand of morality on the law.

MORAL PERSPECTIVES

As explained in Chapter 4, morality is the assessment of conduct in general on the basis of social norms, without regard to specific people in interpersonal relationships. (See Chapter 4.) Throughout the history of welfare and welfare reform in the United States, a central sticking point in the debate about public assistance has been the moral dimension—the morality of welfare recipients themselves and the morality of providing assistance at levels significantly lower than the need. With the passage of PRWOA, the morality of the welfare law itself has received heightened attention. The morality of welfare clients is questioned by the political right; the morality of the welfare law is questioned by the social welfare community.

TABLE 8.1   Classification of Conflicting Values toward Welfare Clients

Parties to the Conflict	Preferred Conceptions of People	Preferred Outcomes for People	Preferred Instrumentalities in Working with People
Political right	Dependent, lazy, promiscuous, irresponsible, bearing illegitimate children, not capable of disciplining children; a drain on the treasury; the locus of the problem and the solution	Independence, taking responsibility, employment, reduction of illegitimacy, marriage	Block grants to states, time-limited benefits, obligation to work, employment programs, no entitlement to welfare, limited training options, deprivation of benefits for nonconforming behavior in critical aspects of life, family cap policy
Social work/ Social welfare	Endowed with human dignity and a capacity for change; victims of repressive economic and social system and of discrimination and racism; capable of supporting and raising children in families; forced into dependency because of inadequacies within the labor market	Independence, responsible parenthood, employment, self-sufficiency, enhanced self-esteem, stable adult relationships, integration into society, attainment of higher levels of schooling as a basis for making a living	*Micro:* Respect, sensitivity, nonjudgmental attitudes, nondiscrimination, advocacy *Macro:* Access to assistance for which there is eligibility; policies and programs to lift women and children out of poverty; ways of providing safe, supportive environments

The conflict between the political right and the social welfare community arises from diametrically opposed views of welfare recipients. Table 8.1 summarizes the conflicting views of welfare clients taken by the political right and by the social work and social welfare community. The conflict reflects the ambiguity felt by most Americans, who are torn between their belief in self-sufficiency and their belief in the need to be compassionate. Client values are not represented in the table because, in this model of analysis, they are the object of the parties' values.

THE POLITICAL RIGHT ON THE MORALITY OF WELFARE RECIPIENTS

The attitudes of the political right toward welfare policy and the welfare system are colored by the way it prefers to view the morality of welfare recipients.

Preferred Conceptions

The political right's preferred conceptions of welfare recipients are best summed up in its own words:

> Isn't it time for the government to encourage work rather than re-warding dependency? The Great Society has had the unintended consequence of snaring millions of Americans into the welfare trap. Government programs designed to give a helping hand to the neediest of Americans have instead bred illegitimacy, crime, illiteracy, and more poverty. (Personal Responsibility Act of 1995, p. 65)

Welfare clients are deemed to be immoral because they are dependent and lazy and do not take personal responsibility for their lives. They contribute to the high rates of crime, illegitimacy, and poverty and are a drain on the federal treasury. The causative factors are the unintended consequences of government programs that encourage dependency and lack of initiative. The noble intentions of the welfare system of the past are viewed not only as failing but also as worsening the problems of poverty and dependency.

Murray (1984), a leading spokesperson of the right, posited the premise that humans respond rationally to economic incentives. The welfare state, he said, has provided exactly the wrong incentives to the poor and the underclass by rewarding nonwork, family dissolution, and out-of-wedlock births. If the economic supports (that is, AFDC) that enable poor single mothers to support additional children are removed, they eventually will abstain from sex, use birth control, or have abortions. The message that should be conveyed to these mothers from their earliest years is that having a baby without a husband entails awful consequences. "If this is not done, the mere existence of a welfare system will create an economic incentive to have children, or will reduce the economic penalty for having one" (Murray, 1984, p. 162).

This viewpoint suggests that the system that intended to address the problem of poverty instead became the problem itself. From the perspective of the political right, welfare was originally created to provide temporary assistance to tide over families undergoing a crisis such as the loss or dis-ability of the breadwinner. Instead, it fostered long-term dependency and fueled a "culture of poverty." The political right's negative preferred con-ceptions of welfare recipients suggest certain preferred outcomes.

Preferred Outcomes

The political right claims that its policy "will change this destructive social behavior by requiring welfare recipients to take personal responsibility for the decisions they make" (Personal Responsibility Act of 1995, p. 65).

The preferred outcome equates personal responsibility with economic independence.

Ellwood (1988) maintains that the political right's preferred outcomes represent core American values and that income support, especially AFDC and general assistance programs, conflict with those values, which include individual autonomy, the virtue of work, the primacy of the family, and the desire for community. Social policy, he believes, must come closer to these American ideals, which hold that people who meet reasonable social responsibilities will be able to achieve at least a modest level of dignity and security.

Preferred Instrumentalities

The political right's preferred instrumentalities in the form of programs and policies are contained in the welfare law. For example, as indicated in Table 8.1, supporters of PRWOA argue that welfare benefits should be time-limited. They predict that cutting off welfare benefits will motivate recipients to seek work and retain jobs.

Another of the preferred instrumentalities is to give states the option of denying assistance to teenage parents if they are not living at home or in an approved, adult-supervised setting. Assistance could also be denied to children whose mothers fail to establish paternity. There is no provision in the PRWOA for federal regulation of the family cap policy (denying assistance to an additional child born after a child has already gone on AFDC). Instead, states have complete flexibility to set policy, and nineteen states have denied assistance to additional children.

In sum, the values of the political right reflect a conservative ideology in favor of states' rights and a diminished federal role in, and responsibility for, human welfare. The political right's abiding belief in individual responsibility, the work ethic, and marriage and family appears to devalue and question the morality of individuals and groups who do not fit this picture. The welfare law reflects this ideology and this preferred conception of welfare recipients.

THE IDEOLOGY AND VALUES OF THE SOCIAL WORK COMMUNITY

The Social Work Community's Response to Welfare Reform

The social work community's own value orientation and ideology have stimulated some critical responses to the welfare law. Mills (1966) argues that the labels associated with AFDC recipients serve as political tools that the political right uses to promote a regressive welfare reform system. He deconstructs those labels, exposing them as signs of prejudice, and reinterprets them into a new paradigm.

According to Mills, welfare dependence was a social and economic category in preindustrial society but has become a moral and psychological category in postindustrial society. When the federal policy to support single women with children was first instituted as part of the Social Security Act, the purpose was to allow women to stay at home and raise their children. Aid to Dependent Children (ADC) discouraged the participation of women in the labor force by reducing the working recipient's grant. Raising children was seen as an important social responsibility (Withorn, 1996). Proper motherhood and control of women's sexuality—not self-sufficiency—were the original goals of the welfare system. Dependence now carries a stigma. Welfare recipients are perceived as lazy women exhibiting deviant behavior, and welfare itself is blamed for these perceived deviancies (Aaronson & Hartmann, 1996).

Mills (1996) also deconstructs the stigma of illegitimacy. There is no empirical evidence that the availability of welfare is a significant motivation to have children (Schur, 1988). There is also no evidence to support the assumption that cutting off benefits will restore a sense of responsibility. Higher welfare grants are not correlated with any increase in fertility.

Commenting on Ellwood's (1988) contention that the conservatives' preferred outcomes for welfare recipients represent core American values, Withorn (1996) argues that the facts belie the ideals. Ellwood underplayed race, class, gender, and ethnicity as dominant factors that determine access to the economic benefits of the society. "He ignored the powerful interference of sexism, racism, and classism" (Withorn, 1996, p. 502).

The political right's preferred outcomes for welfare clients are based on the assumptions that schooling is accessible, that employment that pays a living wage is available, that keeping a job is within the control of each person, and that marriage and family planning are accessible and desirable to all (Segal, 1997). And, the political right would say, if people do not avail themselves of these opportunities, they have only themselves to blame, and they are deficient in character. These assumptions, however, are not based in reality.

Perhaps the major proximate preferred outcome of the welfare law is gainful employment. It is a noble goal, but to achieve it, participants must have the opportunity to be educated and trained for decent-paying jobs. Women who need assistance in obtaining day care in order to work must receive it, and adequate health care must be provided (Segal, 1997). Non-discrimination on the basis of gender and ethnicity must be maintained, and low-cost transportation must make access to job sites feasible. These prerequisites are not in place at this time.

A major conservative preferred instrumentality is to cut off welfare benefits to induce single mothers to seek jobs. The pressure on single mothers to work requires that they balance the role of provider and nurturer. Many welfare recipients, however, do not need an incentive to work. Many worked prior to reaching their current destitute state, and others do not use welfare for long. Many cycle in and out of the work force as jobs fail to pay enough and day care falls through. Many face multiple barriers to employment and will require long-term support. There is an unrealistic assumption that all single mothers with children can work full-time. If, among married women with preschool children, 40 percent are out of the labor force; and if, of women who work, only two out of three work full-time, it is difficult to find a rationale or hold the expectation that low-income single mothers will behave much differently (Ozawa, 1994).

Another preferred instrumentality of the political right is the family cap policy, which states may elect to institute. The family cap, however, will fail because research has shown that welfare benefits have no impact on women's marital and childbearing behavior. A study by Ozawa (1994) showed no relationship between the birthrate of unmarried women 15 to 19 years old and the level of AFDC payments.

The social work community has opposed the new welfare law because the profession identifies with a humanitarian philosophy and the belief that government can provide a safety net to prevent its most vulnerable citizens from destitution. Social workers do not condone all clients' behavior, but they do not condemn welfare clients as immoral because a nonjudgmental attitude is one of the hallmarks of the profession. Social workers, in general, believe that welfare clients are victims of failures and gaps in the social and economic system and should not be blamed for their situations. For social workers, the issue is not the morality of welfare recipients but the morality of the welfare law itself and the adequacy of means afforded to welfare recipients to reduce their dependency.

The Morality of the Welfare Law

As the political right questions the morality of welfare clients, many social workers are questioning the morality of the welfare law. The decision to eliminate the federal guarantee of aid to poor families and children raises moral issues about how a society with ample resources treats its most vulnerable citizens. Traditionally, most societies have felt a moral responsibility to provide for their most vulnerable members. In varying degrees, most societies have faced the problems of poverty, joblessness, physical and mental illness, disabilities, single-parent families, abandonment, and abuse, and governments tried to deal with the problems because citizens felt some responsibility to protect those who could not protect themselves. Now, in the United States, because the system designed to protect the most vulnerable citizens did not work well, responsibility for their welfare seems to have evaporated.

Reforms contained in the new welfare law can be expected to thrust many of these families further into poverty and are not likely to empower them by liberating them from welfare dependence. Rather, according to a recent Urban Institute study, the new welfare reforms may push 2.6 million more people, including 1.1 million children, into poverty (as cited in Aaronson & Hartmann, 1996). Under the rubric of welfare reform, we are creating a society that condemns to poverty, punishment, and isolation anyone found guilty of not playing by the rules—from legal immigrants who see their American dream fade away, to people who have disabilities, to those who cannot keep a job (Withorn, 1996).

The survival of a safety net of income supports and of the women who need assistance requires the social work community's retaking of the high moral ground (Withorn, 1996). The members of this community must affirm an array of values concerning the way they view welfare recipients, what they want for them, and how they work with them. The same holds true for values about the government's role in welfare. These values, listed in Table 8.1, represent what social workers believe to be right and moral and provide an alternative to the social policies and programs of the political right.

Preferred Conceptions

Social workers prefer to view welfare recipients as individuals possessing dignity and the ability to change. They believe that people who are poor and are members of minority groups have been wronged by a social and economic system that discriminates against them and by welfare policies designed to keep recipients below the poverty line. Social workers believe that the fault lies not with the clients but with the way in which the system has maintained and perpetuated welfare dependency. The professional view is that clients want to get off the dole and are capable of doing so. In the words of one among many welfare recipients:

> Two years ago, my husband and I were making $50,000 a year. We both lost our jobs. The people that live here (in a welfare motel) a lot of them are not here because they're lazy, because they have drug problems, or any of that. But that's the general consensus I get and how I'm treated. But, I'm educated.
>
> They (potential employers) tell me I don't look like a welfare recipient. How am I supposed to look? Am I supposed to fit into that stereo-

type that you have, that we're shiftless, we're lazy, we're drug-oriented, we don't care about our children, and all of that? I think that if more people were involved with us, they would begin to understand. (Swigonski, 1996, p. 97)

Social workers see most poor people as moral, as desirous of extricating themselves from poverty, and as having the capacity to do so with the proper assistance.

Preferred Outcomes
Social workers' preferred goals for services to welfare clients are to facilitate their ability to extricate themselves from poverty and become economically self-sufficient, to be responsible parents and maintain stable adult relationships, to gain self-esteem, to become integrated into mainstream society, and to take responsibility for their lives. These preferred outcomes are uncannily similar to those of the political right; the difference lies in the means, the preferred instrumentalities.

The political right starts with a punitive attitude, believing that welfare recipients need to be punished for immoral behavior. Hence, its instrumentalities are critical, punitive policies that attempt to downplay society's responsibility for the welfare of its citizens. In contrast, social workers approach the clientele with a high degree of respect and sensitivity. The welfare recipient, in the view of the social work community, is a product of his or her society. According to this view, the long-term goals of self-sufficiency and economic independence require the prior fulfillment of such proximate goals as job finding and retention, earning adequate income, and preserving housing and family stability.

Social workers' preferred outcomes for welfare recipients parallel what they want for other clients and for all members of society and are shared by the vast majority of Americans. What is at issue is the means to achieve the desired ends.

Preferred Instrumentalities
Most social workers are not employed in public welfare. As of 1995, only 0.8 percent of social workers were working in public assistance (Gibelman & Schervish, 1997). Among the reasons offered for the lower percentage of social workers in public welfare today than in the 1960s, when they headed most welfare departments, are the increased emphasis on case management, the "look" of welfare offices, and the refusal of welfare officials to hire social workers (Gibelman, 1995).

As Table 8.1 indicates, at the micro level, where social workers are involved in public welfare or in family and children's services, working in direct practice with families on AFDC, preferred instrumentalities include showing respect and sensitivity, being nonjudgmental and nondiscriminatory, and advocating for clients. At the macro level, preferred instrumentalities include policies and programs that address welfare clients as a group. Social workers have acquired significant knowledge of the plight of welfare recipients and the impact of social policy on their lives.

Policy Recommendations

Aaronson and Hartmann (1996) offer a series of policy recommendations for enabling welfare recipients to move themselves out of poverty and become integrated into the mainstream of society: increasing the minimum wage, expanding the income and child care tax credits, reducing discrimination in the workplace, providing paid family and disability leave, expanding unemployment insurance to cover more part-time and low-earning workers, ensuring universal access to and portability of health insurance, providing quality child care to families that need it, and providing vocational and other relevant training to enter and remain in the labor force. Similarly, Withorn (1996) posits a series of expansive programs to help lift women and families out of poverty and provide safe, supportive environments for them in which to raise their families. Among Withorn's recommendations are allowing women to retain more of their assets and income from outside sources; increasing child support payments; improving housing; services to combat domestic violence; mental health, substance abuse and job programs; and sheltered workshops.

A major problem with these "shopping lists" is their cost and funding. In the current fiscal climate, many of these expensive programs will not be well received by taxpayers intent on cutting costs and by the federal government. Private funding efforts may provide some relief but are bound to fall short because of the enormity of the expense. Solutions to self-sufficiency must be sought in areas other than government largesse, such as self-help and advocacy/empowerment approaches. Social workers need to provide evidence about what works, to consider what is politically feasible and what is cost-effective.

In sum, the values of social workers include viewing people as having dignity and a capacity for change and wanting a secure way of life based on job and income consistency, family stability, and the self-esteem that accompanies a productive life. Social workers believe that government policies should reflect these preferred conceptions of and outcomes for vulnerable people. Even though social workers are not generally employed in public welfare, they still need to advocate for clients who have fallen through the cracks to help restore their dignity and independence.

MORAL DILEMMAS

While ideological conflicts between the political right and the social welfare community persist over the morality of welfare recipients and the welfare law, moral dilemmas face the state legislators, administrators, and practitioners charged with carrying out the provisions of the welfare law. For a dilemma to be moral rather than ethical, it must focus not on the specific relationship between the professional and the client but on values and behavior that reflect social norms.

Dilemmas Facing State Legislators

Legislators face moral dilemmas as they assume the responsibilities thrust on them by the federal government. As beneficiaries of federal block grants, states must now allocate funds to needy individuals and families. Moral dilemmas arise when legislators have to decide where and to whom to allocate the limited funds. The funds become even more limited when states use federal welfare funding windfalls to defray general budgetary costs. Decisions about priority funding are fraught with value conflicts.

The basic dilemma is whether to allocate the funds to promote self-sufficiency or to raise the basic level of assistance. Promoting self-sufficiency—encouraging people to get jobs—means providing funds for day care and transportation, incentives to employers to hire workers, and disregarding income limits for employed welfare recipients. Raising the basic level of assistance means increasing the basic grant for food, clothing, and rent. The choice is not either/or but balancing these two options. If more is allocated to promote self-sufficiency, then less is available for increasing the basic grant, and vice versa.

The welfare law (PRWOA) has been designed to ensure, during the early years, that most states enjoy a surplus over previous years in their federal grant for public assistance. The dilemma for legislators is how to allocate these surplus funds. Furthermore, when inflation erodes the value of the basic grant, will states divert funds from other sources to maintain recipients' already low standard of living? Because the federal block grant is capped, states that wanted to distribute more would have to draw from their general revenues. The welfare sector of the budget would have to compete with other state priorities. Promoting self-sufficiency and increasing the basic grant are formidable values competing for legislators' moral integrity.

Dilemmas Facing Administrators and Practitioners

A pervasive moral dilemma facing administrators and practitioners in public welfare agencies is whether to adhere to rules and regulations that might result in denial of benefits, or to bend or circumvent the rules in order to meet the desperate needs of clients. This dilemma can also be represented as adhering to a policy of "less eligibility" versus recognizing that the level of benefits is below the poverty line even for people eligible for financial aid.

- The client misses by one day the deadline for submitting an application for benefits. Should the practitioner put down today's or yesterday's date on the form?
- The client, who has four children, earns $10 a week over the amount that makes her eligible for day care. If she becomes ineligible for day care, she could lose her job and be back on welfare. Should the worker report the $10 or advocate for an exception to policy?
- The client is working off the books and is earning more than the welfare law allows. Should the worker report or overlook the infraction?

Individually, each case presents an ethical dilemma because it involves a conflict of values for the practitioner in relation to a specific client. Taken together, however, the cases present moral dilemmas based on two conflicting values.

In the desire to promote bureaucratic efficiency, society advocates that agency rules are to be adhered to for maintaining order and achieving efficiency. Neither society nor particular institutions can long exist if their rules, regulations, and laws are not followed. In the welfare framework, these rules regulate the behavior of millions of people who lack the power and initiative to change them. Flexibility by welfare officials and practitioners in implementing the rules can go a long way toward meeting basic needs for food, clothing, and shelter. The moral dilemma is between adherence to rules and sensitivity to the needs of people who may overstep or evade them. The dilemma can be characterized, on a macro level, as the classic conflict between bureaucratic and professional values. The resolution of the moral dilemma can take three forms.

At one extreme, the practitioner identifies with the agency and applies the law or regulation in the strictest possible way without regard to the suffering it may cause. The defense of this mode of action is that one is ordered to obey the law, to follow the rules. This mentality in the extreme is akin to that of Nazi bureaucrats who sent millions of people to their deaths during World War II while claiming that they were following orders. Following orders or obeying rules at the expense of distraught and suffering clients represents a displacement of goals. The goals of the agency—to serve clients and to help them move toward self-sufficiency—are displaced, and following the rules becomes an end in itself. This action reflects a typical bureaucratic orientation, whose characteristics include identification with, and unconditional loyalty to, the organization, acceptance of the goals and activities of the organization, and career aspirations within the organization. The bureaucrat's reference group is the organization.

At the other extreme, the practitioner identifies with the client and disregards the rules. The professional is "a person who by virtue of long training is qualified to perform specialized activities autonomously—relatively free from external supervision and regulation" (Scott, cited in Gibelman, 1978, p. 2). The professional's primary identification is with the profession. The lines of authority and accountability in the bureaucracy, which represent control, are generally incongruent with the standards of the profession, which represent freedom. Although identifying with the client and disregarding the rules shows compassion and empathy for the client's dire situation, it undermines the agency's bureaucratic structure and authority. No agency can long endure if its rules are disregarded.

In the middle position, the practitioner is involved in a constant moral struggle because he or she identifies with the agency and its social purposes and also with the welfare clients and their needs. Several options are available:

- The practitioner will look for ways to bend the rules, to gain exceptions to policy, and to advocate for agency flexibility toward client need. This presupposes the practitioner's acquiring a thorough knowledge and understanding of the rules, which may contain exceptions or loopholes that are applicable.
- The practitioner also seeks to equip the client with knowledge to appeal an unjust rule while a grant continues. This could include the right to hire an attorney or bring along a knowledgeable friend to represent the client in litigation. It is an effort to empower the client to take charge of his or her own life as much as possible.
- The practitioner could also involve other agencies and organizations in an effort to bring about policy changes on behalf of clients or to meet client needs.

The resolution of the moral dilemma is contingent on the practitioner's priorities in identification and values. A practitioner who identifies with the agency is not likely to have a dilemma, because his or her primary value is adherence to agency rules; hence, clients' violation of rules will negatively affect their eligibility for services. A practitioner who identifies with clients maintains client welfare as a primary value and believes that agency rules should serve client interests and not agency interests; hence, clients' violation of agency rules will not automatically affect their eligibility for services.

Administrators and practitioners who identify both with the agency and with the clients are involved in a moral struggle of conflicting values: promoting agency purpose and promoting client welfare. Decisions in favor of the agency can cut off needed benefits; decisions in favor of clients can threaten agency stability. To resolve the moral dilemma, the administrator or practitioner seeks ways to empower clients, advocates with superiors on their behalf, reinterprets rules, and finds exceptions to policy. With this approach, the administrator or practitioner gains satisfaction in seeking ways to compromise and legitimate the claims of the agency and of the clients.

CONCLUSION

Welfare reform is a very emotional and complex issue in the United States, though welfare consumes only 1 percent of the federal budget. Welfare reform goes to the heart of the basic American values of individualism, the work ethic, and family stability. When pockets of Americans who share these values are prevented from translating them into their lives and, instead, become dependent on the benevolence of others for basic needs, their dependency evokes conflicting assignments of blame. Whose fault is it that millions of Americans cannot succeed on their own? Conflicting answers have been expressed in the ideologies and values of the political right and the social welfare community.

In recent years, there has been a general consensus in the society and among social workers that the previous welfare system did not work as intended in weaning people off welfare. Social workers' ideas about changing the system have not been sufficiently persuasive. Now, a new law is in place that has revolutionized the system, received universal condemnation from the social work community, and gives rise to the prediction of dire consequences for the welfare and immigrant population. The results are not yet in regarding these consequences, although a lack of food and the demands of food pantries have strained the food distribution systems in many cities (Swarns, 1997).

The passage of the PRWOA means that social workers must work harder to renew their commitment to improve the lives of those who have been hurt by the social structure. There is an urgent need to try to change society's preferred conceptions of welfare clients. Persons with low or no incomes are not lazy and ungrateful but, in many instances, exhausted and brutalized. Their struggle for empowerment and liberation from their conditions coincides with social workers' preferred outcomes for them. The two most-preferred instrumentalities in empowering welfare clients are compassion and justice. Compassion means to suffer with clients as human beings in feelings and action. It calls for the elimination of the stigmatization of welfare recipients; support for young mothers, the elderly, and the disabled; and resources to acquire food, clothing, shelter, and health care with dignity. Justice requires that ways be found to create enough jobs to protect workers from exploitation and to reduce the inequalities perpetuated by classism, racism, and sexism (Swigonski, 1996).

To chart the nascent effects of U.S. welfare policy is to "glimpse the American soul, its caring and its callousness, its fairness and its biases, its competence and its neglect" (DeParle, 1997, p. A1). What is taking shape is not just a new program but a nation's definition of itself. If welfare changed in head-spinning ways, the problems of most poor, single mothers did not. "With welfare and without it, the familiar struggles remained: families in poverty and children without fathers. In the end, it might prove easier than anyone imagined to change welfare, and even harder to change people's lives" (DeParle, 1997, p. A16).

This chapter is devoted to people who lack power and the controversies that swirl around them. The next chapter, on managed care, is devoted to power plays among managed-care companies, social workers, and clients. Ethical dilemmas confront social workers who are caught between the policies of the health care companies and the needs of their clients in a chaotic and rapidly changing health care system.

9

MANAGED CARE

Managed care has brought about major changes in the financing and delivering of social services. It has affected most social workers, social agencies, and clients and has created significant moral and ethical dilemmas for social workers. This chapter is divided into two major sections. The first presents an overview of some of the characteristics and functions of managed care. The second analyzes ethical issues raised by managed care in social work practice.

CHARACTERISTICS AND FUNCTIONS OF MANAGED CARE

The term *managed care* refers to a broad and constantly changing array of health insurance and payment programs that seek to contain costs and to ensure the quality of physical and mental health services. Under managed care, decisions regarding reimbursement are transferred from patients and providers to third parties whose presumed incentive is to enhance the delivery of services in cost-effective ways. The central dynamic of managed care involves a significant realignment of power away from medical and other care providers and toward managerial and financial professionals. These new "gatekeepers" decide how, when, and under what circumstances care is to be provided.

The impetus for health care reform in the United States derives from two primary sources: lack of universal coverage and excessive rates of health care spending. Because of public resistance to governmental control of health care, the United States has opted, by failing to enact public policy, for a private market solution in the form of managed care. Managed care appears in many different forms, but its central feature is that someone is "managing the care"—that is, taking an overview (*Ethical Currents*, 1996).

Managed-care organizations are not, in and of themselves, moral or immoral, good or bad. They are neither beneficent nor evil. The way in which they are administered and funded and their effect on clients are the focus of our concern. Managed care is based on the idea that centralizing and coordinating services for patients allows fairer distribution of resources, better preventive care, greater efficiency, more access to primary-care physicians, and more coordination of care between physicians. Although these are desirable goals, the suspicion of most educated laypeople is that the goal of most managed-care organizations is to maximize profits (Wolpe, 1996).

Managed care is changing the health care system in the United States in fundamental ways. It is refashioning the traditional relationships between social worker and client, and social workers' relation to agencies and communities. For social workers in health and mental health settings, the rise of managed care represents the triumph of financial concerns over practically all other considerations. It is not a triumph of which social workers are proud.

Controlling Costs

The need to control the costs of health and mental health services is responsible for much of managed care's prevalence and is a result of three factors: the availability of third-party reimbursement, which insulates the service provider and client from direct concern with the mounting costs of these services; the expansion of private insurance to include mental health services and substance abuse treatment; and the development of new technology. The escalation of health care costs, principally because of the availability of new technology, has far outpaced cost increases in other sectors of the economy and is consuming a growing proportion of the gross national product. This means that less money is available for other goods and services desired and needed by society, ranging from national defense to air purification.

A basic premise of managed care is that costs are more likely to be contained when there is a centralized authority to oversee the service delivery system. One of the most widespread funding control mechanisms is capitation. Instead of reimbursement for each service that is provided, capitation provides a specified and limited lump sum of money to cover whatever services may be required. Capitation-financed programs try to control costs by providing services at a reduced rate and contracting only with providers who agree to deliver the services at that lower cost. Capitation may also control costs by restricting services to conditions that are deemed clinically necessary to treat (Corcoran, 1997). Clinical necessity, however, may not always have a clear definition.

Probably the most common procedures for controlling services and therefore controlling costs are found in utilization reviews. Utilization reviews are designed to determine the medical necessity for treatment and whether the services are covered under the managed-care contract. The control of costs has been instrumental in the loss of 400 emergency departments in hospitals since 1992, mostly in inner cities and rural communities. Managed care has determined where people get emergency care, how much treatment they get, what services hospitals provide, and how services are paid for (Kilborn, 1997).

Medicare and Medicaid Managed Care

The motive for introducing managed care into Medicare and Medicaid—the United States' two largest health plans—has been to control costs. The number of enrollees in these two programs has been increasing with every passing year (Welch, cited in Corcoran, 1997). Among other cities, New York City has developed a plan to move its Medicaid recipients into managed care (*Medicaid Managed Care*, 1997).

Many aspects of managed care and its role in Medicare and Medicaid are of concern to social workers. The rate of increase of enrollment in managed-care arrangements is staggering and is likely to continue to grow. It is difficult to say exactly how the continuing changes in managed care in Medicare and Medicaid will affect the social work profession because there is such variability among and within states. In light of the increased enrollment and anticipated savings, the increase of managed-care arrangements in Medicare and Medicaid could provide additional resources for distribution to other needy members of society "in an effort to promote an agenda of social justice and access to resources, a role ideally designed for social work involvement" (Corcoran, 1997, p. 196). However, the converse effect may also result: the savings may be allocated to the politically attractive goal of tax reductions or be allocated to meet needs defined by politically powerful groups. We simply do not yet know, though the overriding preoccupation with cost containment does not paint an optimistic picture.

Conflict in Mission

In the view of social workers, mental health care is becoming increasingly "corporatized" (Wineburgh, 1997) through the introduction of incentives and mechanisms for reducing costs and managing care. This "corporatization" of managed mental health care is manifest in the conflicting missions of social agencies.

Social workers need to be aware of the fundamental differences in mission between managed-care companies and themselves as providers and the effect of these differences on the treatment of clients. Because managed-care companies primarily serve the funding bodies, their purpose differs from that of social work agencies. They are concerned with controlling capitated risk for groups of people, and therefore any individual's particular need is evaluated in the context of all others' needs. Thus, managed-care companies use gatekeepers to examine intimate details about a person from a distance, and the gatekeeper may use that information to deny rather than to provide needed services. In contrast, social workers' general aim is to work with all who request and need services. *"With managed care the mission is restrictive and generalized, whereas with social workers, service delivery is inclusive and individualized"* (italics added) (Davidson & Davidson, 1996).

Managed health and mental health care represents a highly individual-oriented strategy embraced by lawyers, politicians, and insurance companies that is being imposed on the community of health and mental health providers—social workers, physicians, psychiatrists, nurses, psychologists, and others. The managed-care practice model is at the opposite end of the communitarian spectrum and the systems approaches with which most social workers are familiar. It recognizes only individuals—providers and consumers, formerly known as social workers and clients—and the corporations and partnerships that employ them. It allows no place for social systems such as families, agencies, or communities. In its drive to improve the bottom-line cost of public health and mental health care in the United States, managed care appears to disregard the social cost in lives, pain, and suffering or any other nonfiscal or long-term health consideration. Managed care is the latest in a growing list of signs that, in the long struggle of professions to control health care bureaucracies, others are seizing control in order to advance their own interests at the expense of the professions and health care consumers.

The traditional conflict between profession and bureaucracy has been translated in the managed-care environment as a conflict between two cultures: the professional and the commercial.

> The fundamental act of professional medical care is the assumption of responsibility for patients' welfare—an unwritten contract assured by a few words, a handshake, eye contact denoting mutual understanding or acknowledgment by the physician that "We will take care of you." The essential image of the professional is that of a practitioner who values the patient's welfare above his or her own and provides service even at a fiscal loss and despite physical discomfort or inconvenience. There is no outside invested capital seeking returns from the physician's work.

The fundamental objective of commerce in providing medical care is achieving an excess of revenue over costs while caring for the sick, ensuring profit for corporate providers, investors or insurers. A central feature in enhancing net of income over expense in a competitive market is a reduction in volume or quality of services so as to reduce costs, while maintaining prices to the purchaser. While cost reductions often diminish the quality of services, such economies are not always passed along to the public as lowered prices. (McArthur & Moore, 1997, pp. 985–986)

The culture of medicine is similar to the culture of social work. Social workers operate from a set of core values that include "service, social justice, dignity and worth of the person, importance of human relationships, integrity and competence" (NASW, 1996, p. 5). There appears to be an intrinsic conflict between the values of social workers and the goals of managed-care organizations. For-profit organizations acquire their organizational raison-d'être from the pursuit of profit, whereas nonprofit organizations get theirs from the pursuit of a mission that binds the agency's personnel, supporters, and beneficiaries together in a common purpose (Salamon, cited in Gibelman & Whiting, 1997). It is not insignificant that the largest proportion of social workers are employed in the nonprofit sector (Gibelman & Schervish, 1997).

Romirowsky (1997) refers to a similar dichotomy in the mission of social agencies. Managed care has reinforced the businesslike orientation of social service agencies. There is a strong suspicion among directors of mental health agencies that their organizations will be unable to continue providing services based solely on their social welfare mission. Many mental health agencies that provide counseling may wither away while trying to preserve their original missions, seeing their revenue shrink to insignificant numbers. The shift to becoming dollar driven rather than mission driven has perilous consequences, especially for the ethical stance that social agencies have taken over the years. Social workers tend to work within agency-based practices because they feel they are making a difference, tackling multiproblem cases with the appropriate clinical and financial resources, regardless of the client's ability to pay for services. The agency's conflict between its social work mission and its businesslike mission could be immobilizing. It threatens the very existence of the traditional social work agency.

Impact on the Role of Social Workers in Health Care

"The market-driven, competitive, managed care environment further underscores the need for social work to clearly define its role and function"

(Hendricks, 1997, p. 2). This need has become more urgent because the profession is becoming delegitimated and deprofessionalized in hospitals. In some hospitals, social workers are being replaced by utilization review specialists and nurse case managers on inpatient units. Workers with less education and skill are being trained for specific tasks in discharge planning. New positions such as "patient care associate" are being established that require minimal training (Health Care Policy and Practice Network, 1997).

One of the serious consequences of the deprofessionalization of social work in health care is the elimination of departments and jobs for social workers. The role of social workers, which predominated in the 1970s and 1980s, is rapidly disintegrating under the transformations instituted by managed care. The changes have affected two primary interests of social workers: social work services are less available to patients (consumers), and the integrity of the professional role has been compromised. "The profession must respond to the changes by attempting to restore the role of the social worker as it has been developed or create new models which fit the changing health care system" (Beallor, 1997, p. 1). It is vital that the health care system continues to employ social workers to meet the psychosocial needs of patients in order to maintain the quality of care (*Statement of Principles*, 1997). Social workers face an uphill struggle to articulate their role in a changing health care scenario and to persuade managed-care companies of the effectiveness of social work and the need for social work services to patients.

Social workers in many health care organizations are finding that they are increasingly isolated from each other as a result of the dismemberment of social work departments. Like other health care professionals, they are being required to participate in the continuing negotiations over the costs of services. Energy that they formerly devoted to direct service is being devoted to the "marketing" of the service area or organization in which they are employed.

With the integrity of their profession at stake, social workers have become convinced that they must mount aggressive challenges to the anticlient policies of managed-care companies. Such views are also suggestive of the identified needs and ultimate well-being of the consumers of services. Among the ideas that have been put forth to assist social workers to become more proactive are the following: (1) forming alliances with other professions and consumer groups to protect clients' rights and to lobby politicians; (2) advocating internally for increased decision-making power by professionals at all levels of managed-care systems; (3) documenting critical incidents that demonstrate the difficulties faced by clients and professionals because of managed-care policies, and conducting research projects in support of these claims; and (4) challenging the massive profits being made by stockholders, the huge corporate salaries, the huge administrative costs, and submitting the information to the media (Davidson, Davidson, & Weinstein, 1997).

ETHICAL DILEMMAS IN MANAGED BEHAVIORAL HEALTH CARE

This section is organized around a number of ethical issues that arise out of the relationship between managed behavioral health care companies and social workers. They include client autonomy, social worker autonomy, nonmaleficence, informed consent, confidentiality and divided loyalty.

Every social worker working in managed care or whose clients' care is governed by a managed-care organization is faced with many ethical issues. They are more difficult to resolve now than they were prior to managed care because of the addition of another party to the client–social worker–payer relationship (Corcoran & Vandiver, 1996). The introduction of a third party into the client–social worker relationship has a profound impact. "It becomes a system in which the therapeutic relationship involves three people and, as such, all of our accumulated knowledge of how to develop, understand and utilize the therapeutic alliance becomes obsolete" (Strom, 1992, p. 122). This tension affects the ways in which providers and consumers work with each other. Managed care, in effect, places an intermediary in the therapeutic relationship.

Client Autonomy

Freedom of choice is a basic American value. In health care, freedom of choice has meant that the individual has an open choice of physicians and even hospitals, and in mental health, a choice of providers and agencies. Opponents of managed care argue that it curtails patients' freedom of choice, particularly in regard to access to specialists and choice of treatment (Thomas, 1996). Treatment choice is often driven by the provider alone or in concert with the managed-care utilization reviewer. Respect for personal autonomy may be compromised through limitation of choice, which violates the ethic of self-determination (NASW, 1996, 1.02). It may also be compromised if the client is not fully informed about the parameters of care mandated by the health care plan. In promoting client autonomy, the social worker is responsible for ensuring that the client fully understands the implications of treatment under the managed-care plan.

Threats to personal autonomy that have always existed in social worker–client relationships are potentially exacerbated by the entrance of the third party because of its own agendas, which include quality assurance, utilization review, and reduced forms of treatment in order to gain an economic advantage. Managed mental health care can easily become a bureaucratic and paternalistic impediment to personal autonomy (Blum, cited in Wineburgh, 1997). Clients do not have much say about the limitations on the number of sessions allowed by their insurance plans and whether that number can be increased if necessary. Serious ethical choices abound when social workers participate in the process of silent marginalization and disenfranchisement of large numbers of people (Masters, 1996).

Gag rules, established by managed-care companies to prevent practitioners from disclosing options to their clients, have heightened distrust among the public and have created ethical conflicts for practitioners. It is a violation of the ethics of beneficence and autonomy to withhold from patients information they request or need about alternatives for care. This denial is a form of stealing (Lipkin, 1996).

Adherence to the principle of client autonomy goes beyond social worker responsibility to inform and involve clients in decision making wherever possible. It also involves client responsibility to abide by societal decisions to conserve health care and to make an individual effort to use resources wisely and lead a healthy lifestyle.

Social Worker Autonomy

Because managed care determines the modality, duration, and intensity of treatment, social workers are caught between a client-centered ethic that seeks the best care for the individual and a company-centered ethic that demands explanation, justification, and oversight in order to authorize payment for services. According to Reamer (1997), managed behavioral health care represents a shift of control for intervention from the social worker to the payer and brings about an increase in fiscal management at the expense of clinical management.

Social workers face several major changes, such as loss of professional autonomy, reduction in private practice, increased hours, and reduction of earnings. Further, as reimbursable treatment activities narrow, many essential clinical services such as school or home visits, supportive or emergency telephone contacts, and collateral interviewing are being excluded (Strom, 1992). Generally, health professionals are reporting that managed care means more work, greater stress, and less compensation.

Another limitation on social worker autonomy comes from the managed-care policy of mandating brief therapy. Phillips (1996) contends that many social workers will have to offer a treatment that they believe is against the best interests of, or not the most effective for, the client. Social workers face the dilemma of fulfilling their professional duties to the client while complying with payer regulations.

Nonmaleficence

In professional practice, oversight by managed care has created several ethical issues around the principle of nonmaleficence—do no harm. Two important areas of tension are created by denial of client care and collusion.

Denial of Care

As managed care limits the amount and extent of payments for mental health care, providers are forced to prioritize treatment choices. Doing so is particularly difficult for social workers in situations where cost containment goals are met by placing limits on the length of treatment.

What happens when the client has not improved, the presenting problem remains unresolved, and certification of further reimbursable treatment is denied? What if medication consultation is mandatory for the certification of benefits? Most social workers maintain that medication is indicated when the condition warrants its use, not as a cost containment substitute for client–social worker interaction. What is the practitioner's ethical responsibility if the client refuses medication? What if the client needs hospitalization? What about clients who are eligible only for quite limited inpatient stays and are discharged quite ill (Wineburgh, 1997)?

Many managed-care companies have developed economic incentives to discourage hospitalizations because they are the most expensive and therefore the least desirable kind of treatment (Feldman, 1992). Managed behavioral health care organizations have no referral resources for clients whose benefits have been terminated. These questions challenge the moral and ethical convictions of social workers, as they pit the meeting of clients' needs against the limits of available services. Some may resort to unethical practices by colluding with clients to make or change the diagnosis in order to avoid premature termination of benefits.

Collusion

A second consideration is the fact that some common types of nonreimbursable problems may lead social workers to choose certain diagnoses for the sole purpose of maintaining the service and keep the reimbursement flowing. In a study of social workers' deliberate misdiagnoses, Kirk and Kutchins (cited in Strom, 1992) found that

> fifty-nine percent said that Axis I diagnoses (the major mental disorders) are used for insurance purposes when clinically unwarranted. Seventy-two percent of the respondents are aware of cases where more serious diagnoses are used to qualify for reimbursement. Eighty-six percent are aware of instances when diagnoses for individuals are used even though the primary concern is the family. (p. 400)

Collusion is inherently deceptive and manipulative. Strom (1992) maintains that it corrupts not only the client–social worker relationship but ultimately the entire profession's pact with society to perform in an unbiased and ethical fashion. She offers the example of an insurance plan that recognized only the fifty-minute session, although in the therapist's judgment the client was best seen for sessions twice that long. Does the social worker accept payment for only one session, or does the social worker report that he or she is seeing the client for two short sessions rather than one? Strom concludes that "although this may be accurate according to the spirit of the law, according to the letter of the law it is probably fraud" (p. 401).

Collusion or "gaming" also affects physicians. When a physician exaggerates the seriousness of a patient's condition in the utilization review, he or she will have to record these exaggerated conditions in the patient's chart, thus jeopardizing the patient's future care as well as the physician's future actions (in terms of malpractice or negligence). Similarly, a psychiatrist who labels a patient's illness according to the most serious, best-reimbursed diagnosis may be stigmatizing the patient in other areas of the patient's life (Thomas, 1996). The long-term ethical effect on the character of physicians and on society of dishonesty in the name of beneficence is not a trivial matter (Pelligrino, 1994).

Social workers are caught in a bind. Their code of ethics is clear about their responsibility in these situations. Social workers may not abandon their clients who may need more services (NASW, 1996, 1.16b). They have an ethical duty to treat clients until the presenting problems are resolved, clients are referred or transferred, or they discontinue treatment.

Reamer (1997) asks whether social workers should provide services to clients in need even when managed-care companies refuse to authorize payment. What if clients are suicidal or pose a threat to a third party? He concludes:

> Thus, if a managed care company does not authorize continued payment for services, social workers cannot terminate services abruptly. That is not to say that social workers are obligated to continue providing services gratis. Although social workers may choose to provide some services without reimbursement (such *pro bono* actions are the mark of virtuous professionals), it should not be reasonable to expect them to do so routinely. When social workers choose to terminate services because a managed care company has elected not to pay them, they must (1) carefully assess the extent to which the client is still in need of service, (2) explain to the client the available alternatives, (3) arrange an appropriate referral. (p. 100)

All details should be carefully documented to ensure nonabandonment.

Informed Consent

Client autonomy is assumed when an individual has received sufficient information with which to make a decision. This raises the issue of informed consent in managed care. To preserve their autonomy, clients should be informed about and should understand the rules of the plan they join. The social worker needs their permission—consent—in order to disclose information about them to the managed care company (NASW, 1996, 1.03).

Informed consent is a process through which adequate information is provided to clients in order to help them make decisions about treatment. The client must be told as part of informed consent that the social worker must share information with others. The identity of the office to which the information will be given is made known. The client, on the basis of this information, must give written consent in order to ensure reimbursed coverage for the care provided.

Boyle and Callahan (1995) raise moral questions concerning clients who have impaired judgment that impedes their ability to exercise preferences for treatment. There are reasons to be extremely cautious in requiring informed consent in managed-care settings. Because managed health care shifts the responsibility for care to enrollees, there is more concern about the ability of some mentally ill clients to exercise that responsibility.

Questions arise about the extent of the social worker's responsibility to disclose to clients the reasons they must deny care to them. Thomas (1996) asks whether it is morally permissible to provide only partial disclosure to patients—that is, to recommend only those treatments that are covered through their managed-care program rather than full disclosure of all possible treatments. Clients are entitled to know the extent and limitations of their mental health benefits and treatments. Many clients know nothing about the limits of their benefits or whether they can change to other plans. An ethical issue arises when the policies of a managed behavioral care company restrict social workers' ability to act in the client's best interests and restrict information essential for informed consent (Wineburgh, 1997). The following case illustrates a social worker's sensitivity to the ethical issues in informed consent.

CASE 9.1 Informing the Client of Policy Limitations

Mr. G, a 47-year-old high school teacher, entered treatment at the urging of his wife, who complained he lacked warmth, humor, and sexual spontaneity. He himself complained of chronic low depression and easily induced feelings of shame and humiliation. From a *D.S.M. IV* perspective, he met the criteria for dysthymia and narcissistic personality disorder.

In his initial session, Mr. G stated he felt profoundly cheated out of many crucial developmental experiences by an overprotective mother and a distant father. Mr. G's mother was an ambitious woman who was deeply disappointed in her husband and in her life generally. Mr. G believed that he and his mother had an unnaturally close relationship, one that made him feel special but that was probably bad for him. He remembers that she hovered over him and left him feeling that he couldn't do anything for himself. His father was an unassuming, unambitious man who paid little attention to his son.

After my first session with Mr. G, I contacted his insurance company and was informed that I would be required to provide his case coordinator with a list of specific behavioral goals for treatment (for example, that he talk about his sexual inhibitions or steps to pursue advanced training in his field) and to provide follow-up reports every eight sessions as to whether or not the client had met those goals.

At the next session with Mr. G, I told him of his insurance company's policies. I told him I felt a good deal of concern about the degree of intrusion this requirement for goals and progress would impose on the treatment. Mr. G's response was an angry diatribe about how he felt cheated by his company for turning therapy into nontherapy. He told me I should sue the company. He stalked out and promptly forgot his next appointment.

At the next session, I told Mr. G that I felt treatment under his managed-care plan might seriously undermine his therapy. I told him that, given his history, I had grave reservations about the breach of privacy and amount of control demanded by his company. I told him the treatment might replicate his experience with a controlling, intrusive mother. I wondered what he felt we should do.

At the next session, he reported that he felt greatly reassured by my concern for the quality of his treatment, since he had wondered how committed I was to working with him. He suggested that we go on without insurance. We agreed to a reduced fee and proceeded with the treatment (Masters, 1996, pp. 8–9).

Informed consent requires that the social worker fully inform the client of the parameters of care and that the client understand the implications of the treatment under the plan. If the social worker believes that the client will receive little benefit or could be harmed by the managed-care plan, the social worker is responsible for informing the client and discussing the potential risks to the client's treatment and privacy (Masters, 1996).

Confidentiality

Informed consent is related to confidentiality. In the managed-care system, clients and social workers do not control the right to privacy and confidentiality. Managed-care companies' and government agencies' access to records also limits the control of privacy. The limitation of confidentiality is not unique to managed behavioral health care, although disclosure of mental disorders is arguably worse than disclosure of general health information because of its greater stigma (Boyle & Callahan, 1995). The technological innovations with which social workers must contend—the videotaping, answering machines, fax machines, computers, and electronic transmission of client information over telephone lines—bring social workers into closer contact with machine personnel who may possess a "machine mentality" (Munson, 1996, p. 245). These technological changes challenge social workers' values regarding confidentiality.

Social workers' efforts to maintain confidentiality are in conflict with employers who believe that they have a need and right to information about their employees' treatment. Increasingly, social workers are required to tell clients that there is no confidentiality under managed care (Munson, 1996), because it may not be possible to obtain reimbursement for treatment without some compromising of confidentiality. Clients must be informed that the managed-care utilization reviewer has the power to limit reimbursement and may, and usually does, require the release of confidential information to determine the extent of treatment. Clients find themselves compelled to sign consent forms to release information to the managed-care gatekeeper in the hope that doing so will ensure that third-party payments are made to the provider. Social workers find themselves prevailing on clients to sign these release forms, which, in effect, ends a client's right to privacy in the absence of a valid clinical reason for doing so (Davidson & Davidson, 1996). Ethically and legally, social workers must protect confidentiality unless the client has consented to do otherwise.

Boyle and Callahan (1995) contend that what is morally relevant is not whether managed mental health care plans need to know (they do), but rather how they use and protect this information. The moral obligation of managed behavioral health care is to ensure that all those who have legitimate access to the information use only that which is necessary to accomplish their work and to protect its dissemination.

Boyle and Callahan (1995) see some positive aspects to managed mental health care's attitude toward confidentiality. They point to well-recognized exceptions to the general confidentiality rule that give society a compelling reason to have access to confidential information in certain circumstances. There are social and medical reasons why reviewers for mental health care must have access to privileged information. If we adopt this view, managed mental health care should be seen as part of the confidential relationship.

Corcoran and Winslade (1994) suggest protecting patient confidentiality in four ways. First, the duty to protect confidentiality should be extended beyond the patient and the provider to include managed-care personnel. Second, managed-care organizations should develop ways to protect anonymity by limiting access to patient-identifying information and narrowing the scope of requested information. Third, patients should be informed of the extent to which information will be disclosed to the managed-care organization, and written, informed consent should be obtained regarding the release of this information to the managed-care organization. Fourth, the patient should be involved as much as possible in the utilization review process.

Divided Loyalty

In every professional–client relationship, the professional has a prima facie duty of fidelity to the client and to the agency. This in itself may produce conflict. As one of the parties to the service, the managed-care company expects loyalty because of its contractual relationship with the professional. The social worker must be loyal to the client and at the same time to the employer and the managed behavioral health care company. There is an obvious conflict of values in loyalty split three ways. The social worker's values point to the primacy of the client's needs, whereas the company's values are directed toward its fiscal viability and will often contradict the client's needs. The employing agency may fall somewhere in between.

At the heart of the conflict of interest are two legitimate duties: to provide quality care (the principle of beneficence) and to contain costs and distribute limited societal resources equitably (the principle of social justice). The social worker is an agent of the client but concomitantly is an agent of the managed-care company and the provider of scarce and valuable societal resources. The ethical dilemma pits the best interests of the client against the social justice issue of a fair distribution of costs and services (Corcoran, 1997).

The ethical dilemma for the social worker parallels the ethical dilemma for the physician. Shall physicians follow the dictates of their conscience and the dictates of good practice in giving primary consideration to the aid and comfort of the patient, or shall physicians compromise care in favor of the cost-saving philosophy of their employers (McArthur & Moore, 1997)? For the physician, managed care raises at least two conflicting loyalty issues that are not unique to managed care. This conflict is captured in two contradictory statements:

[P]hysicians are required to do everything that they believe may benefit each patient without regard to costs or other societal considerations. In caring for an individual patient, the doctor must act solely as that patient's advocate against the apparent interests of society as a whole, if necessary. (Levinsky, cited in Sabin, 1994, p. 319)

As a member of this profession, a physician must recognize responsibility not only to patients but also to society, to other health professionals and to self. (Preamble to the American Psychiatric Association Code of Ethics, cited in Sabin, 1994, p. 319)

It is difficult for health care professionals in the managed-care system to maintain primary and exclusive commitment to patients because of divided loyalty. Conflicts of interest are inevitable when professionals feel loyalty to patients and to employing and funding organizations.

Physicians are expected to balance the interests of their patients with the interests of other patients. When deciding whether to order a test or procedure for a patient, the physician must consider whether the resources should be saved for another patient or not used at all. The needs of patients may conflict with their physicians' financial interests when managed care imposes limitations that impact on one or the other. The gatekeeper role is morally dubious because it generates a conflict between the responsibilities of the physician as patient advocate and as guardian of society's resources.

Pelligrino (1994) claims that managed care has compromised patient care by creating economic incentives for physicians to delay or avoid hospitalization, consulting with specialists, or calling for effective but expensive treatments. Economic incentives create irreconcilable conflicts between the physician's obligations to other patients and other health care professionals in the system. Moreover, the needs of the chronically or emotionally ill may be slighted and continuity of care disrupted by competitive advertising. "This division of loyalties undermines trust and makes the physician the patient's adversary rather than his or her ally in obtaining needed care" (Pelligrino, 1994, p. 1169).

For social workers, the division of loyalty arises when a client loses coverage in the process of treatment or when the services a client is receiving are no longer approved for payment. The social worker is "faced with a moral dilemma of his [or her] own economic needs versus client needs" (Paradise, cited in Strom, 1992, p. 400). The social worker must also respect the contractual obligations deemed appropriate by the same payer—obligations that may contradict obligations to clients. Sabin (1994) advises psychiatrists to acknowledge the existence of these contradictions and collaborate with the client in managing the conflicting obligations. He concludes that representing two conflicting values can be ethical if the clinician conducts appropriate forms of disclosure and informed consent. This approach is corroborated by the NASW Code of Ethics (Section 1.06):

> Social workers should be alert to and avoid conflicts of interest that interfere with the exercise of professional discretion and impartial judgment. Social workers should inform clients when a real or potential conflict of interest arises and take responsible steps to resolve the issue in a manner that makes the clients' interests primary and protects the clients' interests to the greatest extent possible.

The code suggests that in the managed-care era, as difficult as it may be, the conflict should be resolved in the interest of the client and not necessarily in the interest of the managed-care company.

CONCLUSION

It is not unethical to control costs through managed care if doing so does not impair the quality of service. But, as noted by Phillips (1996), "practitioners have rarely been able to provide optimal care for their patients, and the provision of continued treatment when insurance plans have expired has long been a problem" (p. 183). Poor management, organizational self-interest, and the search for profit have been associated with the rapid growth of managed behavioral health care.

Though managed care is ubiquitous, no single definition or model of managed care exists. As the industry grows and expands, incremental rescinding of some restrictive policies is occurring, whether through government regulation (Pear, 1996) or consumer movements working along with HMOs (Pear, 1997b). These changes reflect consumers' demand for greater choice in coverage and in physician selection.

As yet, in the social work literature there are no empirical studies of managed care's impact or its implications. There is an urgent need for such research. The evidence that does exist is not all negative by any means. In some plans, there have been reductions of expenditures without sacrificing the quality of care (Lohmann, 1997).

Managed care will continue to transform social work practice by bringing cost considerations directly into the worker–client relationship. The managed-care model raises serious questions about the continuing viability of the social agency model of practice to which social work has been committed for most of twentieth century (Lohmann, 1997).

Managed care will look quite different in the coming years. Bigger firms are buying smaller ones, and providers are forming alliances among

themselves and bypassing managed-care companies altogether by contracting directly with third-party payers, despite the financial risk and possible
economic ineffectiveness of such a move. In Congress, by November 1997
more than 200 legislators had cosponsored the *Patient Access to Responsible
Care Act*, which aims to regulate managed-care companies and establish
comprehensive federal protections for health care consumers (*NASW News*,
1998). This legislative effort reflected the dissatisfaction of many consumers
over the policies and practices of managed-care companies. Professions,
too, are mobilizing and forming coalitions to influence the direction of
managed care (*Statement of Principles*, 1997).

Changes in health care and managed-care policies and practices inevitably affect values and ethics. The dilemmas that arise at one time may be
different from those appearing at other times; context is a critical variable in
any ethical dilemma. Ethical dilemmas will inevitably arise in the health
care system because the values and interests of the parties clash. For social
workers, the central issue for managed-care ethics is what is in the best interests of the client.

On a macro level, the economic power wielded by managed-care companies has affected the health care system in the United States in profound
ways. On a micro level, the power that is wielded by laypeople on the policies and programs of community-based agencies also dramatically affects
agency services. The next chapter studies ethical dilemmas in lay–professional relationships.

10

LAY–PROFESSIONAL
RELATIONSHIPS

Confrontations between lay leaders and professional staff are inevitable in social welfare agencies. The conflicts, which sometimes become power struggles, manifest themselves in a variety of ways, such as in requests to circumvent waiting lists, requests to get jobs for family members, designation of fund-raising allocations, and assignment of the primary responsibility for decision making. This chapter examines some ethical dilemmas in lay–professional relationships.

CIRCUMVENTING THE WAITING LIST

A common issue facing executives of social agencies whose beds and services are limited is the pressure that lay leaders exert to circumvent the waiting list for a close relative's admission.

CASE 10.1 My Mother Needs Admission to the Nursing Home

One of the most serious dilemmas that I frequently confront arises when I get a call from an important person who tells me that his mother has applied to a home for the aged where there is a waiting list. His mother is very sick and lonely, perhaps doesn't have long to live, and the lay leader wants me to get her into the home, which may have a waiting list of 200 people. The ethical dilemma is, What is the right thing to do? Those on the waiting list are also needy and were there first. I have never been able to resolve the dilemma once and for all. Even though I feel very uncomfortable, there are times when I just try to push for this particular person. Sometimes whether I make the effort is a function of the lay leader's wealth and prestige in the community.

Discussion

The underlying values of each option can be classified into two groups: (1) justice versus fiscal adequacy and (2) conceptions of clients as strangers or intimates.

Justice versus Fiscal Adequacy.   Denial of the lay leader's request can be justified by relying on the value of justice. Acquiescence to the request can be justified by the value of fiscal adequacy. The value of justice includes such notions as fairness and fidelity, mutual respect, and beneficence. According to Rawls (1981),

> The main idea is that when a number of persons engage in a mutually advantageous cooperative venture according to rules, and thus restrict their liberty in ways necessary to yield advantages for all, those who have submitted to these restrictions have a right to a similar acquiescence on the part of those who have benefitted from their submission. We are not to gain from the cooperative labor of others without doing our fair share. (p. 112)

The waiting list is regulated by the principle of fairness—first come, first served. By agreeing to be placed on a waiting list, applicants restrict their freedom and must wait their turn for openings. They have a right to expect similar acquiescence by the home for the aged, which benefits from their submission by having a steady stream of clients available to fill beds. The home agrees that, as openings occur, it will restrict intake to the waiting list. Outsiders who want to circumvent the waiting list are not to gain from the "cooperative labor of others without doing their fair share," which is to await their turn. Thus, the principle of fairness would deem lay leaders' political and economic pressure unethical because it violates the value of justice.

A contrary value is the fiscal viability of the agency. A donor with financial clout and leadership acumen contributes to the ongoing vitality of the agency. The positive effects of coddling influential donors are their continued financial support and ongoing leadership role. The negative effects are yielding to their power and influence and refraining from criticizing their actions when they violate moral norms. Acquiescence to the lay leader's request reflects preference for the value of fiscal viability over the value of justice.

Clients as Strangers or Intimates. Toulmin (1981) distinguishes between ethics toward family members and ethics toward strangers. We relate differently to families, intimates, and neighbors than we do to complete strangers. In transient encounters, our moral obligations are limited to not acting in an offensive manner. For example, when waiting to see a movie, one does not go to the head of the line but awaits one's turn. Families might look the other way when a moral error has been committed by a family member. "So, in the ethics of strangers, respect for rules is all, and the opportunities for discretion are few. In the ethics of intimacy, discretion is all, and the relevance of strict rules is minimal" (p. 34). In this scenario, the lay leader's mother desiring admission is a stranger to the nursing home, and the lay leader is an intimate to the professional. Toward strangers, "respect for rules is all" and the rule is to abide by the waiting list. Toward intimates, "discretion is all" and the rules may be bent. For the social worker, what is the ethical thing to do?

Because the home has jurisdiction over its admissions policy and is filled to capacity, all the people on the waiting list may be categorized as strangers—not yet clients—who will have to abide by the institution's rules and policies. The lay leader and the social worker are distant players on this stage who may not ethically influence decisions on admission. Because there is a waiting list of "strangers," respect for rules is paramount. The waiting list may not be circumvented.

Ethical Theory

The ethical dilemma is whether the social worker should support the lay leader's request to circumvent the waiting list. Several variables are operative: the security of the social worker's job, the degree of power being exerted by the layperson, the consequences of nonacquiescence, and the quality of the professional's relationship with the layperson. These variables are based on different assumptions.

A social worker who feels insecure in the job is more likely to succumb to the pressure of circumventing the waiting list than is one who feels secure in the job. Yet even the secure individual may not be able to resist the repeated demands of a powerful layperson. The consequences of refusal may be the loss of one's job, reduction or withdrawal of the gift, and resignation of the lay leader from the agency's board. The strength of the layperson's power is a function of his or her status in the community: the higher the status, the greater the power, and the more wrenching the refusal. Refusal is also a function of the relationship between the layperson and the social worker: the deeper the relationship, the greater the obligation to acquiesce. Ultimately, the central question is, What is the right/good thing to do? Ethical principles and theories are essential in order to clarify the choices in this dilemma.

**TABLE 10.1   Application of Ethical Principles and Theory
to Circumventing the Waiting List**

Ethical Theory	Circumvent	Do Not Circumvent
Deontological	Duty of nonmaleficence; duty of gratitude to donor	Duty of fidelity to people on waiting list; principle of justice: "first come, first served"
Utilitarian	Retain lay leader's involvement in agency; preserve agency's financial viability; prevent loss of professional's job	Person waiting may die—greater harm principle; public protest

To deontologists (see Table 10.1), it would appear that circumventing the waiting list is simply wrong because others were there first and the duties of justice and fidelity prevail. Yet "first come, first served" may not be the only principle operating in this situation. It is conceivable that the person being pushed to the front of the waiting list is more needy than the others. If that is known to be the case, the decision might incline in that direction because of the prima facie duty of nonmaleficence, which supersedes the duty of fidelity.

On the other hand, the prima facie duty of gratitude could be operating here. Agency executives often convey to large contributors and board members that they can expect preferential treatment for members of their families, whether in the use of agency services or in gaining employment. There is an implicit—at times, explicit—promise that they may be served ahead of others. The majority of board members at one agency indicated that they expected such "perks." Thus, the social worker feels a sense of duty to fulfill these unwritten promises.

To utilitarians, at issue are the possible consequences of refusal. The individual might die. The social worker may lose his or her job. The lay leader may reduce or eliminate the gift, may sever the friendship, may resign from the agency. Since these negative consequences may be harmful to more people than the refusal to place one person at the head of the list, the principle of utility suggests giving in to the lay leader's demand. Acquiescence can be viewed as the lesser of two harms. It could also be supported by the duty of gratitude to donors.

There may also be negative effects of acquiescence. It is conceivable that the person superseded on the waiting list is in more dire need than the layperson's relative, and the delay in institutionalization may hasten death.

Moreover, though such decisions are usually made with discretion and in private, the action may become known in the community and generate public protest. Thus, to avoid these negative consequences, it is necessary to resist the pressure. By insisting on an ethical standard of fairness, the social worker adds to the credibility of the agency and the profession. "It is important to impress upon the leadership that there is a special duty to uphold the integrity of the agency and that a proper ethical response is consistent with the agency's mission" (Yaffe, 1996, p. 199). Ideally, ethical instincts will tell social workers that the waiting list is inviolate, but they may find it difficult to withstand the pressure of influential laypeople.

Resolution
The dilemma of circumventing the waiting list highlights the power conflict in professional–lay relationships. If the request is denied on ethical grounds, the social worker and the layperson can meet with the prospective entrant to explore alternative possibilities. Other opportunities should be created for the layperson to continue his or her leadership role in the agency.

In some communities, two waiting lists are formed. Most of the admissions come from the "regular" waiting list. The remainder are reserved for lay leaders who helped to create the facility. Communities need to be innovative in accommodating the needs of the people on the waiting list and the relatives of lay leaders.

CASE 10.2 Threatening the Executive's Job

A board member of long standing has an ailing mother in need of residential placement. She calls me to get her mother into a nursing home. Upon calling the executive of the home, I discover that there is a waiting list between six months and a year long. I inform the board member of this fact and add that I cannot replace someone on the waiting list with her mother. The board member, chair of the personnel committee, states that, although I have been doing an excellent job as executive director, she could have some input into my annual appraisal, and whether she chooses to do so depends "on your performance." I apprise the president of this conversation, and we arrange to meet with the board member. At the meeting, I make every effort to find an alternative placement for her mother. She drops her threat.

I was able to handle the situation in this way because I was feeling good about my job and was not insecure. By involving the board president, I demonstrated that this matter was not my problem. Our ethical stance persuaded the board member that she was wrong to threaten me with repercussions.

Discussion

In contrast to the previous case, in which the social worker displayed initial ambivalence, the demand and threat by the lay leader are unequivocally resisted in this case. Security in the job helped, but what was more helpful was the involvement of the president and the authority inherent in the president's role.

CASE 10.3 *Giving a Job to My Daughter*

A daughter of a board member graduated from a fine MSW program. Knowing that the agency is looking for new staff, the board member submits her résumé "for consideration." He intimates that because funding for the program and the position is often tenuous, he is prepared to make a significant donation "for the continuity of the program."

After I and the director of clinical services interviewed the daughter, I said she had some positive credentials but we couldn't hire her for the position. I never hire someone whom I can't fire.

Discussion

In this case, the executive involves another person in assessing the candidate's credentials. There are no threats, but the possibility of resources to continue the program is offered. The executive feels secure enough to say "no" to the daughter's application because she is not suitable for the job as measured by professional hiring criteria.

CASE 10.4 *Establishing a New Service*

A board member who is active on the agency's planning committee suggested at a committee meeting that the agency get involved in a new area of service. I knew that the consequence of this involvement could be that the board member would derive personal gain, thereby creating a conflict of interest. When asked about this possibility by a committee member, he denied being in the business. I knew he was lying.

Resolution

I informed the president about the board member's conflict of interest. The president and a trustee called him separately and said that although his intentions were noteworthy, he might have a conflict of interest. At the next board meeting, he said that he had made an error by being overzealous and had rethought his position, and he withdrew his suggestion. He made the withdrawal look like his own decision.

Discussion

This situation ended amicably because the board member trusted the president and the trustee who approached him after the social work executive placed the problem in the president's lap. Both lay leaders, through their influence, impressed on the board member the unethical features of his plan.

In sum, the social work executives in these three cases consciously decided not to deal with the conflict situation by themselves but to employ an important practice principle: involving another person in authority, preferably the board president, in the problem and not taking ownership of the problem upon oneself.

FUND-RAISING

Of the many ethical issues that emerge in the course of raising funds, four have been selected for analysis. The first two deal with wealthy individuals whose power contravenes agency policy. The last two present dilemmas for the professional working with bequests and endowments.

Wealth and Power versus Agency Policy

CASE 10.5 "Money Talks"

A major contributor has given us millions of dollars and solicited millions more, and his wife has become the associate director of an agency that we fund. Although we are cutting back our agency allocations, this contributor wants his wife's agency to get a 100 percent increase in its grant. From the point of view of equity, it is unfair for an agency to receive a 100 percent increase when other agencies are being cut. But this person has made it very clear that he will walk away from our agency if we refuse. We stand to lose millions of dollars. The ethical dilemma is made slightly less unpalatable by the fact that his wife's agency provides good services. If it did not, it would be a devastating ethical dilemma because it would be more difficult to justify the increase. To resolve this, I talked to three supervisors. One of them said, "We are being held up. This is a robbery, and I am not sure there is anything we can do about it." The other supervisor characterized it as a question of the old joke, "Where does the 600-pound gorilla sit?" "Wherever it wants." The third person said, "Sometimes you just have to lie back and enjoy it." The fund-raising department urged us to do whatever this contributor wants because we cannot risk the impact on the campaign. Knowing that the wife's agency's program is decent enables me to rationalize that we are not losing funds that help people, but I am still troubled. I would probably make the same decision.

Discussion

This case is about a donor asking for an increase for his wife's agency, but such dilemmas take other forms too. Examples include lay leaders who demand that the agency purchase supplies from their companies, take out insurance through their firms, or hire their relatives for jobs. This case is a paradigm of the layperson's exercise of power for personal and family gain.

The social worker's resolution applied utilitarian reasoning. Staff was persuaded that the individual would carry out his threat to leave the agency if his request were denied. The agency stood to lose a great deal of money by not acceding to his request. The greater good was served by granting the increase, although doing so violated the agency policy of across-the-board allocation reductions. The donor's contributions, as well as those he solicited, outweighed the cost of the inequitable decision. The prima facie duty of gratitude took precedence over the prima facie duty of justice.

Another approach would have been to assist the agency to secure resources from other sources. This might not satisfy the donor, but if his major concern is to increase the budgetary allotment to his wife's agency, he might be persuaded to pursue other available resources.

CASE 10.6 *Taking Advantage of a Good Deal*

The funding agency offered to cover an end-of-year deficit of up to $25,000 in one of its member agencies. The executive director of the member agency projected that the agency would be able to balance its budget by the year's end. Several lay leaders then suggested that the member agency purchase supplies up to the $25,000 and let the funding agency reimburse those expenses. What should the executive director do?

Discussion

At first glance, the proposal seems to have merit. The deficit would be real, and the funds spent would be used to meet legitimate agency needs. The purchase certainly would be legal as far as the funding agency was concerned.

But, at second glance, is this the right thing to do? Is it honest? Spending the money and seeking the reimbursement would be legal but would not be ethical because the spirit of the funding agency's guarantee would be violated. The deficit would be falsely created in order to qualify for the reimbursement. The use of the money for legitimate agency purposes was a rationalization that could not justify such an action (Yaffe, 1996). The lay leaders' proposal was dropped. Although the plan was legal, it was unethical.

Bequests and Endowments

To raise much-needed funds and guarantee continued income in future years, large agencies sometimes invest heavily to procure bequests and endowments that raise ethical issues.

CASE 10.7 Investing in a Trust

I will oftentimes turn down a gift if I think it is ethically questionable or not in the best interests of the donor even though it may be wonderful for the agency. A donor wants me to invest his money in a trust that would provide a regular income for him. I believe that this is not in his best interests, for he may want to take a trip or buy a home and his capital would be tied up in the trust. In the long run, our relationship will be better served by my telling him that it is not good for him, because he will invest it anyway in another form. The trust is always in the organization's best interest, but it may not always be in the donor's best interest.

Discussion

The ethical sensitivity of the professional is demonstrated here. It is always in the interests of the agency to receive investments, but it may not always be in the interests of donors to give them. Donors tend to be unsophisticated in financial planning and vulnerable to deception. The professional used his knowledge of consequences to help the client anticipate the outcomes of his decision. Practically, the agency lost the investment, but the professional did the right thing. His ethical reasoning prevailed.

CASE 10.8 Adding One's Daughter as a Beneficiary

A 65-year-old man, ill with terminal cancer, wanted to create a charitable trust. The transaction was approved by our lawyer and his lawyer. While in the hospital, he decided to add his daughter, whom he had wanted to disinherit, as a secondary beneficiary. We really anguished about this. On the one hand, it was a completed, irrevocable trust with $500,000 to $600,000 for the agency. But naming the daughter as a beneficiary meant that the money would be deferred for perhaps fifty years. Do I allow that trust to be amended, or do I not? I could not decide.

The agency said not to change it. My humanistic half said I should. My committee chairman and I decided that because we are serving this donor and this was his request and his doctors said he is competent, we should do it. I gave up the value of half a million dollars.

Discussion

The professional's ethical dilemma is based on a conflict of values. The value of self-determination supports the client's ethical right to change the designation of his beneficiaries, though legally he could not because he had created an irrevocable trust. Support for client autonomy is based on fidelity to the relationship.

The agency also values fiscal stability, a value that could support denial of the request to change the trust. Lawyers for both parties had set up the irrevocable trust, making it a "done deal." Support for fiscal stability is based on fidelity to the agency and fulfilling a promise. Not amending the trust would also redound to the benefit of many more people in the community.

The dilemma was resolved in favor of the donor. The professional and the chairman emphasized the prior relationship with the donor and the need to respect his autonomy. They were not driven by greed. The decision was very costly to the agency but was deemed to be the ethical thing to do. The moral traces that remained in the decision not taken were very costly indeed.

CONCLUSION

The impact of wealthy donors on agency policy is profound and far-reaching. Social workers are faced with serious ethical dilemmas over circumventing waiting lists and agency policies, increasing funding to one agency when other agencies are being cut, or hiring board members' families. The decision to accommodate donors' requests appears to be rationalized in order to maintain fiscal stability, but it can also be resisted ethically.

Fund-raisers do not generally become involved in family dynamics, estate plans, or the financial conditions of donors. In the area of bequests and endowments, intense relationships tend to develop between professionals and donors, so that professionals may feel a deeper commitment toward donors' interests in doubtful situations. The ethical bulb illuminates the appropriate response, usually in favor of the donor.

This chapter concludes Part II, which discussed ethical dilemmas in diverse social problems and fields of service. Part III, consisting of four chapters, concentrates on one major theme in applied ethics: the autonomy–paternalism dilemma, with particular focus on the elderly.

AUTONOMY AND PATERNALISM

11

AUTONOMY
VERSUS PATERNALISM

Part III is devoted exclusively to the conflict between autonomy and paternalism. This emphasis reflects the centrality of client self-determination and agency beneficence in social work practice. This chapter provides an overview of the ethical and social work literature. The following three chapters illustrate the conflict through presentation of a variety of cases. The Epilogue integrates the themes of the book.

THE PRINCIPLE OF RESPECT FOR AUTONOMY

At the core of the concept of autonomy is oneself, free from control by others and from personal limitations that prevent meaningful choice (Beauchamp & Childress, 1994). For a choice to be real, it must be freely made and based on understanding, not helplessness and resignation. It must be open to examination and evaluation (Chachkes, 1986). Autonomy is reliance on one's own powers in acting, choosing, and forming opinions (Gillon, 1985). By contrast, a person with limited autonomy is in some respects controlled by others or incapable of acting, choosing, and forming opinions on his or her own (Beauchamp & Childress, 1994). Although freedom from control by others and from personal limitations is an idealized version of autonomy, rare in its occurrence, it offers a standard toward which to strive. Autonomy is expressed in the rational choosing among clearly defined and understood alternatives.

Miller (1981) distinguishes among four types of autonomy:

1. *Autonomy as free action:* Action that is voluntary, not the result of coercion or undue influence, and intentional—the conscious object of the actor.
2. *Autonomy as authenticity:* Action that is consistent with the person's attitudes, values, character, and life plans.
3. *Autonomy as effective deliberation:* Action that is based on an awareness of alternatives and the evaluation of consequences.
4. *Autonomy as moral reflection:* Action that reflects one's moral values. Much of the literature and the cases that follow reflect Miller's types of autonomy.

AUTONOMY AS SELF-DETERMINATION

In social work, the principle of autonomy has been equated with self-determination. "The principle of client self-determination is the practical recognition of the right and need of clients to freedom in making their own choices and decisions in the casework process" (Biestek, 1957, p. 19). Autonomy as a right implies an obligation on the part of others. In social work, the autonomy of the client implies an obligation on the part of the social worker "to provide the positive means, i.e., give full information and viable alternatives from which to choose, and negative means, i.e., refrain from duly influencing or coercing" (Abramson, 1983, p. 48).

One of the issues that confronts social workers is the distinction between respecting the client's self-determination and influencing the client. Does influencing the client reduce self-determination? Influence is appropriate when the social worker shows respect for the client. Influence becomes manipulation when the social worker tries to move a person in a direction that the person would not voluntarily choose (Salzberger, 1979).

Self-determination has been recognized as a primary factor in health care ethics. In a study of hospital social workers, most ethical conflicts were found to arise between social workers' pursuit of what they deemed as in their clients' best interests and fostering maximum client self-determination (Proctor, Morrow-Howell, & Lott, 1993). In another study (Rothman, Smith, Nakashima, Paterson, & Mustin, 1996), pursuit of clients' best interests was defined as directiveness modes or helping strategies. The study found that social workers use a wide range of directiveness modes in the reported case vignettes. These include "reflective"—the social worker explores a problem without indicating a direction to solve it; "suggestive"—the social worker states a tentative direction for resolution; "prescriptive"—the social worker clearly indicates a specific course of action; and "determinative"—the social worker takes an independent action on behalf of the client without the client's awareness.

Autonomy may be restricted only if doing so is necessary to prevent harm to other people and to oneself. If the restriction is justified, it must rest on a competing moral principle such as beneficence.

THE PRINCIPLE OF BENEFICENCE

Morality requires not only that we treat people autonomously and refrain from harming them but that we contribute to their welfare. These actions fall under the principle of beneficence. General obligations of beneficence, or the "reciprocity theory of obligations of beneficence" (Beauchamp and Childress, 1989, p. 203), are in response to the benefits we receive from others. Specific obligations of beneficence derive from special moral relationships in social roles such as parent, spouse, and friend.

One principle of beneficence requires that benefits be provided to people, and a second requires the balancing of benefits and harms. Because in the course of producing benefits we also create risks, the second principle, based on utility, is an essential addition to the principle of positive beneficence. For example, in Chapter 14, in the discussion of coercing elderly or incompetent patients to accept nutrition and hydration or acquiescing to withhold it from them, we note the importance of weighing the treatment's probable chance of success and benefits against the probable costs or risks to the patient. In social work there is an obligation to provide benefits to clients and to promote their welfare. Clients, however, may not always view the social worker's services as beneficent and may resent intrusion into their lives. Situations arise in which beneficence leads to paternalism.

PATERNALISM

Paternalism is the overriding of a person's wishes or actions through coercion, deception, or nondisclosure of information, or for the welfare of others. Paternalism occurs when the social worker seeks to benefit the client without the client's consent. It is considered an affront to the dignity and independence of the client (Linzer & Lowenstein, 1987). All definitions of *paternalism* contain the element of coercion or interference that is justified for the good of the individual (Reamer, 1983b). Childress (1981) contends that paternalism is prima facie wrong and needs to be justified.

Abramson (1985, 1989) offers a model of paternalistic beneficence that she defines as protective interventions (at times made despite the client's objections) intended to enhance the client's quality of life. Such interventions can range from limited to extended involvement in a client's affairs. Murdach (1996) adds selective beneficence as a middle range between limited and extended beneficence.

Abramson (1989) cites four reasons to justify paternalism: acting on behalf of a child who is too young to make decisions; treating a person who is mentally incompetent; preventing an irreversible act such as suicide; and a temporary interference with a person's liberty that will ensure future freedom and autonomy. Reamer (1983b) cites four attributes of clients that warrant paternalistic interventions: (1) clients lack information that, if available, would lead them to consent to interference—for example, the client is about to commit suicide mistakingly thinking that her spouse has died; (2) clients are incapable of understanding relevant information, either temporarily or permanently—for example, a client who is mentally impaired raises the knotty issue of how to determine competence; (3) clients consent to an intervention prior to the interference—for example, a client consents to restrictions on alcohol intake when he is admitted to an alcoholism treatment center, though he may resent the restrictions later; (4) clients are likely to consent to an intervention after the interference—for example, an individual whose judgment is temporarily impaired approves of the paternalistic interference against self-destructive behavior that saved his life.

In addition to attributes of clients, Reamer cites attributes of situations that warrant paternalism: (1) the harmful consequences that are likely to occur without interference are irreversible—for example, the client who plans to injure himself permanently; (2) a wider range of freedom for the client can be preserved only by temporarily restricting the client's freedom—for example, drug and alcohol abuse and suicide; (3) the immediate need to rescue overrides prohibitions against interference—for example, a client who is about to jump off a bridge.

The conflict between autonomy and paternalism presents itself in a variety of settings, including elder abuse victims and patients who have Alzheimer's disease, reside in nursing homes, or refuse medication. Moody (1992) argues that it is dangerous to apply the principle of beneficence to the treatment of Alzheimer's patients, for patient autonomy cannot serve as a counterweight because of their condition. "With no barriers from autonomy, an appeal to beneficence may persuade us that euthanasia is the best course for the patient" (p. 48). He cautions against the subtle tendency to demean human beings through beneficence.

Despite every effort to enhance the self-determination of nursing home residents, in actual practice the nature and organizational structure of medically oriented nursing homes lead staff to make many decisions for residents, thus thwarting their personal autonomy (Reshen, 1992).

Thus, the setting of practice may pose a barrier to enhancing client self-determination.

DECISION-MAKING CAPACITY

Conrad (1987) cites a patient's noncompliance with taking medication as a conflict between patient autonomy and physician paternalism. Roberts (1989) reasons that noncompliance is due to ambivalence about living under the treatment plan. Schwartz, Vingiano, and Bezirganian (1988) concluded that psychiatric patients' refusal of medication, for the most part, was a manifestation of their illness and not a reflection of autonomous functioning. Their study suggested that decisions supporting the right to refuse treatment based on personal autonomy should be subject to clinical rather than judicial review.

In *Rivers v. Katz* (1986), the New York Court of Appeals ruled that institutionalized psychiatric patients and prisoners cannot be deemed to lack capacity to refuse psychotropic drugs merely because they are committed or incarcerated or carry a psychiatric diagnosis that suggests diminished capacity. Thus, even the *judicial* standard for assessing capacity is based on functional considerations, not on diagnostic categories or placement.

Treatment decisions with involuntary aged clients become even more difficult in protective service cases. Concern for the individual's safety often clashes with self-determination (Linzer, 1996; Lewis, 1984). Client self-determination has positive features (freedom to do as one wishes) and negative features (freedom from coercion). In protective service cases, the client's self-determination is expressed as freedom from coercion to enter a nursing home or to receive home care. "Achieving a realistic balance between personal autonomy and protective care is the defining challenge of social policy for impaired persons" (Kennedy, 1993, p. 177).

A major reason for placing elderly involuntary clients in nursing homes is the assessment of their lack of decision-making capacity. Determining mental incompetence is difficult and often subjective. For example, a person may be confused in the emergency room but able to function well at home, or a person may endanger herself at home by not turning off a stove but may appear well oriented in an interview. Confusion in some areas may not preclude competence in others. Thus, the social worker may intervene in some areas and respect the client's right to make decisions in others (Burstein, 1988). For the social worker and other health care professionals, the question is not whether the person is competent but whether the person is capable. Most people might fail the global test of competence, but they could pass the test of capacity in specific areas of daily functioning.

Decision-making capacity is seen on a continuum or sliding scale, not in an absolute sense. "A patient's capacity to make a decision may fluctuate, or a patient may be capable of making decisions about her own health care but not be able to make decisions about her bank account" (High, 1992, p. 9). The capacity to participate in care decisions is almost always decision-specific, relative to specific tasks, and may fluctuate over time (High 1989; Levinson, 1990).

One must sense when a client cannot make decisions and resist the tendency to assume that most older people lack this capacity. Usually, a determination of decision-making capacity is based on functional considerations. The capacity for health care decision making depends on the ability to (1) understand the nature of the treatment choice, (2) understand the implications of the various alternatives, and (3) make and communicate a reasoned choice (AARP, cited in Kane, 1993).

Paternalism—exaggerated beneficence—directly challenges the principle of autonomy. Should the principle of respect for client autonomy have priority over the principle of professional beneficence? Beauchamp and Childress (1989) conclude that neither principle can override the other.

COMMUNITY AS A COUNTERPRINCIPLE

Veatch (1984) champions the supremacy of autonomy over other principles. Callahan (1984) questions the supremacy of autonomy over such considerations as community. As a system of values for individual welfare, autonomy may be the answer. But as a system of values for life in community, autonomy may not do as well. Autonomy "will inevitably diminish the sense of obligation that others may feel toward us and shrivel our sense of obligation toward others" (p. 40). When we juxtapose autonomy with community, we introduce constraints and limits and a vision of the self that is part of a wider collectivity. Autonomy is *a* value, not *the* value.

Community, of which the social agency is a major representative, may be a counterprinciple to autonomy. The value of community is advocated by the "Communitarians," a group of social thinkers who "emphasize the importance of community, the moral claims staked by shared needs and futures, as distinct from the claims of various subgroups and individuals" (Etzioni, 1991, p. A22). Community is an important part of external reality with which clients must contend when they come to the agency for service. Social workers can use it as a counterbalance to client self-determination and autonomy when they help clients to consider the effects of their decisions and actions on family, friends, and neighbors in the community.

TABLE 11.1 Ethical Principles, Ethical Theories, and Social Work Practice

| Ethical Principles | Ethical Theories | | Social Work Practice |
	Deontology	Utilitarian	
Autonomy	People possess unconditional worth and have the right to determine their own destiny	People should develop their own potential in the future	Supports self-determination and clients' right to make decisions affecting their lives; advocates informed consent
Beneficence (Paternalism)	People are obligated to respond to others' kindness and to fulfill their social roles	Leads to improved living conditions and better society	Agency is responsible for clients' welfare; community serves as a countervalue to self-determination

AUTONOMY AND PATERNALISM IN SOCIAL WORK PRACTICE

The principles of autonomy and beneficence can be supported by ethical theories and applied to social work practice (see Table 11.1). Each principle can be independently supported by both deontological and utilitarian theories. When the principles confront each other—that is, when autonomy is juxtaposed with beneficence—they carry equal weight. In supporting autonomy, the focus is on the client; in supporting beneficence, the focus is on the agency and the community. When beneficence turns into paternalism, autonomy usually has the upper hand and is difficult to overrule.

CONCLUSION

The conflict of autonomy versus paternalism confronts social workers in a variety of settings. Social workers' respect for client self-determination and autonomy sometimes clashes with their and their agencies' beneficence toward clients' best interests, a beneficence which may become paternalistic.

The theoretical dimensions of the autonomy–paternalism dilemma serve as an introduction to the next three chapters. Though the cases involve mainly elderly clients, the dilemma occurs with other age groups and types of human problems and in a variety of settings.

12

REFUSAL OF SERVICES

Refusal of services creates quandaries for social workers because it raises questions about autonomy and beneficence, paternalism, and the determination of decision-making capacity. The conflict is explored in the five cases in this chapter.

ILLUSTRATIVE CASES AND ANALYSIS

CASE 12.1 Elder Abuse

Mr. S is a 73-year-old Caucasian male who has multiple chronic illnesses and is confined to a wheelchair. His appearance is disheveled and dirty, and he smells of urine and alcohol. He lives in a rundown tenement that is a well-known drug location. He has a boarder, a drug-addicted younger man who has stolen money from Mr. S and has physically assaulted him on several occasions. Mr. S was referred to the agency by the police precinct after they responded to several of his 911 calls. Mr. S stated that his life was in danger and no one would help him. The social worker ascertained that Mr. S had "run the gamut" of crime victims services—including the police, courts, and conflict resolution centers—and was considered to be "foul-mouthed, uncooperative, and resistant." The client's psychiatric evaluation indicated no cognitive impairment.

During the initial interview, Mr. S revealed that he was terminally ill with cancer and his one desire was to leave his only son with an inheritance. Having no money (his income from SSI was limited), he used the money he got from renting out an extra bedroom to gamble, hoping to "hit it big" and leave his son "comfortable." However, this plan had not worked out as he expected; he was now in arrears on his rent and telephone and utility bills. He had been pressuring his boarder to come up with money that he claims was owed to him, and an argument ensued. The boarder knocked Mr. S unconscious and fled with his television and stereo. Mr. S was now afraid to return to his apartment and was staying with his son. However, his son asked him to leave after an argument over his drinking. As a last resort, the client agreed to contact us. His opening remark to the social worker was an offensive ethnic epithet.

The social worker is repulsed by the client. She confides to her supervisor that during the initial interview she at times felt like hitting him. She determines that Mr. S requires an order of protection, a police escort to get him back into his own apartment, an emergency grant for rent and utility arrears, and home care for personal care, meal preparation, and chore services. Mr. S uses strong language to refuse all options, accusing the agency of wanting to take away his freedom. Because the intervention plan requires the client's consent and Mr. S is not mentally incapacitated, his refusal creates a dilemma for the social worker. She wants to help Mr. S, an elderly victim of abuse, but she also needs to respect his right to self-determination and freedom of choice.

Discussion

In recent years, federal and state laws have been enacted to detect, prevent, or remedy mistreatment of the aged. Among the programs and systems that have been instituted are the criminal justice system, domestic violence laws, Adult Protective Services, and programs offered through the Older Americans Act (Welty, 1995). Social workers in many fields of practice are confronted with cases of elder abuse. Levine (1993) notes that intervention is based on the social worker's assessment of the client's situation, the client's competence, and the available appropriate resources. "The major challenge to social workers is working with a competent victim who refuses assistance" (p. 49). The case of Mr. S presents such a challenge.

The ethical principles of autonomy and beneficence and their related social work values of self-determination and agency responsibility are relevant to this case. They offer a constructive framework for the practitioner's decision. This discussion will apply the ethical decision-making model of values, action, rules, principles, and theory to justify the social worker's decision.

Table 12.1 illustrates the ambivalence of the client and the dilemma for the social worker. The client values independence and brooks no interference in his life that would restrict his freedom, but he also reaches out to the agency for assistance. The social worker values client independence but

TABLE 12.1   Model of Ethical Decision Making in a Case of Elder Abuse

Parties to the Conflict	Values	Action	Rules	Principles	Theories
Client	Being independent; being protected	Seeks help; refuses restrictive interventions	Consent must be obtained before services are rendered	Respect for autonomy	*Deontological:* Clients have inherent right to choose
					Utilitarian: Autonomy leads to self-actualization
Social worker	Being independent; freedom from mistreatment; safety of elderly clients	Respects refusal of interventions; intervenes to stop mistreatment	Consent is necessary before services are rendered Social workers must prevent elder abuse	Respect for autonomy; duties of beneficence and nonmaleficence	*Deontological:* Prima facie duty of fidelity to client *Utilitarian:* Prevention of harm to elderly leads to a better society

also prefers that clients be safe and not mistreated. She is ambivalent about whether to respect the client's refusal of services or intervene to protect him from abuse.

The social worker is conflicted between two rules: to require the consent of the client before rendering services (Matlaw & Mayer, 1986; Beauchamp & Childress, 1994) or to prevent elder abuse even without the client's consent. Requiring consent is justified by the principle of respect for autonomy, and preventing abuse is justified by the principles of beneficence and nonmaleficence. Deontologically, autonomy is supported by the prima facie duty of fidelity. Beneficence is supported by the utilitarian principle of least harm. Beneficence often becomes paternalism when social workers attempt to protect elder abuse victims from harm against their will. Levine (1993) acknowledges that

> An abused older person might choose to remain in a dangerous environment despite the social worker's attempt to protect the older adult. The client might also refuse various services that the practitioners believe will improve the victim's situation. In relating to the elder abuse victim, human service practitioners who deal with elder abuse must perform a delicate balancing act weighing the community's interest in

protecting its citizens against their client's desire to live with dignity and independence. (p. 23)

The dilemma is intensified when the case involves a competent adult victim who refuses intervention. In dealing with competent adult victims, Quinn (1985) contends that the social worker must respect the client's right to refuse services and that safety and protection should be secondary to the client's right to self-determination. However, what if the client—Mr. S—voluntarily seeking assistance, is in imminent danger but refuses assistance?

Resolution

Both options are ethically sound and the decision could go either way, so it behooves the practitioner to look more deeply into the situation to determine whether one side weighs more heavily than the other and whether there is room for a compromise. Linzer (1996) suggests that an ethical dilemma can sometimes be resolved by applying a practice principle that integrates both ethical principles, thereby obviating the need to choose between them.

The ethical principles are client autonomy and social worker beneficence. Since the client was deemed competent, Mr. S's autonomy was respected, and the social worker did not implement her intervention plan immediately. However, she did not close the case; she advised the client that she would remain available for him to call or drop in to talk. The social worker's willingness to listen was the "hook" that successfully engaged the client. He called her daily, venting his frustrations, and after two weeks he agreed to the original plan that she had recommended. The social worker arranged for an order of protection, a police escort to get him back into his own apartment, an emergency grant for rent and utility arrears, and home care for personal care, meal preparation, and chore services. The boarder, who had taken over the apartment, was arrested when he refused to leave.

Mr. S has been calling the social worker weekly, at which time she provides supportive counseling. She plans to conduct monthly visits to monitor the home environment. The client–worker relationship is totally changed; there is mutual respect and understanding based on trust and acceptance. Although Mr. S continues to be belligerent at times, he is no longer offensive to the social worker and she now considers him to be "a character but one of my favorite clients."

"Imposed decisions should be avoided when practice solutions may be found to justify a decision acceptable to the parties involved" (Linzer 1996, p. 140). The social worker's efforts to engage the client by listening, accepting, and encouraging him to maintain contact were successful in obtaining a positive resolution of the client's presenting problem and the ethical dilemma.

CASE 12.2 Elder Abuse in Daughter's Home

An 88-year-old widow moved into her daughter's house because of increasing frailty. The daughter, separated from her husband, was only marginally able to cope with life and stress. Living with her was an 11-year-old son who had behavioral problems and learning disabilities. Mrs. R attended the day center three days a week. We noticed that she came in with a fracture and a few bruises on her scalp and legs. The family said she lost her balance because of early stages of dementia. But when she came in with multiple bruises on her thighs and breasts, we suspected sexual abuse. The family claimed that the child was playing ball with Grandma and that the marks and bruises were due to the ball hitting her body. The decision was made that this woman could not return to her home, and we informed the family.

We called Adult Protective Services and the police and took the case to court. The client was placed in the hospital until a guardian could be assigned and nursing home placement arranged. The woman died in the hospital. We saw that as a blessing in disguise for her own safety, because we feared that the daughter would continue to want to keep her mother at home in order to receive her income.

We overrode the client's wish that nothing should be done to change her situation. Good social work practice respects a capable client's self-determination, but in an elder abuse situation, when the assessment was made that the client was not safe at home because of her dementia and frailty, we felt we needed to make decisions for her, for this was a matter of life and death. We were united in the need to provide a safe haven for this individual.

Discussion

The NASW Code of Ethics (NASW, 1996) limits client self-determination when it poses "a serious, foreseeable, and imminent risk to themselves and others" (p. 7). Though the agency was guided by the principle of respect for client autonomy, it was also guided by the principle of beneficence (Proctor, Morrow-Howell, & Lott, 1993).

Support for the client's self-determination is weakened by her physical and mental condition, lack of family support, and perceived incompetence. The agency felt a strong need to protect the client from physical abuse and possible death. There is considerable support for overriding self-determination and autonomy when life is perceived to be at stake (Reamer, 1983b; Loewenberg & Dolgoff, 1992). The principles of beneficence and nonmaleficence combined to override the client's autonomy. While the decision appears to be paternalistic, it was made not to deliberately override the client's will but to protect her from abuse.

CASE 12.3 Deciding for Alzheimer's Patients

A bright, independent woman who has been coming to the community center several days a week was diagnosed with Alzheimer's disease. For the last year and a half, she has denied any assistance. Denial is her survival kit in her deteriorating condition. The family has not told her that she has Alzheimer's because it would not be good for her to know. She has her own defense mechanism for her memory losses and her increased inability to care for herself. She is at risk because she lives alone, though her children visit and shop with her.

The son insists, and we concur, that she needs someone to take care of her. The daughter suggests we need to wait until her mother is ready because if somebody is put in without her approval she is going to sabotage the appointment. The practice issue is, How do I as a case manager help the family to deal with this situation? The ethical issue is whether to override the woman's self-determination and place an attendant in the home against her will.

The woman was beginning to lose the ability to drive a car, but the family was unable to convince her not to drive. One day she drove to the hospital and crashed and walked into the doctor's office totally bruised. At that point, she made a decision not to drive a car any longer. For this client, something drastic had to happen for anything to be put into place. Today, for the first time, there is going to be a home attendant, whom she interviewed but does not recall. The dilemma was resolved through the involvement and agreement of all the parties.

Discussion

This case demonstrates that an ethical dilemma can be resolved by opting for one action over the other. This case also demonstrates that an ethical dilemma can be resolved by applying a practice principle that integrates two ethical principles, thereby avoiding having to choose between them. As in Case 12.2, the ethical principles are client autonomy and agency beneficence. Because the client was deemed somewhat competent, her autonomy was respected and the agency's beneficence was not activated.

The key event that resolved the dilemma was the car crash. By deciding to stop driving, the client admitted that she was incapable of maintaining the same degree of independent living as heretofore. The staff involved the entire family in a decision-making process to cope with the situation. This practice principle was effective in helping the client to seek assistance with the tasks of daily life. By participating in the decision to have a home health aide, the client maintained a modicum of autonomy. The agency acted in a beneficent manner, and the ethical dilemma was resolved through the integration of autonomy and beneficence.

CASE 12.4 Refusal of Home Care Services

The R family was referred to the family service agency by Mrs. R's physician. He worried about her increasing frailty and dementia and believed she needed home care services. Mr. and Mrs. R live in a two-bedroom garden apartment with two grown sons. One son works and one collects disability. Neither contributes financially or helps with the household tasks.

When the social worker visited their apartment, Mr. R, age 85, was disheveled, dirty, and dressed in an undershirt and trousers. He was obviously cognitively impaired. Mrs. R, age 80, was greatly depressed and indicated that she wanted to die. The apartment was dirty and piled with papers. The floor was covered with various other items. A closet filled with laundry smelled of urine. Mrs. R told the social worker that she sends out the laundry once a year. The younger son's possessions were everywhere, including the floor of his parents' bedroom. Mrs. R also indicated she hires a housekeeper once a year.

Clearly, Mrs. R is trying to do more than she is physically or emotionally able to handle. She can barely walk and needs to hold onto furniture. She has fallen out of bed many times. Yet she does the cooking for the entire household.

Although their income indicates that they could afford to pay for help, Mrs. R refuses to pay even a subsidized rate. This family needs case management, counseling, and home care services but is unwilling to consider making any changes. Should Mr. and Mrs. R be left to maintain their autonomy? When do issues of safety override their right to live as they choose?

Discussion

The present generation of older persons in the United States is healthier, more active, and in better financial condition than any previous cohort of elderly aged 65 and over. Only 5 percent require institutional care, and only 10 percent require community assistance. Seniors who are physically healthy have the lowest rates of anxiety, depression, and substance abuse among adults. However, the proportion and the average age of the elderly will continue to increase well into the next century. The fastest growing segment of the elderly is the 85 and older group, in whom the incidence of dementia approaches 50 percent. "The prevalence of both mental and physical disability increases with advanced age not because age is an illness but because illnesses that occur late in life are persistent, less lethal, and thus accumulate" (Kennedy, 1993, p. 171).

Historically, when a family could not care for the elderly with mental and physical disabilities, nursing home care was the only available solution. However, in the mid-1970s, the United States introduced home health care services to provide less costly, more personal help than what is available in nursing homes. Over the years, the costs of home health care have ballooned out of control (Berger, 1996). Experts agree that costs have to be reduced, but they point to the significant benefits that accrue to the clients and caregivers participating in the program. The elderly are maintained in their own homes, they live longer, and the quality of their lives is better. In addition, home health care has provided jobs for many minorities. For these reasons, the agency would like to introduce home care to this family.

This case, typical of elderly who refuse home care services, evokes the autonomy–paternalism dilemma and the knotty issues regarding the decision-making capacity of elderly persons. The values of the couple appear to clash with the values of the agency represented by the social worker. However, the couple's behavior may reflect not values of self-determination but a pattern of coping with the exigencies of longevity. From the facts on hand, it is difficult to know whether the pattern displayed is an expression of a preferred way of life or an accommodation to the travails of aging. If the latter, there is no ethical dilemma but a clinical challenge to maintain their viability as a family. If the pattern can be said to reflect their values, these values appear to both coincide and clash with those of the agency, which respects client self-determination but is also responsible for the health and social functioning of its elderly clients.

The ethical dilemma is whether to respect their autonomy or override it. Is Mr. and Mrs. R's refusal of home care and case management services the autonomous decision of "mentally competent" persons who are aware of their circumstances and the possible consequences of their decision? The social worker describes Mr. R as "cognitively impaired" and Mrs. R as "depressed." The physician worried about Mrs. R's "increasing frailty and dementia." Degrees of mental incompetence but not total incompetence seem to be corroborated by the physician and the social worker.

Supporting this judgment is the condition of their apartment. The urine contamination of their living quarters is clearly unhealthy and probably contributes to their deteriorating mental state. But even under these conditions, Mrs. R is able to cook for the entire family. They have managed to live this way for years and are not harming anyone else. Who are we to step in and, under the guise of beneficence, shower them with a battery of services that they don't want? Perhaps we should follow the prevailing ethos and support even their diminished autonomy, for they are able to make decisions. Their decision-making capacity should be viewed as decision-specific, relative to specific tasks, and likely to fluctuate over time (High, 1989; Levinson, 1990).

On the other hand, the couple's decision to refuse home care and other services may be attributed to their mental illness and not to a consistent pattern of autonomous decision making (Schwartz, Vingiano, & Bezir-ganian, 1988). Their decision-making capacity may be impaired by their mental state. The issue, therefore, is competence, not lifestyle or environment. If their competence is impaired, beneficence may legitimately override autonomy (Abramson, 1985), and the agency may not be morally neutral toward the inevitable deterioration of the family.

Considerations of autonomy and beneficence differ in acute care settings and home care. In the acute care hospital setting—an alien and intimidating place—the competent patient is the decisive moral agent. The patient's choice supersedes the choices of family members, even when they seek only the patient's well-being, as well as the choices of physicians and institutional and state interests. The patient is the key decision maker.

In the home care setting, the client is on familiar ground, and the professional caregiver is the foreigner. The home setting can diminish caregiver authority and encourage, even embolden, patient autonomy. It can also camouflage incapacity. "When clients are seen only intermittently in surroundings where they are bolstered by family and familiar routines, it can be difficult to assess levels of understanding, independence of judgment and decisional capacity" (Collopy, Dubler, & Zuckerman, 1990). The autonomy of clients runs headlong against the autonomy of caregivers.

Emboldened autonomy is not the rule in home care. For many frail elderly, long-term care at home leads toward a progressive erosion of autonomy. When people are dependent on others on a long-term basis and need assistance with the basic activities of daily life, their dependency can be viewed as the absence of autonomy. "Executional incapacity is thus confused with decisional incapacity" (Collopy, Dubler, & Zuckerman, 1990, p. 8). The authors offer a model of autonomy for home care along the continuum between emboldened and eroded autonomy. There is a middle ground where clients develop mutually accommodating and reciprocal relationships with caregivers, whether they be family members, professionals, or formal caregivers. The various tensions among clients, families, and caregivers require more than a strict ranking of autonomy and authority. Who wins is not the issue. What matters is the necessity of protecting autonomy by accommodation, by the recognition of interdependence, mutuality, and shared burdens within a limited resource system.

Resolution

The dilemma has not been resolved as work with the R family progresses. Data concerning the history and health of the family members are being gathered. The social worker and the agency continue to ask whether the family members should be left on their own. It behooves the agency to find the middle ground between the emboldened and eroded autonomy of the family and the beneficence of the agency.

Should the R family's capacity conclusively be determined to be severely diminished, the agency could readily invoke communitarian principles to override their autonomy. The pendulum has swung toward autonomy and away from the moral community that takes responsibility for its members' welfare. Social work agencies are permeated by a beneficent orientation toward individual and communal welfare that also respects autonomy but overrides it when warranted in order to promote community betterment. In the words of Callahan (1981):

> Hard times require self-sacrifice and altruism—but there is nothing in an ethic of moral autonomy to sustain or nourish those values. Hard times necessitate a sense of community and the common good—but the putative virtues of autonomy are primarily directed toward the cultivation.of independent selfhood. Hard times demand restraint in the blaming of others for misfortune—but moral autonomy as an ideal makes more people blameworthy for the harms they supposedly do for others. Hard times need a broad sense of duty for others, especially those out of sight—but an ethic of autonomy stresses responsibility only for one's freely chosen, consenting adult relationships. (p. 19)

The ethic of autonomy needs to be balanced with an ethic of community.

CASE 12.5 Refusal of Nursing Home Placement

Mr. and Mrs. W have severe physical disabilities that require nursing home placement or chronic hospitalization. They refuse and are adamant about remaining in their own home. Despite the fact that the agency is providing as much support as its resources allow, the couple still remain at risk. There is no extended family that can be relied on. The community is aware of their plight and is concerned about their welfare. Do we, as a family agency, have a right to tell this couple that we will withdraw our services after a time-limited period in the hope that doing so might move them into accepting the institutional plan they so desperately need?

Discussion
The conflict among the parties is embedded in values that lead to particular actions (see Table 12.2).

The Couple
The couple's values are to retain their independence by remaining at home with its attendant security and familiarity. They expect the social worker to affirm their wish to remain at home and continue to provide services.

TABLE 12.2   A Values–Practice Paradigm

	Couple	Social Worker	Agency
Values	Home-security, familiarity, belonging; self-determination	Client self-determination; preservation of life and the quality of life; equitable distribution of resources	Preservation of life and the quality of life; just and equitable distribution of resources; community sanction
Practice	Remain at home; continue to receive agency support services	Offer choice and abide by the couple's decision; refer couple to protective service agency or nursing home	Refer couple to protective service agency or nursing home

The Social Worker

The social worker subscribes to the two contradictory values of client self-determination and preservation of life and a quality of life. A third professional value is the equitable distribution of limited resources to benefit the maximum number of people. Available information suggests that the couple would require additional funds as their physical condition deteriorates, thus making these funds unavailable to others.

The social worker is faced with an ethical dilemma. If she supports the client's right to self-determination, she should give the couple a choice to remain in their home or to enter a nursing home. If the couple choose to stay at home, the social worker is ethically bound to honor this decision because it is consistent with the value of client self-determination. If the social worker supports the preservation and quality of life, she could refer the couple to Adult Protective Services, suggest institutional placement, or provide twenty-four-hour care. The couple's wish to remain at home would be overridden.

The Agency

The agency values protection of its clients' lives, justice, and the equitable distribution of resources to reach as many needy people as possible. It also values community sanction. Supported by community funds, the agency feels duty-bound to implement the dominant community value: preservation of life. The agency's options are to refer the couple to protective placement or to a nursing home.

Resolution

Self-determination and preservation of life may be viewed not as irreconcilable values but as progressive values: a value that may be dominant at one time may be superseded by another value at another time. While the couple are subsisting with limited agency assistance, the value of self-determination may command more attention. As their health deteriorates, however, the value of protection may become more dominant. If medical knowledge attests to their increasing deterioration, it supports the social worker's preference for protection over self-determination.

Progression of values and knowledge of changing circumstances seem to support Lewis's contention that "an approach that depends on an evaluation of consequences is likely to yield a tentative choice of action, subject to revisions or modification during the entire service transaction, constantly responding to new data generated by the service process itself" (Lewis, 1984, p. 208). As new information becomes available from physicians' testimony about the couple's physical condition, the utilitarian approach may advocate a shift from respecting the couple's right to remain at home to assuming a more protective role. The theory could support the principle of nonmaleficence, which could justify the rule that people who cannot take care of themselves should be protected by the community. In the absence of such information about their physical debility, the mandate may not be as clear.

Deontologically, the principle of respect for the couple's autonomy is equivalent to the prima facie duty of fidelity. Contrariwise, the responsibility to protect the couple's health and life stems from the prima facie duty of nonmaleficence. The duty to prevent harm takes priority over the duty of fidelity. Protection of life is a greater duty than respecting autonomy.

In discussing the options of placing an elderly man in a nursing home based on formalist (deontological) and consequentialist (utilitarian) theories, Lewis (1984) offers numerous possibilities that are determined by consequences. If the consequences may not be lifethreatening, Lewis advises following the formalist approach: respecting the person's autonomy. If they are life threatening, the greater good is to place the individual in a nursing home. Where there is ambiguity, the choice may be either to respect autonomy or to place in an institution.

It is apparent that a theory cannot tell practitioners what to do in an ethically ambiguous situation. It can frame the question and provide the context for the principles, values, and knowledge. The resolution of the dilemma is to be found not in the objective situation, which can have different interpretations, but in the social worker's careful weighing of principles and values.

Theory cannot prescribe. Principles are required to guide practitioners in ethically ambiguous situations. Loewenberg and Dolgoff (1992, p. 60) offer an "Ethical Principles Screen" of priorities in ethical decision making (see Table 12.3). This screen can serve as an objective guideline for practitioners who may be unable to decide between competing principles. It is a

TABLE 12.3   Ethical Principles Screen

Ethical Principle 1	Principle of protection of life
Ethical Principle 2	Principle of equality and inequality
Ethical Principle 3	Principle of autonomy and freedom
Ethical Principle 4	Principle of least harm
Ethical Principle 5	Principle of quality of life
Ethical Principle 6	Principle of privacy and confidentiality
Ethical Principle 7	Principle of truthfulness and full disclosure

useful but not absolute index of priorities. Even Ethical Principle 1—the protection of life, which is the supreme value—may not be a priority when the threat to life is ambiguous. Practitioners should have the freedom to re-arrange these priorities if, in their judgment, the situation warrants doing so.

The agency had asked whether it was ethical to remove its services in order to force the couple to enter a nursing home. Having already put the services in place, the agency, in effect, had made a promise to the couple to support them in their home. In medical ethics, it is deemed unethical to re-move life-sustaining treatments once they are in place (Beauchamp & Childress, 1994). Here, too, it would be unethical to remove "life-sustain-ing" services to the couple. This obligation, however, did not imply that the agency supported the couple's autonomy; it merely delayed the agency's intention to remove the services. The agency was seeking ways to encour-age the couple to enter a nursing home, and the couple did go. The di-lemma was resolved when the agency decided that it was more important to try to preserve the couple's lives than to respect their wish to stay at home.

CONCLUSION

The five cases in this chapter illustrate the conflict between autonomy and beneficence. In each case, it was not an arbitrary decision that resolved the dilemma but a number of variables that gave weight to the resolution.

In Case 12.1, the client's experience of abuse and his refusal of services encouraged the worker to wait for the client to be ready and not to try to impose services. He eventually did reach out to the agency and was wel-comed. In Case 12.2, the client's perceived incompetence, plus the physical abuse to which the client was being subjected, convinced the professional team that her life was not safe in her daughter's home. In Case 12.3, the client's modicum of competence, pride, and independence, along with her family's cooperation with the agency coalesced in the joint decision to accept a home health aide. A practice solution was found to justify a decision acceptable to the parties involved. In Cases 12.4 and 12.5, the determination of capacity was the issue, and it was not entirely clear that autonomy should be overridden.

The autonomy–paternalism dilemma is especially prominent in work with the elderly because their increasing frailty raises questions about their decision-making capacity. No objective guidelines exist to help social workers decide whether to honor autonomy or implement beneficence/paternalism in these ambiguous situations. The resolution should be based on a judgment of what the "equity" of the situation demands, which calls for skilled appraisal based on practical judgment (Moody, 1983). This includes the gathering of as much information about the situation as possible, the ordering of the values and rules of each party to the conflict, and the application of ethical principles supported by theories. The "Ethical Principles Screen" offers an objective set of priorities. Although some of the social workers in these cases were able to override self-determination, they did so hesitantly. Others were not ready to take such a bold step. A decision is ethical when it is based on professional values.

Another focus of the autonomy–paternalism dilemma is assisted suicide. Although the issue has been debated primarily by physicians and philosophers, social workers are directly involved because they engage patients in discussions about pain, death and dying, and family. They also provide group counseling to their colleagues who work with AIDS patients, some of whom desire to commit suicide. In the next chapter, assisted suicide is discussed from legal, religious, medical, and professional perspectives.

13

ASSISTED SUICIDE

The issue of physician-assisted suicide (PAS) continues to be debated across the United States even though the Supreme Court voted to uphold two states' bans on it ("Excerpts," 1997). PAS is profoundly affected by the conflicting values of the autonomy–paternalism dilemma. It is a subject with which social workers in hospitals, nursing homes, and other health care facilities are also involved because they discuss it with patients and families. This chapter focuses on legal, religious, medical, and social work issues raised by assisted suicide.

THE PHILOSOPHERS' BRIEF

With an intent to influence the U.S. Supreme Court's decision, a group of six liberal philosophers submitted a brief on the PAS bill. They urged the Court to uphold two federal appeals court rulings, one in New York and the other in California, that said that mentally competent, terminally ill patients have a constitutional right to a doctor's aid in killing themselves. The brief's fundamental principle was that in deeply personal and momentous decisions—how one dies falls into that category—each person must be free to follow his or her own religious or ethical convictions, without government interference beyond the minimum needed to ensure that those decisions are not irrational, ill informed, coerced, or unstable.

Much of the brief sought to situate a constitutional right to PAS in previous Supreme Court rulings on abortion and on the refusal of life-sustaining treatments. At the heart of the philosophers' case were ideas about the autonomy of the individual and the neutrality of the state. "Most of us see death as the final act of life's drama, and we want that last act to reflect our own convictions, those we have tried to live by, not the religious or ethical convictions that a majority forces on us in our most vulnerable moments" ("Assisted suicide," 1997).

Sandel challenges this view. "Despite their claim to neutrality, the philosophers' argument betrays a certain view of what makes life worth living," but there are other views that do not see each person as his or her own ultimate scriptwriter but as a participant in a larger drama. There are "a wide range of moral outlooks that view life as a gift, of which we are custodians with certain duties." Far from being neutral, Sandel maintained, the ethic of autonomy invoked in the brief departs from many religious traditions (cited in Steinfels, 1997, p. 12).

RELIGIOUS PERSPECTIVES

The ethical considerations in the care of dying patients are theologically seen not only as issues of technological, medical, or institutional management, but more fundamentally as a sign of a deeper crisis of meaning in the culture. Society seems unprepared to assess the significance of suffering, dying, and death as part of the whole of human life.

While much of the discussion on legal assisted suicide has focused on the autonomy to make end-of-life decisions, theistic religious traditions have emphasized that such choices are limited by the ultimate sovereignty of God over human life. Life assumes the character of a "gift" or "trust" rather than private property. This status invests human life with sanctity and militates against killing. Some see death as an enemy to be conquered. Others see death as one of the life processes created by God and believe that human beings have a responsibility to respect the integrity of these processes.

The central theological understanding of the person in the Judeo-Christian legacy is expressed in the concept *imago dei*, the idea that human beings are deserving of a fundamental awe and respect because of their creation "in the image of God." "A moral community emerges not by contractual agreements made by otherwise unencumbered individuals making rational choices based on self-interested preferences . . . but through our common presence to each other in relationships of interdependency. The model of the self as chooser seems to be alien to who we know ourselves to be" (Campbell, 1991, p. 270).

THE SUPREME COURT DECISION

After listening to the pro and con arguments regarding physician-assisted suicides, the Supreme Court upheld the bans on assisted suicide in the cases of *Washington* v. *Glucksberg* (1997), and *Vacco* v. *Quill* (1997). The Court argued that states have an unqualified interest in the preservation of human life, in protecting such vulnerable groups as the poor, the elderly, and disabled persons from abuse and neglect. It rejected the claim, in the New York case (*Vacco v. Quill*) that equated assisted suicide with the right to refuse treatment; the Court distinguished between assisted suicide, which is deemed to be "killing," and refusal of treatment, which is "letting die." The Constitution does not grant a generalized right to commit suicide ("Excerpts," 1997).

The case of "killing," the *Vacco* case, hinged on Dr. Timothy Quill's admission that he prescribed a lethal dose of sleeping pills to a patient suffering from leukemia, knowing that she intended to use the pills to end her pain-riddled life. The New York grand jury's decision to acquit the doctor was overturned by the Supreme Court. The *Washington* case also concerned a physician prescribing a drug to hasten his patient's death.

In the case of "letting die," *Cruzan* v. *Director, Missouri Department of Health* (1990), the parents of a young woman in a persistent vegetative state who was being kept alive artificially requested that nutrition and hydration be terminated and said that their daughter would have concurred. The Supreme Court decided that artificial feeding tubes could be removed and that a person's right to refuse treatment is guaranteed by the Constitution. It was as a result of the *Cruzan* case that the Court distinguished between killing and letting die. The upshot of the Supreme Court's decision is that states' prohibition against assisted suicide does not violate the equal protection and due process clauses of the Fourteenth Amendment. States still retain the right to legalize or ban assisted suicide.

MEDICAL PRACTICE

Dr. Jack Kevorkian, though indicted a number of times for his assisted-suicide practices, has never been convicted. It is rare for a physician to be convicted for this offense, because the evidence to prosecute is hardly ever available and the act itself is protected by the persons closest to the person who allegedly wanted to die. The circumstances preclude prosecutors from bringing a case to trial.

The practice of "passive euthanasia" appears to be widespread in hospitals. What might be called managed deaths, as distinct from suicides, are currently the norm in the United States. The American Hospital Association reports that about 70 percent of deaths in hospitals happen after a decision has been made to withhold treatment. There is less information on the deaths that occur in nursing homes and in private homes (Kolata, 1997). Passive euthanasia occurs when doctors decide not to provide antibiotics to treat an infection, withdraw drugs that maintain a patient's blood pressure, or remove a patient from a ventilator. Cases in point are those of Mrs. P and Mrs. B.

CASE 13.1 Treatment for Ovarian Cancer (A)

Mrs. P developed ovarian cancer in her 50s. At first, she responded to chemotherapy but later, because of her lack of response to the drugs, developed bowel obstructions. Her doctor could operate to try to remove the obstructions, but the procedure is not likely to be effective. He could insert a tube to drain her stomach to prevent her from throwing up, but he would have to ask Mrs. P if that is what she wants, and she would have to live with the tube for the rest of her life.

The doctor told Mrs. P that he wants to focus on her symptoms rather than on the underlying disease. Thereupon, he sent her home with pain medications to take if she is in pain and antinausea drugs to take if she is nauseated. Because of the obstructions, she will never eat or drink again. She will not return to the hospital for any aggressive treatment. The doctor said that he never bluntly tells the patient that there is no hope and that she is going to die, but he acknowledged that they both know what is going to happen soon.

CASE 13.2 Treatment for Ovarian Cancer (B)

Ovarian cancer had spread to the liver of Mrs. B, a 40-year-old woman. She was jaundiced and in such agonizing pain that she could not sit up. She did not want to die, but death was near and she was living in agony. Mrs. B's doctor sent her home with a morphine drip, which soothed her pain, sedated her, and hastened her death. Mrs. B's death was peaceful.

Discussion

Would these doctors' actions be characterized—as assisted suicide, assisted death, or relief of suffering? Is there a difference among them? The doctors' intent is to relieve suffering. Can actions such as these be separated into discrete categories?

Doctors give different signals that it is time to die. They might say to the patient, "Do you want to go home and be with your family?" Or, "I can see you're in pain; let's start a morphine drip." The patient may not pick up the clues contained in these statements. The patient may be thinking, "I don't want this pain, but if the medication will shorten my life, I can live with the pain." Sometimes there is a lack of candor in the communication between physician and patient. The patient is being invited to make a choice without understanding its ramifications. In the words of one woman who wasn't prepared for the decisions she had to make and who thought morphine would make death easier but cause more pain, "Morphine-induced death isn't a pretty, floating-off-on-a-cloud kind of quiet death. It, too, is a struggle. Dying is as hard as birth. . . . morphine eased my terminally ill husband's pain but hastened his death" (Campi, 1998, p. A19).

Though doctors are relatively open about their practices with the dying, and they make life-and-death decisions all the time, they anguish over them. The managing of death—a modern phenomenon—creates moral traces for doctors and other health professionals. It is not easy to live with oneself knowing that one helped a person to die. To assuage their distraught feelings, doctors tell themselves that they are assisting individuals to die in peace.

Surveys of attitudes toward assisted suicide suggest that most Americans believe that doctors should be allowed to help terminally ill patients to end their lives. A poll by the *Washington Post* in 1996 found that 51 percent of the adults surveyed favored legality and 40 percent opposed. The better-off financially and the better educated were more likely to favor legal assisted suicide. Demographically, 70 percent of blacks and 58 percent of people over 70 were opposed. They were not asked why they were opposed (Kolata, 1997).

These polls show support for legal assisted suicide in the abstract. But the support dwindles when people are asked about permitting it for reasons other than unremitting pain, such as in the case of a terminally ill patient who feels that life is meaningless or is worried about being a burden. Legislators understand that deep down the public is ambivalent, and that ambivalence partly explains why thirty-five states have laws that explicitly criminalize euthanasia and assisted suicide (Emanuel & Emanuel, 1997).

The problem with the opinion surveys is that they do not address the wrenching specifics with which doctors, lawyers, theologians, and philosophers are wrestling. What if the patient has years to live? is paralyzed but not in pain? is of sound mind but too feeble to take the pills? signed the statement but is now unable to express his or her wishes?

These knotty questions led Sandel to view physician-assisted suicide as one of the rare issues in which ambiguity is preferable to moral consistency, in which judgments on a case-by-case basis are better than strict laws or guidelines about what is right or wrong. "Sometimes it is better to leave things murky" (cited in Rosenbaum, 1997).

Despite the cautions against its institutionalization, efforts are under way to develop protocols and guidelines for assisted suicide. Questions once thought to be unthinkable are being asked: Who is an appropriate candidate? Should patients put their requests in writing? Should a second opinion be obtained? Should there be witnesses? a waiting period? reports to the coroner (Stolberg, 1997)?

The New York State Task Force on Life and the Law concluded that when a patient requests assisted suicide or euthanasia, a health care professional should explore the significance of the request, recognize the patient's suffering, and seek to discover the factors leading to the request. These factors may include insufficient symptom control, clinical depression, inadequate social support, concern about burdening family or others, a sense of hopelessness, spiritual despair, loss of self-esteem and abandonment. These issues should be addressed in a process that involves both family members and health care professionals. . . . Any response to a request for assisted suicide or euthanasia is morally weighty. Ready agreement to the request could confirm a patient's sense of despair and worthlessness. (cited in Bopp and Coleson, 1995, p. 241)

THE SOCIAL WORK APPROACH

The policy adopted by the delegate assembly of the National Association of Social Workers in 1993 states:

Social workers should not promote any particular means to end one's life but should be open to full discussion of the issues and care options. As a client is considering his or her choices, the social worker should explore and help ameliorate any factors such as pain, depression, need for medical treatment, and so forth. Further, the social worker should thoroughly review all available options including, but not limited to, pain management, counseling, hospice care, nursing home placement and advance health care directives. (Client, 1993, p. 60)

The policy provides a comprehensive guide for social workers in end-of-life decisions. It encourages the exploration of life options, the acquisition of knowledge of living wills, powers of attorney for health care, and legislation about health care directives. The role of the social worker is to help patients to express their thoughts and feelings, to facilitate exploration of alternatives, to provide information for making an informed choice, and to involve family members and significant others. If a social worker is unable to help with decisions around assisted suicide, he or she should refer patients and their families to competent professionals who are available to address these issues.

It is inappropriate for social workers to deliver, supply or personally participate in the commission of an act of assisted suicide when acting in their professional role. Doing so may subject the social worker to criminal charges. If legally permissible, it is not inappropriate for a social worker to be present during an assisted suicide if the client requests the social worker's presence. (Client, 1993, p. 60)

The NASW delegate assembly did not take a stand on whether assisted suicide is moral or immoral.

Social workers need to be aware of some of the reasons why people seek to commit suicide or desire assisted suicide: (1) Their depression may prevent them from making rational decisions, but if diagnosed, it may be alleviated by prompt treatment. (2) Many physicians are not trained in pain management and therefore let their patients endure pain that could be avoided. (3) People may be suffering from social isolation and require continuing care. (4) People may be under psychological pressure to think that their lives are not worth living. Though armed with this knowledge, social workers are still likely to find it difficult to work with clients who have requested assistance with, or who desire to commit, suicide. The following case is excerpted from the process record (a record describing the group process) of the facilitator of a support group of social workers who work with HIV/AIDS patients.

CASE 13.3 Should Tom Help His AIDS Client to Commit Suicide?

The facilitator asked the group to think about the most challenging client with whom they have ever worked. Tom answered that he had a client with end-stage AIDS who decided to take his own life and asked Tom to direct him to one of the places where people are helped to kill themselves. At first Tom was shocked and attributed this emotional outburst to depression and deteriorating health. He wanted time to think about the client's request and told him they would continue the discussion next week.

Tom said he was lost after that and could not find any guidance about what to do because this subject had not been discussed in case review or staff meetings. He was bringing his request for support and guidance to the group. Several members validated Tom's experience and echoed a similar theme—that support for social workers was limited and guidance was nonexistent.

Tom said he believed that it was the patient's right to make that decision. He just did not want to be the person to tell the client that it was all right, because his role as a social worker was not to tell clients what to do. Another group member commented that the choice of when to die was a matter of self-determination and that's what social work is about. He had provided information about such groups to clients who requested assistance with suicide, but he told these clients about the limitations of his helping with the request. He treated such requests just like any other piece of information the client might request. A heated discussion ensued.

The facilitator then asked how far does obligation to support client self-determination extend. Do we have an obligation to protect clients from themselves? One member commented that she could never support or agree to discuss a client's desire to commit suicide. She would seek supervision and then inform the client that this was not an issue she felt comfortable discussing. She realized that clients would be left to fend for themselves, but to assist a client to access the services of assisted suicide would be unethical and against her professional role.

As the group was coming to an end, the facilitator suggested that, in addition to bringing this issue to the support group, the members might benefit from a prearranged agreement that in this situation at least two other group members be convened for a review of the case. The purpose of this dialogue would be supportive in deciding how to proceed with this client. No single social worker should be asked to make these decisions by himself or herself. We can take steps to ensure that the treatment and support we provide is exhaustive and within the ethics of our profession.

Discussion

The social worker's hesitation to support and even refer the client for assistance to commit suicide was a mark of the gravity of the act and her personal anguish. Although another group member seemed to have no hesitation in supporting the client's self-determination, most members felt that the issue was especially complex and that they would not want to assume the responsibility themselves. The facilitator, therefore, suggested that they consult with each other so that no one had to shoulder the decision alone.

In the course of the discussion, the social worker explored the contributing factors—the client's pain, depression and concerns. But, as put forth in the NASW delegate assembly policy statement (Client, 1993), the social worker refrained from assisting in the suicide. In the group, there was legitimate disagreement about whether social workers should support client self-determination in committing suicide.

Antisuicide laws aim to keep physicians as healers committed to curing and not killing their patients; to protect elderly and infirm persons from psychological pressure to consent to their own deaths; to protect poor and minority persons from exploitation in order to reduce the cost of public assistance; and to protect persons with disabilities from societal indifference and antipathy ("Excerpts," 1997).

Kass (1990) argues against those who advocate PAS based on the principle of autonomy:

> Euthanasia for one's own dignity is, at best, paradoxical, even self-contradictory: how can I honor myself by making myself nothing? Even if dignity were to consist solely in autonomy, is it not an embarrassment to claim that autonomy reaches its zenith precisely as it disappears? For the choice of death is not an option among other options, but an option to end all options. . . . Is it dignified to ask that someone else become my killer? . . . I think I sufficiently appreciate the anguish of their parents—Karen Ann Quinlan or Nancy Cruzan—or their children and the distortion of their lives and the lives of their families. I also know that, when hearts break and people can stand it no longer, mercy killing will happen and I think we should be prepared to excuse it—as we generally do—when it occurs in this way. But an excuse is not yet a justification, and very far from dignity. (p. 42)

CONCLUSION

Bopp and Coleson (1995) argue that assisting people to commit suicide is not an appropriate response to the life crises that cause people to desire death. The message conveyed is that they are of such little worth that we agree with their often depression-influenced views that they are better off dead. The Constitution does not require society to stand by while those seeking self-destruction pursue assisted suicide or suicide. Nor does it permit a state to protect only some of its citizens from threats that face all. People who are terminally ill are just as susceptible to depression-induced desires to die as the general population. Moreover, few terminally ill patients want to commit suicide, and those who express suicidal urges are likely influenced by depression. As a result, people seeking suicide need life-affirming treatment, not assistance in death. People who are poor, infirm, and older, the disabled or minorities—all those who are particularly vulnerable in our society—deserve our help in living, not in dying.

Patients who seek physician-assisted suicide can be viewed paradoxically as both asserting and relinquishing their autonomy. The assertion of autonomy is expressed in declaring the desire to die and enlisting a physician to assist in the process. The relinquishing of autonomy occurs when the patient passively accepts the physician's decision to send the patient home with or without morphine drips, as in the cases cited, when death is imminent. The autonomy–paternalism dilemma is more murky when the patient does not question the physician's decision. In the next chapter, the autonomy–paternalism dilemma is explored in the case of an elderly woman who refused nutrition and hydration.

14

SPIRITUALITY, ETHICS, AND SOCIAL WORK IN LONG-TERM CARE

The central focus of this chapter is a case presentation of an elderly female nursing home patient who refuses nutrition and hydration against the wishes of her physician. The case was presented as part of a conference on spiritual and ethical issues in working with the elderly. A panel of clergy caregivers representing five of the world's major religions was invited to discuss the spiritual and ethical issues raised by the case. The social work perspective was contributed by the author. Three subject areas that permeate work with the elderly introduce the case: determination of capacity, refusal of nutrition and hydration, and spirituality and religion.

DETERMINING CAPACITY

Competence is the capacity to perform a specific task. In a medical context, the word refers to the ability to make a reasoned and intentional choice among alternative courses of action to reach a treatment decision. Competence is the central ethical issue in geriatrics because an evaluation of competence is the foundation for every other ethical consideration, such as withholding or withdrawing treatment. Evaluations of competence are also the foundation from which residents exercise their rights under nursing home regulations (Levinson, 1990).

To assess competence, it is necessary to focus on the specific cognitive abilities the patient possesses and uses in the actual decision-making situation and whether the patient's behavioral disturbances interfere with passing the tests of capacity. Five tests of capacity exist: indicating a choice, factual understanding, rational reasoning, appreciation of the nature of the situation, and reliable outcomes of choice (McKinnon, Cournos, & Stanley, 1989).

Competence and autonomy are closely allied but not identical. Incompetent patients may act autonomously, without external coercion or manipulation. Autonomy presupposes self-governance, the freedom to make one's own decisions; competence presupposes the ability to make one's own decision in a reasoned and conscious way. Internal factors such as fear, neurotic obsessions, or drug addiction can impair both autonomy and competence.

Competence is related to capacity; a decision is the product of capacity. Ordinarily, a patient capable of making conscious and reasoned choices can be expected to make a competent decision. But the "competence" of a decision is not necessarily synonymous with the "competence" of the patient. A decision may be considered harmful when it is not in conformity with the physician's recommendations, but that does not ipso facto mean that the patient is incompetent. On the other hand, a totally incompetent patient could make the "right" decision—for example, by agreeing with medical recommendations—but lack the capacity for consciously reasoned choices.

When a competent person makes a decision that may bring harm or death, that decision is usually the result of differences in values or an error in logic. The key question is: Which should be the dominant principle—the patient's freedom to choose according to his or her best interests, or the doctor's freedom to intervene when he or she thinks the patient has made a harmful or dangerous choice? Some have tried to resolve this dilemma by relating the criteria of competence to the gravity and consequences of the decision. When the decision is one that could save the patient's life—for example, transfusion for severe blood loss—physicians would recommend that the more stringent criteria for competence be applied, and if the patient cannot meet those criteria, then the treatment should proceed (Pelligrino, 1991). This approach is confirmed by Roca (1994).

The physician does not always arrive at conclusions about capacity with complete confidence. It is sometimes difficult to be certain that psychiatric symptoms are interfering with choice. In such cases, the dangerousness of the patient's decision enters into consideration: the more dangerous the decision, the more inclined the physician is to lean toward safety and find the patient incapacitated (Roca, 1994). It is usually the attending physician who determines capacity and who recommends treatment. If the physician is unsure, a psychiatrist is consulted. If the decision is that the patient is incapacitated, the proxy goes into effect.

In a study of decisions to withhold treatment to incompetent patients, Hanson, Danis, Mutran, and Keenan (1994) found that incompetent patients were far more likely than competent patients to have life-sustaining treatments withheld. Most of the decisions were made by a consensus of physicians and family surrogates, so major conflicts rarely occurred. Treatments withheld included nasogastric feeding, dialysis, and intravenous hydration. A likely explanation for the strong association between patient incompetence and a decision to withhold treatment is that physicians and family members consider the meaning and probability of survival when deciding about life-sustaining treatments.

In health care delivery generally, and in nursing homes in particular, a fear of liability dominates the thinking of many health care providers. This fear contributes to a bias toward reliance on surrogates—particularly family members—to make decisions. The presence of family members often substitutes for a careful assessment of the patient's own functional capacity to engage in rational decision making. It is much more efficient to deal with an articulate relative who serves as proxy than to do a thorough evaluation of an impaired older nursing home patient.

Achieving an appropriate balance between patient autonomy and professional beneficence in the nursing home population is particularly difficult. The growing number of frail and dependent elderly requiring decisions about medical procedures poses a special problem for health care professionals. To deal with this problem, efforts are being made to validate objective criteria for assessing competent decision-making capacity. However, no one set of measurements has been agreed on, nor is it likely that a single set will suffice (Fitten, Lusky, & Hamann, 1990).

The capacity to participate in care decisions is almost always decision-specific and relative to specific tasks, and it may fluctuate over time (High, 1989). Health care professionals should assume that an adult patient has decisional capacity. Patient depression or anxiety should not be taken as prima facie evidence of decisional incapacity. The health care professional has the ethical duty to counter depression or anxiety as much as possible in order that a patient's capacity be exercised as fully as possible. However, if, after reaching for the patient's cognitive abilities through questions and a verbal understanding of the possible decisions and their consequences, the physician determines that a particular elderly patient is decisionally incapacitated, the physician and other health care professionals should respect the patient's rights of autonomy by facilitating proper surrogate decision making and provide optimal care while guarding against paternalism. Decision-making capacity can be viewed on a continuum (High, 1989).

Patients who refuse medication have had their self-determination supported by recent court decisions that reviewed petitions to involuntarily medicate a patient. In *Rivers* v. *Katz* (1986), the New York Court of Appeals ruled that "in situations where the State's police power is not implicated, and the patient refuses to consent to the administration of anti-psychotic drugs, there must be a judicial determination of whether the patient has the capacity to make a reasoned decision with respect to proposed treatment before the drugs may be administered pursuant to the State's *parens patriae* power" (McKinnon, Cournos, & Stanley, 1989, p. 1159).

The refusal of nutrition and hydration calls into question a patient's decisional capacity. Determining capacity is a complex matter that touches on assessments of competence, the interface between patient self-determination and physician beneficence, and the values underlying the decision.

REFUSAL OF NUTRITION AND HYDRATION

Artificial nutrition and hydration (ANH), also called tube feeding, is the provision of artificial nutrients and fluids by means of a tube inserted through the nasal passages into the stomach (nasogastric) or via an incision through the abdominal wall into the stomach (gastrostomy) or small intestine (jejunostomy). Tube feeding is indicated in the short term to provide nutrition and hydration for seriously ill patients who are recovering the ability to eat. In the short or long term, it supplements oral feeding in patients who are unable to take in adequate nutrients to maintain or regain their health or functioning (Ahronheim, 1996).

Patients are increasingly devising advance directives that refuse service or forbid heroic measures to be operationalized in case they become incapacitated. They have been empowered to do so by the Patient Self-Determination Act of 1990, which requires all hospitals participating in Medicare or Medicaid to ask all adult inpatients whether they have advance directives and to document their answers and provide information on hospital policies and state laws. Other health agencies such as hospice and home health have instituted similar requirements (cited in "Excerpts," 1993). Morally, the advance directive serves as a means for maintaining autonomy. Autonomy is not only a basic moral and legal right but also an instrumental good. Individuals are better able to determine what is in their own best interests, given their values, beliefs, and circumstances, than someone else.

Situations may arise in which it may not be in the best interest of a person to follow a specific directive, particularly in the short term. For example, it may be appropriate to treat despite a nontreatment directive, in situations in which hydration may be necessary for comfort and tube feeding is needed to improve poor nutritional status. The nature and intent of such interventions are primarily for temporary relief or to provide additional time for assessment and diagnosis. These interventions should not be continued if they provide no long-term benefit and if the person had expressed a clear wish to avoid prolonged provision of life-sustaining treatment (Van Allen, 1988). Reasonable medical judgment may thus indicate that a certain treatment modality is needed for a person's comfort or that additional time is required for better assessment of long-term prognosis.

The New Jersey Supreme Court allowed in principle the removal of feeding from Claire Conroy, an 84-year-old nursing home resident with advanced Alzheimer's disease, whose nephew petitioned the court on her behalf (*In re Conroy*, 1985). In Massachusetts, Paul Brophy, a 45-year-old firefighter who was permanently comatose after a ruptured cerebral aneurism, was allowed to die by removal of feeding (*Brophy v. New England Sinai Hospital*, 1986). These decisions were based on the weighing of benefits and burdens (*Conroy*) and on respect for self-determination (*Brophy*)—classical analytical approaches of ethics.

In the *Conroy* case, the evidence of the woman's wishes was indirect. She "did not like the doctors," according to her nephew. The pain and suffering of continued life and her inability to understand the burdens of treatment played a large role in the court's decision. In the *Brophy* case, there was a clear living will in the form of prior knowledge of the patient's explicit wishes not to be maintained by life-support technology in this kind of situation. In spite of court rulings in both cases, however, the institutions caring for the patients refused to allow withdrawal of feeding (Cassel, 1987). Physicians have been wont to disregard such directives when they deem it necessary. They may persuade the family that the insertion of a feeding tube after a stroke, for example, is temporary in order to await the progress of recovery. In the nursing home, professional staff meet with the family to ascertain the patient's wishes and will respect those wishes if the family affirms them as the patient's own.

The decisions in the *Conroy* and *Brophy* cases were in contrast to the Missouri Supreme Court's ruling in *Cruzan v. Director, Missouri Department of Health* (1990). Upheld by the U.S. Supreme Court (June 25, 1990), the Missouri court ruled that Ms. Cruzan's feeding tube could not be discontinued even though she was in a vegetative state, because evidence regarding her wishes was inherently unreliable.

Faced with a patient like Conroy, Brophy, or Cruzan, most of us would recognize an ethical dilemma. For example, we want to preserve life but also to respect self-determination. We want to do no harm, yet both treatment and nontreatment seem harmful. One must choose the most right or the least wrong of these options.

Food and water decisions are usually of the "least wrong" sort because to allow or, worse, cause the death of a person by starvation or dehydration seems wrong. Yet increasing numbers of voices are saying that that is sometimes right—or at least less wrong—than the alternative, which is continued life (Cassel, 1987). The question remains: Should it ever be permissible to withhold or withdraw food and nutrition? The answer should acknowledge the different meanings that food has to people—a spiritual connection to a divinity, ethnic belonging, a psychological connection between feeding and loving and between nutritional satisfaction and emotional satisfaction.

The President's Commission for the Study of Ethical Problems in Medicine and Biomedical and Behavioral Research in 1982 suggested that artificial feeding interventions need not be continued for patients with permanent loss of consciousness. There is controversy over how to classify artificial nutrition and hydration. Court decisions are contradictory (Meilaender, 1984). Lynn and Childress (1983) appear to classify ANH as a medical treatment; given that definition, it would be legal to withhold ANH just as it is legal to disconnect a respirator for a comatose patient (Zerwekh, 1997). Though withholding ANH may be legal, however, it is not necessarily moral and ethical. Another view is that ANH is a humanistic act, not a medical one. "It seems, rather, to be the sort of care that all humans owe each other. . . . When we stop feeding the permanently unconscious patient, . . . we are withholding the nourishment that sustains life" (Meilaender, 1984). Given that definition, feeding is no different from washing and bathing and therefore is mandated regardless of the patient's condition or wishes.

The debate about classifying ANH as a medical or humanistic act focuses mainly on patients who do not show capacity for decision making and are severely demented or comatose. Other patients, as in the case to be presented later in this chapter, who do possess capacity may prefer not to be fed or hydrated. In such cases, should we adhere to the patient's wishes (McCann, Hall, & Groth-Juncker, 1994)? For an increasing number of noncomatose patients, the benefits of continued life are perceived to be insufficient to justify the burden and cost of care, death is the desired outcome, and the role of the physician is to participate in bringing death about (Siegler & Weisbard, 1985).

For those who hold that it is intrinsically wrong not to feed another person, the logical question that follows is whether feeding always improves patients' well-being. The absence of food and hydration could be severely detrimental to the health of some patients. But the absence of food and nutrition could diminish the incontinence, painful bowel movements, and other maladies of other patients. Sometimes, when ANH is medically contraindicated, health care practitioners must individualize patients. What should be our moral response to withholding or withdrawing nutrition?

A competent patient's decision not to accept the provision of food and water by medical means such as tube or intravenous feeding is unlikely to raise questions of harm or burden to others (Lynn & Childress, 1983). Even in the cases of incompetent patients, the authors conclude that "in most cases such patients will be best served by providing nutrition and fluids. Thus, there should be a presumption in favor of providing nutrition and fluids as part of the broader presumption to provide means that prolong life. But this presumption may be rebutted in particular cases" (p. 21). "The feeding of the hungry, whether because they are poor or because they are physically unable to feed themselves, is the most fundamental of all human relationships. It is the perfect symbol of the fact that human life is inescapably social and communal" (Callahan, 1983, p. 22).

In a study comparing decisions by older patients and physician-selected proxies, some respondents, commenting on the tube feeding vignette in the study, felt that the patient was "just depressed" (Zweibel & Cassell, 1989). They did not believe that the patient's refusal of food was intended to avoid the suffering caused by chronic hip pain; they believed instead that, once fed, she would be grateful for the physician's intervention. This reaction could illuminate the ambiguity surrounding the case presentation to follow. Was the patient depressed and perhaps incompetent when she asked not to be fed, or did the request represent the rational thinking of a competent person who wants to die? The case, and practically all end-of-life decisions about artificial nutrition and hydration, is replete with uncertainty.

SPIRITUALITY AND RELIGION

In addition to the issues of competence and artificial nutrition and hydration that arise in working with the elderly, the issue of spirituality and religion has assumed prominence in social work practice. For many years in social work, the spiritual dimension of human functioning was not discussed or written about. It was felt to be the province of the clergy, an area about which social workers knew little and was therefore off limits. Siporin (1985) found an antireligious bias in much of psychotherapeutic literature. Loewenberg (1988) contends that "the social work literature has generally ignored or dismissed the impact of religion on practice" (p. 5). He believes that we need to prepare social workers to practice with religiously oriented clients. This trend has lately been reversed. Greater emphasis on spirituality and religion has been placed in social work practice because they tend to be vital areas of human functioning and service to clients is incomplete when they are overlooked.

Spiritual areas of care offer opportunities for growth and healing. Canda (1988) suggests that the client can be helped to transform suffering into an opportunity for growth. The social worker can help the client find meaning in suffering and should not discredit or eliminate anxiety or guilt. The search for meaning usually encompasses the spiritual dimension of life. Groups in which the spiritual dimension is particularly meaningful include minorities, the elderly, and other special populations (Canda, 1988). Pinderhughes (1989) suggests that it is important to recognize religion in order to understand ethnicity.

Almost all of the religious and nonreligious social work respondents who participated in Millison's study (1994) of their approaches to practice used some spiritual approaches to help their clients, though many shied away from religious approaches. Similar findings occurred in the study conducted by Sheridan, Bullis, Adcock, Berlin, and Miller (1992). "As a whole, [social work] respondents were found to value the religious or spiritual dimension in their own lives, to respect the function it serves for people in general, and to address, to some extent, religious and spiritual issues in their practice with clients" (p. 200). Joseph (1988) studied the significance of religious issues and the notion of God as they emerge in clients' situations. For the purposes of her study, religion was defined as

the external expression of faith (the inner beliefs and values that relate the person to the transcendent or God). It is comprised of beliefs, ethical codes, and worship practices that unite an individual with a moral community. . . . Religion is differentiated from spirituality which is at the ground of our being and strives for meaning and union with the universe. The spiritual dimension seeks to transcend self and relate the individual to the ultimate. For those with theistic beliefs, the ultimate reality is God. (p. 444)

Canda (1989) is critical of social workers' lack of preparation to help clients with religious and spiritual matters. He advises that it is necessary, both personally and professionally, for social workers to come to terms with religious and spiritual issues of their own and in the lives of clients in order to be effective practitioners.

This review of the literature on determining capacity, refusing nutrition and hydration, and the spiritual component in social work with the elderly introduces the case of the nursing home patient who refuses nutrition and hydration, and the reactions of clergy caregivers and a social work professional to the spiritual, ethical, and practice issues raised by the case.

CASE STUDY FOR PANEL DISCUSSION*

CASE 14.1 Resident's Refusal to Eat and Drink as a Means of Ending Her Life

Mrs. S, 89 years old, was admitted to a skilled nursing facility for long-term care with a number of medical ailments, including rheumatoid arthritis, osteoporosis, Raynaud's disease, mild dysphagia 2 esophageal motility (difficulty in swallowing), hiatal hernia, peptic ulcer, hemiparesis 3/94 (stroke—left-sided weakness improved), and depression. A college graduate and teacher in the New York City public school system for many years, Mrs. S used to love reading and sewing; now she watches television, particularly news programs, and is articulate. Widowed twice, her first husband was a general practice physician and the second was the dean of a medical school. She has a daughter, son-in-law, two grandchildren, and one great-grandchild. Mrs. S describes her family as supportive of and close to her and demonstrates great pride in their intellectual achievements and in their identification with their religion.

After her second husband died, Mrs. S lived independently for a number of years until, because of declining health, she moved in with her daughter's family. They refurbished part of their house to suit her needs. The daughter describes her mother as fastidious, demanding, difficult to please, a "control freak." The daughter felt it necessary to photograph parts of the mother's room so that caregivers would know precisely how everything should be in its place.

When Mrs. S's condition worsened, the family agreed to placement for long-term care. Throughout Mrs. S's stay at the nursing home, she voiced multiple complaints about the environment, the other residents, and the quality of care she received, and she exhibited symptoms of anxiety, depression, and increasing suspiciousness. Although she occasionally participated in activities, she spent most of her time in her single room and did not form any lasting relationships with her peers. There were a few staff members, however, with whom she became somewhat close.

The family maintained daily contact with her and visited frequently. Mrs. S freely voiced her numerous complaints to her daughter.

---

*This case, as well as the clergy responses that follow, was presented at a panel discussion at the conference "Whose Life Is It Anyhow? Spiritual/Religious Values and Clinical Ethics in Long-Term Care," cosponsored by the New York City Long-Term Care Ethics Network and the Wurzweiler School of Social Work, Yeshiva University, on December 9, 1996. The clergy responses are presented alphabetically. The social worker's response is the author's.

After a while, the patient learned that the room in her daughter's house that was prepared just for her had been converted into a home office for her son-in-law's use.

During her three-year stay at the nursing home, Mrs. S's physical condition continued to deteriorate, rehabilitative efforts to strengthen her mobility and functionality did not succeed, and her complaints about swallowing and appetite became more frequent. Two days after reaching her 89th birthday, the patient announced to her family and to the nursing home staff that she had decided to stop eating and drinking altogether for the purpose of bringing about her death. She warned the staff that she did not want to be "harassed" about her decision.

Prior to her admission, she had executed a series of advance directives, including two living wills and a health care proxy, appointing her daughter as her health care agent. These documents made it clear that if she became terminally ill or sustained irreversible brain damage from which there was no likely prospect of recovery, she wanted all life-sustaining treatments withheld or withdrawn. Mrs. S's daughter supported her mother's decision to end her life by refusing food and water. Some staff felt she was a bit too enthusiastic about the decision. The daughter observed, as did other staff members, that the patient became more serene and peaceful after she announced her decision.

The patient's attending physician recorded that she had full capacity to make this decision and he would honor her wishes. The staff psychiatrist felt that Mrs. S understood the nature and consequences of her decision, but he also believed her to be depressed and recommended antidepressant medication. The patient refused this medication, claiming that it had caused her unwanted side effects in the past and did not help. The patient offered various reasons for her decision: "I've had a good life. My children are well established in their own lives, and my responsibilities to them have ended. I've been looking for a good way out for some time. I can't stand eating in the [nursing home's] dining room anymore. I hate those people who sit near me. They are so coarse and unfeeling. I find that my swallowing is getting worse."

The ethics team met with the daughter and son-in-law. They insisted on supporting the patient's wishes and did not believe that Mrs. S might be suffering from depression and might benefit from further evaluation and treatment.

The patient continued to refuse food, requested small amounts of water and ice chips, and grew progressively weaker. After a few days, she refused all medications. She was placed in the hospice program. Her fast lasted for thirty-seven days, after which she decided to end it because (1) her plans to die were not succeeding; (2) the process was taking too long and no end was in sight; (3) her dry mouth was becoming intolerable; and (4) she appreciated the extra attention she was getting from the hospice and nursing home staffs. The daughter supported her mother's decision to begin eating and drinking again and said that she and her family were "shaken up and surprised." Her mother's protracted attempt to die had put her family's life on hold, and she had felt obligated to visit her every day. The daughter stated that she hoped her mother would understand that she and her family could no longer visit every day, that it was time for her and her husband to get on with their own lives, and that they had decided to go away for the weekend.

The patient agreed to receive IV fluids for two days and is now being treated with Prozac for what her physician now considers "significant depression."

QUESTIONS FOR THE PANEL

1. What is (are) the ethical dilemma(s) posed by this case?
2. If this patient were a member of your faith, would your faith tradition tilt in favor of supporting this patient's freedom to choose to end her life, or would it seek to support and improve the quality of that life? Provide some principles drawn from your tradition to buttress your answer.
3. What spiritual resources would you bring to bear in attempting to reduce the suffering of this person?
4. How far would you go on religious grounds to attempt to dissuade the patient from her decision?
5. How would you interpret God's role in this scenario?
6. How would you as the caregiver decide to respond to the patient in this case on religious grounds?

THE PROTESTANT PERSPECTIVE*

Few of us call ourselves ethicists, but most of us are called to do real-life ethics every day. Those of us who are engaged in the lives and deaths of residents of long-term-care facilities know that the ethical dilemmas we face together are rarely clear-cut situations that can be addressed simply by the judicious application of principles. Rather, as this case illustrates, we are engaged in a dynamic process involving complex and evolving situations that are subject to interpretation and differences of perspective.[1]

---

*Amy Furth, staff chaplain, The Healthcare Chaplaincy, Florence Nightingale Health Center, New York.

As a pastoral caregiver I have learned that the life stories of our residents are human texts that have as much to teach us as our scholarly tomes on theology, philosophy, or psychology.[2] Before assigning these women and men to categories or diagnoses, we would do well to pay close attention to their life stories in their own words. The woman whose case is under discussion can teach us a great deal about the experience of suffering. The woman lives in chronic pain due to a multiplicity of physical ailments and has been stripped by layer after layer of loss. She has lost two husbands, her home, her professional and personal roles and place in the community, her proud independence, and her sense of control over her body and her life. She has even, in the process of this case study, lost her name. To me she is Mrs. Leiden, a woman who knows what it is to suffer.

As a patient, Mrs. Leiden's medical diagnoses are well documented. Her emotional condition can be inferred from her psychosocial history, which details the richness of the life she has lost and describes her unhappiness with life in the nursing home. She is described as being depressed, isolative, suspicious, anxious, and demanding. Although no specific reference is made to her spiritual condition, it is not difficult to assess that, in addition to her physical and emotional distress, Mrs. Leiden is a woman in the midst of a spiritual crisis.

Spiritual issues are those that deal with the dimension of transcendence or being connected to something beyond ourselves. In the practice of pastoral care, spiritual assessment is concerned with issues of meaning and purpose of life, relationship and community, reconciliation, and sources of hope.[3] Mrs. Leiden feels that since her responsibilities to her family are ended, she has no role in life. She has lost her sense of meaning and purpose. Since she moved out of her own home and then out of her daughter's house, the nursing facility has become the place in which she is intended to live out her remaining days, but she feels alienated from the other members of the community. Mrs. Leiden is lonely and feels abandoned. She cannot reconcile herself to her situation in the nursing home. She is hopeless and in despair—looking for a way out.

It is in the context of great physical, emotional, and spiritual distress that Mrs. Leiden states her intention to stop eating and drinking so that she might hasten the approach of her death and be relieved of her pain and suffering. It is not hard to imagine the potential impact of Mrs. Leiden's despair on staff members engaged in her care. Concern or even righteous indignation are likely to be expressed openly. Anxiety, anger, and guilt are more likely to be felt but unexpressed. Mrs. Leiden is not an easy or pleasant person to be with as a caregiver. Both her suffering and her response to her suffering are an affront to the sensibilities of the community.

We are to imagine ourselves as Mrs. Leiden's immediate community. The ethical deliberations regarding her situation will need to take into account not only the multiple dimensions of Mrs. Leiden's suffering but also how we relate to her as a member of our community. It is Mrs. Leiden, and other residents like her, whose needs have called us together into a community of caregiving. From this perspective, our first concern is not to judge whether Mrs. Leiden is right or wrong to feel that her life is not worth prolonging. Rather, our immediate challenge is to discern what our responsibilities are to Mrs. Leiden as one to whom we are related in the covenant of a caring community.

Mrs. Leiden's life crisis does not present us with an abstract exercise in choosing between conflicting ethical principles. We are not faced with making a choice between *either* respecting Mrs. Leiden's right to make decisions about her own care and treatment *or* intervening to improve the quality of Mrs. Leiden's life in the nursing home. Our immediate moral mandate is both to respect Mrs. Leiden and to care for her. There is no question of Mrs. Leiden's capacity to make her own decisions, and there certainly is no question of whether or not to care.[4] The only practical question is *how* to care. Mrs. Leiden's positive response to the enriched care she receives from hospice and nursing home staff suggests the kind of care that has been lacking in her life. Receiving more adequate and appropriate care, she no longer seeks to hasten death.

The presentation of Mrs. Leiden's case does suggest some potential ethical dilemmas in which religious principles may be considered. Mrs. Leiden indicates that she intends to exercise control over her life by refusing to eat. We may imagine that her determination is an offense to many of the nursing home staff. Some might argue on religious grounds that Mrs. Leiden would be morally wrong to hasten her death by refusing nutrition and hydration. However, Mrs. Leiden's right to make decisions about her care and treatment is protected as a matter of public policy.[5] Does it follow, therefore, that legal protections such as the Patient Self-Determination Act (1991) are threats to the values of religious authority and community?

The concept of autonomy as a matter of public policy is consistent with Protestant Christian religious beliefs and, far from being a threat, protects our freedom and that of all other people to live according to those authorities we recognize for guidance in our lives. These may include religious teachings and teachers, family members, cultural values, physicians, or other guides. But the determination of authority rests with each of us individually.[6]

Some religious leaders lament that so many within their own faith communities do not choose to follow their authority or the teachings of their own tradition. For various reasons they may feel alienated from the traditional doctrines or the traditional authorities. However lamentable this may be, these are concerns to be addressed from within our faith communities. They cannot be legislated as a matter of civil law. Our American heritage of religious freedom means that we look to the law neither to prohibit nor to enforce religion but to preserve our individual freedom *for* religion. Especially in a pluralistic society, respect for personal autonomy is not the enemy but the safeguard of authentic religious life.[7]

Protestant Christians affirm liberty of conscience as a religious principle that is both scripturally based and affirmed by tradition and experience. Individual conscience is understood to be a gift from God, an authority greater than human beings or human institutions. In the Christian scriptures the apostle Paul claims to speak the truth, according to his conscience, confirmed by the Holy Spirit (Romans 9:1). And he recognizes individual conscience as a witness within all humans, a "law written on the human heart" (Romans 2:15). Pauline conscience is not freedom from God but sensitivity to the voice of God.

By recognizing the authority of personal experience, Protestantism may be seen to promote individualism. But it would be a mistake ever to imagine an individual apart from the context of community. We understand ourselves to be born into community and called into relationship. The communal dimension of personal existence is a given, but it is also a challenge to anyone who would presume to live in isolation. We are accountable not only to ourselves but to God and our neighbors also.

Protestant Christians use the language of covenant to express our binding relationship to God and to every other human person of all ages, tongues, and races.[8] In this we are guided by Jesus' reverence of the *shema*, the Great Commandment, which he linked with love of neighbor (Matthew 22:34–40). In the last days of his ministry in Jerusalem, Jesus made his meaning even more explicit in the vision of a judgment day when each of us will be held accountable for the care that we have shown to those who hunger and thirst, those who lack shelter and clothing, those who are sick and imprisoned. He taught his disciples, "Just as you did it to one of the least of these who are members of my family, you did it to me" (Matthew 25:31–46).

Jesus modeled an ethic of care in his life and ministry. Making a distinction between curing and healing, the gospel of Luke, especially, contains many accounts of healing. Jesus often emphasized the power of faith and forgiveness in healing the whole person. In the parable of the Good Samaritan he makes clear that the ethic of care extends beyond family and friendship to include strangers. Jesus' bias is clearly based on need rather than kinship or stature. In the parable of the great dinner he commands that invitations be sent to the poor, the crippled, the blind, and the lame (Luke 14:21).

Jesus' invitation list might describe the residents who make up the majority of our long-term-care communities. To be faithful to Jesus' model of ministry, Christians are called to take into account the whole person: treating not only physical pain and other distressing symptoms but also responding to the social, emotional, and spiritual dimensions of human suffering. We are called to listen more attentively and respond with greater empathy. We are called to be compassionate—to share another's pain. To provide such care in a long-term-care setting may require us to open ourselves and be willing to become more engaged in our relationships with our residents. This is hard to do.

At an institutional level, the determination of staffing patterns has obvious ethical dimensions related to the quality of care offered to residents. Promoting healing relationships takes time and resources. But it is in such relationships that healing takes place. Nurses and social workers, doctors and therapists are often torn between the needs of more residents than they can attend to with the time available to them. Surrendering clinical detachment for attachment to someone in pain is humbling and makes us vulnerable. The inclusion of clinically trained chaplains to the interdisciplinary team can support other staff members in providing holistic care for residents in long-term care settings.

Mrs. Leiden's religion is not identified. If she were a Christian, I would hope to minister to her as one whose presence might provide comfort and encouragement for her to lament, reminisce, grieve, and tell her own story. I would hope to become her companion in a process of reconciliation with her life as she has lived it. Reading from the Psalms together might help us to share the experience of God's presence in the midst of suffering. I would invite Mrs. Leiden to participate in religious services in the hope that the familiar prayers and songs might kindle a feeling of connectedness both to her religious heritage and to other residents with whom she might feel a special kinship.

As her chaplain, I would neither condone nor condemn Mrs. Leiden's stated intention to stop eating, but I would attempt to address the feelings of isolation, alienation, and suffering that contribute to her feeling that life is not worth living. I would want to talk about how painful it is to lose one's illusions of independence and control over one's life, and to help her to recognize the human reality of interdependence. But I would not presume to counsel Mrs. Leiden regarding the morality of her decision.

Christian faith affirms that nothing, not even death, can separate us from the love of God (Romans 8:38). Among Protestant Christians the sanctity of life is not generally interpreted to mean mere biological existence. Death is not welcomed, but neither is it our worst enemy, to be avoided at all costs. We are each of us granted only a span of years in this world. Reverence for life may sometimes call for us to stand back and forgo attempts to control our mortality.

In the actual telling of Mrs. Leiden's story, it would seem that the enriched care offered to her by the hospice team and nursing home staff was such that she ended what, in retrospect, might be interpreted as a hunger strike. Bringing her desperation to the attention of the community, Mrs. Leiden developed with her caregivers relationships that apparently helped her to overcome her feelings of alienation and disconnectedness and made her life bearable.

The introduction of hospice care to long-term care facilities is providing new models for relating to our residents. For one thing, hospice teams coming into our nursing homes relate to staff caregivers as "family" and recognize that doctors, nurses, social workers, and therapists are personally affected by the affliction of those for whom we care. Without dealing with our own anxieties, we cannot become a nonanxious presence for our residents. Acknowledging our own feelings may also help staff members to relate to sons and daughters of residents and other family members who are often overlooked as fellow sufferers. They also need our compassion and our support.

Mrs. Leiden's case does not contain enough information to develop much understanding of her family relationships. Her daughter is portrayed as a truly horrible, scheming person: planting the idea of suicide by starvation in her mother's mind, urging her on, and abandoning her when she forgoes the attempt. The ominous portrayal of the daughter is so extreme as to suggest that her persona may be colored by projection of the unresolved feelings of the staff from whose perspective the case is described. Mrs. Leiden's daughter may or may not be the monster the staff describes. It is not altogether clear from the facts as presented. But it is clear that she, too, is in need of care to help her deal with her own feelings and issues in relationship to her aging and dying mother.

What, then, does Mrs. Leiden have to teach us about ethical issues in long-term care? First, ethical deliberation is not so much about decision making as about engaging in a dynamic process involving a whole community of care. Second, Mrs. Leiden's story tells us that she needed to be reassured of the value of her life not by our judgment but by our respect and our compassion. From a pastoral perspective the moral of this story seems to be that even more than she wanted to die, Mrs. Leiden wanted to be loved.

Notes

1. Arthur Caplan, director of the Center for Bioethics at the University of Pennsylvania, affirms the validity of "hands-on ethics." "We are also in the trenches, doing real-world, real-life ethics here. And that's what philosophy ought to be: about real people, speaking to human concerns—not armchair fantasies about right and wrong" (Dreifus, 1996, p. 42).

2. The paradigm of the patient as a "living human document," first suggested by Anton Boisen in the infancy of the clinical pastoral education movement,

has become a guiding image in the training and practice of pastoral caregivers and pastoral counselors (Gerkin, 1984, chap. 2).

3. Many tools for spiritual assessment have been developed not only by pastoral caregivers but also by nurses, who have shown a long-standing concern for their patients' spiritual needs. For an introduction to spiritual assessment, guidelines for evaluating models of spiritual assessment, and some examples of existing tools see Fitchett, Burton, & Sivan (1997).

4. Despite the clinical determination of capacity agreed to by both the physician and the psychiatrist, some might suggest that Mrs. Leiden's determination to end her life is per se an indication of a lack of capacity—that is, that there can be no such thing as "rational suicide." For an extensive treatment of this issue, see Battin's chapter "The Concept of Rational Suicide" (1995, chap. 4). For a discussion of the issue in the context of beneficence and the conflict of paternalism and autonomy, see Beauchamp and Childress (1994, p. 286).

5. The principle of informed consent in modern medical practice in the United States was established by Judge Benjamin Cardozo in his 1914 opinion in the case of *Schloendorff* v. *Society of New York Hospital*. For an annotated bibliography including reference to both the *Schloendorff* case and to contemporary articles on informed consent, see Fins and Bacchetta (1994).

6. The Fellows of the Calvin Center for Christian Scholarship, while noting that "autonomy has not had a good press among Reformed thinkers," document that the principle of individual responsibility is firmly grounded in the Protestant tradition from the writings of John Calvin (Bouma, Diekema, Langerake, Rottman, & Verhey, 1989, p. 59). For a more general discussion of the issues of autonomy, authority, and community, see Beauchamp and Childress (1994, pp. 124–126).

7. Joseph J. Fins, director of medical ethics at New York Hospital, draws from his clinical experience to illustrate the principle of autonomy in action, "the accommodation that secular bioethics makes for religious diversity" (Fins, 1994).

8. This particular wording is taken from the United Church of Christ Statement of Faith, which affirms belief in the "Holy Spirit . . . binding in covenant all faithful people of all ages, tongues, and races" (Miller, 1990, p. 12).

References

Battin, M. P. (1995). *Ethical issues in suicide.* Englewood Cliffs, NJ: Prentice Hall.

Beauchamp, T. L., & Childress, J. F. (1994). *Principles of biomedical ethics* (4th ed). New York: Oxford University Press.

Bouma, H., Diekema, D., Langerak, E., Rottman, T., & Verhey, A. (1989). *Christian faith, health, and medical practice: By the fellows of the Calvin Center for Christian Scholarship, Calvin College.* Grand Rapids, MI: Eerdmans.

Dreifus, Claudia (1996, December 15). Who gets the liver transplant? *The New York Times Magazine.*

Fins, Joseph J. (1994, Spring). Encountering diversity: Medical ethics and pluralism. *Journal of Religion and Health, 33,* 23–27.

Fins, Joseph J., & Bacchetta, Matthew D. (1994). *Annotated bibliography I (Core curriculum).* New York: New York Hospital, Medical Ethics Committee.

Gerkin, Charles V. (1984). *The living human document: Revisioning pastoral counseling in a hermeneutical mode.* Nashville: Abington Press.

Metzger, B., & Murphy, R. (1991). *The new Oxford annotated Bible: New revised standard version*. New York: Oxford University Press.

Fitchett, G., Burton, L. A., & Sivan, A. B. (1997, May). The religious needs and resources of psychiatric inpatients. *Journal of Nervous and Mental Disease* 185 (5) 320–326.

Miller, A. O. (1990). *The United Church of Christ statement of faith: A historical, biblical, and theological perspective*. New York: United Church Press.

THE CATHOLIC PERSPECTIVE*

It is clear that the woman's religion and the practice thereof had very little to do with the way she was acting (which could be an essential part of the dilemma she caused). I also think that the woman isn't the only "patient" in this case; her daughter easily qualifies as a patient as well.

The ethical dilemmas posed by this case are best summarized by these questions: Whose life is it anyway? Do individuals have the right to die? Are life and/or death decisions now to be reached by a kind of progressive consensus—patient; patient and daughter; patient, daughter, and son-in-law; patient, daughter, son-in-law, and attending physician? How does the family's (and the physician's) ready acceptance of her decision differ from assisted suicide? Does the control that only doctors used to have but that patients now seem to have presage a cultural shift that requires careful analysis? Do the faith traditions have a word, prophetic or otherwise, to contribute?

Catholic moral and ethical teaching could not support either this patient's decision to end her life or the way in which she reached her decision. Although the individual conscience is the primary moral and ethical arbiter, it's what we call an "informed" conscience—one that is formed by Scripture and tradition—that enjoys such primacy. Our perspective is summed up in the introduction to a document entitled *Donum vitae*, an instruction dated February 22, 1987, from the Congregation of the Doctrine of the Faith:

> Human life is sacred because from its beginning it involves the creative action of God and it remains forever in a special relationship with the Creator, who is its sole end. God alone is the Lord of life from its beginning until its end: no one can under any circumstance claim for himself [sic] the right directly to destroy an innocent human being.

The more recently published *Catechism of the Catholic Church* (1994) carefully distinguishes between medical treatment that artificially prolongs

*The Reverend James Gardiner, S.A., board member, Village Center for Care; president, AIDS Interfaith New York.

life and steps taken to hurry the moment of death. The former is permissible; the latter, it says, is "morally unacceptable":

> Thus an act of omission which, of itself or by intention, causes death in order to eliminate suffering constitutes a murder gravely contrary to the dignity of the human person and to the respect due to the living God, his Creator. The error of judgment into which one can fall in good faith does not change the nature of this murderous act, which must always be forbidden and excluded. (2277)

Although the patient's life wasn't being artificially prolonged, what the *Catechism* has to say about this subject might be helpful in clarifying our opposition to hastening the moment of death:

> Discontinuing medical procedures that are burdensome, dangerous, extraordinary, or disproportionate to the expected outcome can be legitimate; it is the refusal of "over-zealous" treatment. Here one does not will to cause death; one's ability to impede it is merely accepted. The decisions should be made by the patient if he is competent and able or, if not, by those legally entitled to act for the patient, whose reasonable will and legitimate interests must always be respected. (2278)

The *Catechism* continues:

> Even if death is thought imminent, the ordinary care owed to a sick person cannot be legitimately interrupted. The use of painkillers to alleviate the sufferings of the dying, even at the risk of shortening their days, can be morally in conformity with human dignity if death is not willed as either an end or a means, but only foreseen and tolerated as inevitable. Palliative care is a special form of disinterested charity. As such it should be discouraged. (2279)

If the patient were Catholic, one of the first things I would do is arrange to celebrate the sacramental Anointing of the Sick, not privately or furtively but "publicly" with family and others (such as, her physician and the staff members with whom she has become "somewhat close") present and participating. On the basis of theology and experience, I'm convinced that the ritual laying-on of hands and anointing with oil, properly celebrated and properly interpreted, can have an effect far beyond its intended spiritual good. I would also recommend to the patient and her family prayer, especially the Psalms as well as familiar devotional exercises, because, as one of the Fathers of the Church suggested, "Prayer changes not God but man."

How far I would go on religious grounds to attempt to dissuade the patient from implementing her decision is difficult to determine in the abstract. I think, however, that I would be guided by two things: first, the insights of her family and those who have been getting to know her almost as intimately as her family—those staff members with whom she has become "somewhat close" and her doctor; and second, particular care not to add to her burdens by imposing guilt on top of everything else that seems to be oppressing (probably depressing!) her.

What is God's role in this scenario? God's role as Creator—author and "sole end"—of human life, has already been invoked. It is our firm belief, one that we share with others as well, that God's judgment is so tempered by God's mercy that the latter all but defines the former. Even in the case of suicide, the *Catechism* points out that "Grave psychological disturbances, anguish, or grave fear of hardship, suffering or torture can diminish the responsibility of the one committing suicide" (2282). It continues: "We should not despair of the eternal salvation of persons who have taken their own lives. By ways known to Him alone, God can provide the opportunity for salutary repentance" (2283).

As a pastoral caregiver, I would want to remind myself of four things. First, in every situation that elicits pastoral care, there may be more than one patient; in the case that we are considering, there are at least two—the woman and her daughter—who are in desperate need of pastoral care if not pastoral intervention. Second, caregivers are as susceptible as anyone else—doctors in particular—to the notion that they can somehow "make things better" again; in the context of pastoral caregiving, this notion is a bona fide temptation. Third, there are very few "cases" that require pastoral care; individuals, each one created in the image and likeness of God and reflecting something of God, require pastoral care. Fourth, the pastoral caregiver has a responsibility that is at least professional if not moral to authentically represent the patient's tradition and not simply "bless" a decision that's untenable.

Then, as mentioned previously, I would speak with the woman and her family and with those who have been getting to know her as intimately as her family—the staff members with whom she has become "somewhat close" and her doctor. I would recommend sacramental anointing, not so much as a way of "blessing" her decision to hasten her death, but as a way of confronting the eventuality of her death within an authentic religious context. I would keep her, her family, and her various caregivers in my own daily prayer.

Postscript: The religious community has to be vigilant about how the definition of life is subtly, almost imperceptibly, undergoing change in our culture. The horizon is shrinking. Many of us would not be able to meet some of the criteria that are currently gaining acceptance in our society—criteria like youthfulness, athletic, sexual, and social prowess, political and fashionable correctness, to name a few. My own involvement with persons living with HIV and AIDS over the past twelve years has taught me that there is so much more to life than meets the eye. My still-vivid memories of how my father was able to care for my late mother during the seven years that Alzheimer's disease complicated all our lives proved to me beyond the shadow of a doubt that the human spirit is incredibly resourceful and resilient. Our respective traditions challenge us to continually resist any attempts to shrink that horizon.

Reference

Catechism of the Catholic Church. (1994). Washington, DC: United States Catholic Conference, Inc., Liberia Editrice Vaticana.

THE MUSLIM PERSPECTIVE[*]

This interesting case raises at least two ethical issues of importance to the Muslim: What power do we have as human beings to control the length of our lives? What does Islam offer the person who no longer sees any reason to live?

This woman's desire to stop eating as a way of hastening her death falls clearly within the Islamic definition of suicide. Islam is very clear that any attempt to shorten one's life by either passive or active means is an attempt at suicide. There is no distinction in Islam between passive and active euthanasia. The Muslim is taught that anyone who commits suicide will be immediately condemned to hellfire. There can be no extenuating circumstances.

As in all other things, Muslims rely on the teachings of the Qur'an to guide them. The Holy Qur'an is the last revelation (holy book), which Muslims believe is the record of God's very words conveyed to Prophet Muhammad Ibn Abdullah (peace and blessings be upon him) by the Angel Gabriel more than fourteen hundred years ago. To this day, its text in the original Arabic language has not been altered and it continues to guide approximately one billion people throughout the world.

The Qur'an teaches clearly that our physical bodies are gifts from God. They are totally under God's control. God knows everything that will happen to us, and nothing takes place without His consent. Nothing happens except that which God wills. One of the basic tenets of Islamic belief is that

[*]Imam Yusuf Hassan, BCC, staff chaplain, The Healthcare Chaplaincy, New York.

only God can give and take life. It is clearly against God's will to try to either lengthen or shorten one's life. The Qur'an says:

> To every people is a term appointed; when their term is reached, not even an hour can they cause delay, nor an hour can they advance it in anticipation. (HQ 7:34)

> Nor can a soul die except by God's leave, the term being fixed as by writing. (HQ 3:145)

> What God out of His mercy doth bestow on humankind none can withhold: what God doth withhold none can grant apart from God. (HQ 35:2)

The second issue involves the woman's lack of will to live and her feelings of worthlessness. Here again, the teachings of Islam are very clear as they apply to her situation. Muslims believe that God is our sustainer as well as our creator. He abides with us and is sufficient for our continued existence. The woman could be reminded that she is never alone and is never without worth in God's eyes. No matter what happens to her physically or psychologically, she remains God's creation and has value. God will not abandon her or place on her any burden she cannot bear. Again the Holy Qur'an teaches us clearly:

> No burden do we place on any soul but that which it can bear. (HQ 7:42)

> Those who are righteous and mend their lives, on them shall be no fear, nor shall they grieve. (HQ 7:35)

Ministry to Muslim patients in situations like this embraces the same principles of pastoral care as are used in other traditions. We are present with the patient, listen to the patient's situation, and share the patient's feelings and concerns. Not unlike some of their more traditional Christian and Jewish counterparts, Muslim believers rely heavily on the teachings of their sacred text, in this case the Holy Qur'an, to bring them the comfort of knowing God's will for them. Being reminded of this will and of God's plan brings the Muslim tremendous comfort and relief. The bringing of this message from the Qur'an then constitutes the essence of ministry to the Muslim patient and family member.

Reference

Koran. Tr. by N. J. Dawood, rev. ed. Thomas Wyatt. NY: Viking Penguin, 1990.

THE JEWISH PERSPECTIVE*

Three ethical issues are raised in this case study:

1. Does a person have the right to refuse nonthreatening treatment that is most probably beneficial—in this case, for depression?
2. What are the obligations of the patient's daughter to her mother under Jewish law (*Halakha*)? Is she living up to them?
3. Does Judaism sanction a conscious decision by one in command of her faculties to stop living—that is, to commit suicide?

Judaism considers the highest duty of any human being to preserve and cherish life. Therefore, Judaism does not recognize a right to refuse a nonthreatening, beneficial treatment.[1] There are numerous citations in the Talmud that indicate that one is commanded to seek treatment for illness, whether physical or mental.[2]

The relationship between the patient and her daughter brings up the question of Jewish law (*halakhic*) obligations of the daughter. Judaism takes very seriously the commandment to honor one's father and mother.[3] For our purposes, we can concentrate on the filial obligation to care for the physical and emotional needs of one's parents. The Talmud and codes make it clear that even deviations from normal parental behavior do not alter the child's obligation to honor the parent, no matter how difficult a burden that may seem.[4] This does not preclude the placing of a parent in a nursing home, if this is seen to be the best course for the parent, but it does mean that the child should always have the parent's best interests at heart. Judging only from the case study, it would seem that the daughter was not making decisions regarding her mother's actions and care in the mother's best interest but was considering first and foremost her own interests. Her seemingly too willing acceptance of her mother's decision to stop eating, in fact her encouragement of that decision, her apparent lack of concern over her mother's refusal to accept treatment for depression when even the psychiatrist, aware of the older woman's distress, had suggested treatment, and her "punishment" of her mother for ending her suicidal fast are actions that are contrary to the *halakhic* mandate to honor one's parent. To that extent, she was not acting ethically in the Jewish tradition.

Judaism regards suicide as a criminal act and as strictly forbidden by *Halakha*. This view holds across the spectrum of religious belief, from Orthodoxy to Reform.[5] The classic source for this attitude is the Talmudic story of Rabbi Hananiah ben Teradyon, who was burned alive by order of the Roman government. He was wrapped in a Torah scroll; then wood was

*Rabbi Marion Shulevitz, chaplain, Amsterdam Nursing Home, New York.

placed around him and set on fire. The Romans also put water-soaked tufts of wool over his heart to prolong his agony. When his students pleaded with him to open his mouth and breathe in the fire so as to die more quickly, he refused, saying that one is not allowed to hasten one's own death.[6]

Judaism regards life and the preservation of life as a cardinal principle.[7] The goal of Jewish law is "You shall live by them" (*v'chai bahem*).[8] Saving a life overrides all commandments in the Torah—including Kashrut, Shabbat, and the observance of Yom Kippur—except for the injunctions against murder, idolatry, and sexual offenses.[9] Life is a sacred trust, given to us by God, which only God can remove. Although traditional Judaism recognizes the autonomy of each individual, such autonomy is not unlimited. A person's life is not his or her own possession but belongs to God. We are the stewards of our life and our bodies, charged with preserving them. Specifically with reference to this case, we are obliged to seek food and water.[10]

No streams within Judaism would support this patient in her decision to end her life. The Jewish obligation to heal extends to healing of soul (*refuat hanefesh*) as much as it does to healing of body (*refuat haguf*). Supporting and improving the quality of the life left to the patient is as much a divine commandment (*mitzvah*) as the imperative to cherish life itself. Loving-kindness (*Hesed*) is a strategy of caring that aims to alleviate the suffering that might impel one to consider suicide as a viable option. It is the obligation of all the caregivers in this case—doctors, nursing home staff, and family members—to assuage the psychological and spiritual symptoms of distress to which the patient's very wish to commit suicide attests.

The Jewish chaplain, in his or her dual role as pastoral caregiver and rabbi, can call on a wealth of spiritual resources for the patient in a long-term-care setting. First is an active, empathic presence. Sometimes just being there, holding her hand, is enough to ease the suffering caused by loneliness and a feeling of abandonment. Listening not just to what she says but to what she means, what her body language and even the appearance of her room tell us, is another way of helping the patient out of the feelings that are causing her such pain.

Judaism can provide us with many spiritual resources. First, it affirms, as we have seen, the supreme importance of human life, worth, and dignity. Human beings are created in the image of God. As Rabbi Irving Greenberg has taught in the name of Rabbi Joseph B. Soloveitchik, one aspect of this creation is that human beings share in God's power. Indeed, it is this empowerment that distinguishes them from animals, who do not have the consciousness or the reason with which to manipulate and control the environment. Thus Judaism can address directly the issue of self-determination, of empowerment. Hospital patients, as well as residents in a nursing home, often tend to feel infantilized and powerless.[11] If this patient could not control the aspects of her living, perhaps she was, through this wish to cause her own death, trying to control at least her dying. It would be my responsibility as chaplain, as well as the responsibility of all her caregivers, to give her the maximum voice in her treatment and living conditions, to help her to achieve the power over her own life and condition that makes for human dignity.

Prayer is a powerful resource for helping this woman find meaning and fulfillment in her life. Prayer is a way of connecting with her tradition, with God, and with her people. It can be a way of venting anger and fear, or it can be an articulation of hope. Prayer is also an affirmation of life. As the Psalmist says, "The dead do not praise God."[12] Whether it is the traditional prayer for healing, a part of the daily or Shabbat service, or perhaps a creative effort by the rabbi or the patient herself, prayer can serve as a comfort to the patient as well as a potent antidote to depression and despair, easing her suffering and distress.

If the patient were Jewish, I, as a rabbi, would represent the Jewish community symbolically to her. The state of aloneness, of a deep feeling of loneliness that is not necessarily lightened by simply being with others in the nursing home, can be mitigated by a sense of connection between this woman and her people, her heritage, and her tradition. I bring all that into the patient's presence when I enter her room. Prayer, ritual and holiday observance, assistance in identifying and doing *mitzvot*—religious commandments—as well as reminiscences of childhood and early years are all ways of effecting the connection that can negate the feeling of loneliness.

Finally, a powerful and valuable spiritual resource is hope: not false reassurances but the sense that there is meaning to life, that one can pull out of even the experience of suffering and illness what Victor Frankl called "a tragic optimism."[13] Her comments to the nursing home staff indicate that she has no sense of hope: "I've had a good life [it's over] . . . my responsibilities are ended . . . looking for a good way out." Reinstilling in this woman the sense that there is something to live for, a sense of hope, could do much to reduce her emotional and spiritual suffering.

Rabbi Avram Reisner has stated: "Unlike the absolute autonomy recommended by secular ethicists, this autonomy [the autonomy recognized by *Halakha*] only inheres in the patient choosing life-giving treatment. It cannot reach to the autonomous choice to seek death. . . . the patient's own judgment whether to undergo risk is determinative unless medical certainty in the efficacy and low risk of a treatment is exceedingly high and the patient's objection is clearly irrational or suicidal."[14]

On the other hand, we can never know with certainty why a patient chooses to reject a treatment, whether out of fear, despair, or a wish to die. It is the duty of the rabbi to present the case of Jewish law and ethics to the patient but not to judge the morality of the final decision. We may counsel, suggest, and attempt to persuade with all the skill and passion in our power, but ultimately the patient has the autonomy, the free will first exhibited by Adam and Eve in the Garden, to reject God's commands. In this case in particular, where the patient is alert, responsive, and not acting irrationally or in a disturbed manner, we have no right to force her to change her mind, let alone to force nutrition on her. We are bound by *Halakha* to do all we can, using the spiritual resources at our command, to convince this patient to reconsider.

I find it interesting that there is no mention of God at all in the case study. Surprisingly, even the most common lament, "Why me?"—which usually means,"Why is God doing this to me?"—does not appear. Where was God for this patient? There is a story of a rabbi who came home from the synagogue one day to find her little daughter crying. She asked the child what was wrong, and the girl told her that she and her friends had been playing hide-and-seek and when it was her turn to hide, she hid so well that the other children gave up and went off to play another game. The little girl waited and waited for them to find her, and when she finally emerged, she was all alone. The rabbi thought to herself, "Isn't this what we do to God? We hide so well, that God cannot find us—and then when we seek God, it is we who cannot find God."[15]

But God was in that patient's room, as God is in the presence of each person who is ill. As Abraham Joshua Heschel has pointed out, many Jewish texts refer to God's presence at the patient's bed.[16] Jacob on his sickbed bowed his head, acknowledging the invisible presence of God.[17]

We are made in the image of God, who has commanded us to choose life.[18] God is a partner with the doctor and the chaplain in the struggle for life; indeed, as Heschel has commented, "Religion is medicine in the form of a prayer; medicine is religion in the form of a deed."[19]

As the caregiver, I would try to alleviate this patient's suffering and despair, her loneliness and feeling of abandonment, through spiritual resources and any others that I could bring to bear. I would certainly try to dissuade her from her decision. A crucial factor seems to be the relationship between the patient and her daughter. I would try to explore that relationship with a view to improving their mutual understanding and if possible bring about a real reconciliation between them. The staff seems to be very supportive of the patient, but it is clear from the outcome that she felt she was not getting the attention and loving care she needed. This too would be a goal—to help this patient feel loved, wanted, and cared for in this setting.

Notes

1. A. Reisner (1991), A halakhic ethic of care for the mentally ill, *Conservative Judaism*, 43, (3), 54–55, citing *Arukh Hashulchan, Yoreh Deah* 339:1. See also Jacob Emden, *Mor uketzia* 228.

2. TB *Baba Kamma* 46b; *Yoma 83b*. See Maimonides, *Mishneh Torah, Hilchot Deot* 4:1; and F. Rosner (1991), *Modern medicine and Jewish ethics* 2nd rev. ed., Hoboken, NJ: KTAV, 7, citing *Malbim*.

3. Exodus 20:12, *Mishnah Peah* 1:1, Proverbs 3:9, TB *Kiddushin* 30b.

4. TB *Kiddushin* 31a, 32a; Maimonides, *Mishneh Torah, Hilchot Mamrim* 6, 7, *Shulchan Aruch, Yoreh Deah* 240:1–25.

5. Cf. S. Freehof (1975), Relieving pain of a dying patient, *American Reform Responsa, 85*, 83–85; E. Dorf (1991), A Jewish approach to end-stage medical care, *Conservative Judaism, 43*, (3), 17; Reisner; Rosner, 259.

6. TB *Avodah Zara* 18a.

7. TB *Sanhedrin* 17a.

8. Leviticus 18:5; see also TB *Avodah Zara* 27a.

9. Maimonides, *Mishneh Torah, Sefer Hamada* 5:5–7; *Shulchan Aruch, Orach Hayyim* 329:3.

10. *Shulchan Aruch, Hoshen Mishpat* 420:1–30. See also J. D. Bleich (1979), The obligation to heal in the Jewish tradition, 1–4, citing Ezekiel 18:4, *Shulchan Aruch Harav VI, Hilchot Nizkei Guf* 4, in *Jewish Bioethics*, ed. F. Rosner and J. D. Bleich, New York: Sanhedrin Press, 18–19. *Shulchan Aruch Harav* is a nineteenth-century hasidic *halakhic* treatise by Shneur Zalman of Liadi.

11. I. Greenberg (1986), A covenantal ethic of medicine, in *Jewish Values in Bioethics*, ed. L. Meier, New York: Human Sciences Press, 130–131.

12. Psalms 115:17.

13. V. E. Frankl (1986), The meaning of suffering, in *Jewish Values in Bioethics*, ed. L. Meier, New York: Human Sciences Press.

14. Reisner, 60–61.

15. H. Kushner (1989), *Who needs God?* New York: Summit Books.

16. Psalms 41:4; *Shulchan Aruch, Yoreh Deah* 335:3.

17. Genesis 47:31.

18. Deuteronomy 30:19.

19. A. J. Heschel (1966), The patient as person, in *The Insecurity of Freedom*, New York: Farrar, Strauss.

THE HINDU PERSPECTIVE[*]

An 89-year-old woman is admitted to a skilled nursing home. She suffers from polymyositis, rheumatoid arthritis, osteoporosis, Raynaud's disease, esophageal motility, hiatal hernia, and depression. She is not in good physical condition, and her bodily functions deteriorate gradually. She frequently complains about swallowing and appetite. She exhibits all the natural problems associated with advancing age. Her extended family is very supportive of her. She is well educated, hails from an upper-class fam-

[*]Babu Suseelan, Ph.D., president, American Hindu Mission.

ily. She is twice widowed with two grandchildren and one great-grand-child. She had a very productive and successful personal and social life.

The patient had decided, on her own, to stop eating and drinking for the purpose of speeding her final stage of life (death). She made a living will directing family, friends, and medical personnel not to prolong her life with artificial life-sustaining treatments. Her daughter supported her decision. Family and nursing personnel found her happy and peaceful in her decision. However, the staff psychiatrist felt she was depressed and recommended antidepressant medication. The 89-year-old woman refused this medication, saying that she had had a good life and was ready to leave this material life. After thirty-seven days, she decided to end her fasting. Her family was perplexed at her sudden change of mind to end her fast. At this stage the staff psychiatrist decided to treat her with Prozac for depression.

According to Hindu tradition, ethical dilemmas exist in this case because there is no spiritual preparation for her to face death. In this case we observe an attempt to solve a spiritual problem with a technical (medical) solution. Unless one is spiritually trained, it is not easy to face old age, death, and dying. Spiritual training is required from early childhood. The Hindu religion prescribes that elderly people completely devote their time and energy to understanding spiritual life. We do not become spiritually mature by growing old or hearing a sermon in old age. Happiness and comfort do not mean sense gratification, physical health, and artificially prolonged mechanical life. If the patient were Hindu, Hindu tradition would conditionally support her freedom to choose to end her life. A brief summary of Hindu beliefs and spirituality will illustrate this position.

Hindus believe in One-All-Pervasive Supreme Being who is both immanent and transcendent, both creator and unmanifest Reality. The universe undergoes endless cycles of creation, preservation, and dissolution. All souls are evolving toward union with God and will ultimately find Moksha (liberation), spiritual knowledge and liberation from the cycle of rebirth. Not a single soul will be eternally deprived of this destiny. Hindus believe in Karma, the law of cause and effect by which each individual creates his or her own destiny by thoughts, words, and deeds. The soul reincarnates, evolving through many births until all Karmas have been resolved.

Hindus believe in Dharma (duty), Artha (wealth), Kama (family life), and Moksha (liberation). Hindus also believe in Purusharthas (stages of life) and in issues, problems, needs, duties, and responsibilities associated with each stage of life. These stages are Kaumara (infancy and childhood), Brahmacharya (adolescence), Grahasta (adulthood), Vanaprastha (retirement), and Sanyasa (old age). This 89-year-old woman has successfully completed all her life stages and is ready to face the last phase of her life.

Hinduism says that death is not the stoppage of life. One simply transmigrates. In *Bhagavat Gita,* Sri Krishna says:

As the embodied soul continuously passes, in this body, from boyhood to youth to old age, the soul similarly passes into another body at death. The self-realized soul similarly passes into another body at death. The self-realized soul is not bewildered by such a change. (2:13)

This case illustrates that the patient is moving through a constant transition from desire to satisfaction, to frustration, and then to a new desire, to happiness, and to the slow course to sorrow. It is this constant flux from desire to satisfaction, from happiness to sorrow, that is characteristic of the phenomenal world. Medication and life support systems can only prolong agony and pain, not life.

Her voluntary attempt in fasting and asceticism is the first step in the denial of the will and the person behind the will to live. In this case, I may say that her will is directed toward sense satisfaction (avoiding life at the nursing home). She has forgotten the spiritual field of willing.

According to Hinduism, voluntary, ascetic preparation to liberate from material existence is not suicide. It is not the will itself that is denied. While denying the will for material happiness, we must assert the will for spiritual happiness. These are acts based on the understanding of Dharma, Artha, Kama, Moksha, and the transmigration of the soul. When one who is spiritually inclined accepts death, he or she attains Mukthi (liberation):

Whatever state of being one remembers when he quits the body, that state he will attain without fail. (*Bhagavat Gita* 8:6)

Material life is momentary, and there is another life in the spiritual world. Hindus envision a spiritual life attainable after death.

Hindus believe that the body changes but the soul remains eternal. Our material body is changing from childhood to youth to old age, yet the soul remains the same. When the body dies, the soul takes on another body:

Never was there a time when I did not exist, nor you, nor all these kings, nor in the future shall any of us cease to be. (*Bhagavat Gita* 2:12)

We are individuals in the past, present, and future. Our individuality is always there, but in the quantity we are not as great as God. In the real sense all are immortal:

The living entities in this conditioned world are My eternal, fragmental parts. Due to conditioned life, they are struggling very hard with the six senses, which include the mind. (*Bhagavat Gita* 15:17)

In this case, the woman's struggling is part of her life, inevitable, and should be accepted with grace and ease.

Suffering and enjoyment take place according to the body. As explained in the *Bhagavat Gita,*

> The nonpermanent appearance of happiness and distress, and their disappearance in due course, are like the appearance of winter and summer seasons. They arise from sense perception and one must learn to tolerate them without being disturbed. (2:14)

Further treatment will not improve her life. Hindus do not believe in prolonged intense treatment in old age if there is no reasonable probability that one's life can be comfortably prolonged. The family and friends should show more compassionate sympathy and love for the suffering woman. Through compassionate love she will be able to be free to choose liberation (Mukthi). Her material mind is not fixed on God and spiritual liberation. Her mind is constantly rejecting and accepting. Since these material pleasures and pains arise from this material combination, the best course is to discontinue prolonged nonvoluntary treatment.

Her painful and traumatic experiences can be repressed by engaging in the devotional service of the Supreme Personality of Godhead. When one is God conscious, old age, death, and dying are not to be feared.

As long as her decision to fast is not a case of active suicide but a passive preparation for her inevitable final stage of life, I would not dissuade her from her will to discontinue treatment. Hindu philosophy and literature are replete with cases of active ascetic life and renunciation in preparation for Mukthi (liberation). She may be suffering the material pain of living at this stage. When you give her better transcendental things to contemplate, she will forget inferior problems in living.

> The embodied soul may be restricted from sense enjoyment, though the taste for sense objects remains. But, ceasing such engagements by experiencing a higher spiritual taste, people will concentrate in transcendental bliss. (*Bhagavat Gita* 2:59)

Her decision should be supported by constant spiritual redirection in preparation for her liberation. Fear, anxiety, frustration, worry, stress, and confusion are created when one is not God conscious. This is a characteristic of the conditioned soul and diseased body. As soon as one is God conscious and ready to accept the final stage of life (Moksha) in the name of God, one's fears and anxieties automatically vanish.

Friends, relatives, and nursing staff live to relieve the suffering of elderly people by enlightening them about the eternal nature of the soul. This enlightenment brings more than philosophical satisfaction; it relieves the bewildered soul of the agony of material existence. As she passes through a difficult, final stage of her life, everyone should encourage her to be in contact with God.

Reference
Bhagavat Gita. Tr. by Gita-Swarupananda. Hollywood, CA: Vedanta Press, 1982.

THE SOCIAL WORK PERSPECTIVE

This case presents a number of social work practice issues as well as ethical dilemmas. The practice issues include the patient's status as an ill person, her relationship with her daughter, and alternatives to suicide.

Social Work Practice Issues

It is apparent from the details of the case that the patient is not terminally ill. A person who has difficulty swallowing but is capable of swallowing with difficulty is not about to die. Even the inability to swallow at all does not categorize patients as terminally ill because artificial nutrition is available. Many residents, particularly those with Alzheimer's disease, can live for many years with a feeding tube.

Advance directives become operative only when the person no longer has the capacity to make health care decisions. Someone who cannot swallow—perhaps because of a stroke or throat cancer—may still possess the mental faculties to make an informed decision, in which case the proxy would not be involved. Residents in nursing homes have the right to make their own decisions, even to refuse medical treatment. When this occurs, the staff must document that the residents have been informed, presented with the options, and understand the consequences of refusal.

The patient in this case was not terminal and could still take in food. She simply made up her mind that she wanted to die (if that was really her intent). The dilemma was whether the nursing home could stand by and allow her to starve herself. If she were at home, she could do what she wanted; however, in a health care facility, efforts must be made to prevent her from committing suicide, even if those efforts include committing her involuntarily to a psychiatric hospital because she is a danger to herself. Moody (1983) suggests that if the act is described as a decision to commit suicide, we are likely to think that psychiatric help is called for.

Moody presents a case somewhat similar to this one, except that the social worker is privy to the announcement and agonizes over what to do. He offers no resolution, but the questions are instructive for the social worker's way of thinking.

A seventy-eight-year-old resident of a nursing home for three years an-
nounces to the social worker that she no longer wants to live, that she
wants the worker's help in obtaining excess doses of sleeping pills in
order to end her life quietly. Should the social worker report this request to a psychiatrist or medical director? Should the social worker
keep it confidential and do nothing? Should the social worker attempt
to talk the resident out of her depression, provide counseling, and so
on? Should the social worker help the patient carry out her express
wish to end her life (e.g., obtain doses of sleeping pills)? (p. 101)

The main issue in both cases is whether the patient should be permitted
to end her life. We may assess her action as a response to her lack of control.
This woman is educated and intelligent, has lived well, and has had prestige and social honor. She has experienced serious losses in her life—the
death of two husbands, physical agility, and friends. She has lost control
over her life and does not even have a home to which she can return. There
is an awareness of finality about residence in the nursing home that de-
pletes any sense of hope for the future. As a patient, she has lost control
over her environment. Food intake appears to be the one area over which
she feels she can exercise some modicum of control; hence her refusal to eat.

We should not condemn the daughter for supporting her mother's decision. The daughter appears to be drained and exhausted from the daily
visits. She has been there for her mother all this time, has converted a room
in her house, and has been a devoted daughter. She would have liked
her mother to fight harder, and she may have been angry at her for trying
to control her life in this way, but she is prepared to accept her mother's
decision.

The psychiatrist believed that the patient was suffering from depression and recommended further evaluation and treatment. Persistent efforts
need to be expended through counseling and medications with fewer side
effects. Greater attention should be paid to her distress and to more creative
efforts at rehabilitation. This woman continues to live, even against her
will. Her life could be made more pleasant.

The patient appears to relate better to staff than to other patients—a
pattern that exists among better-educated patients. If she is still able to use
her abilities and talents, they should be put to use for the benefit of others
to give her a sense of worth and accomplishment. She might be encouraged
to read to other people or lead a culture group or a current events group.

The Ethical Dilemma

The ethical dilemma revolves around the scope and parameters of individual autonomy. The patient expresses her autonomy by signing a series

of advance directives, including two living wills, and appointing her daughter as a health care proxy. She is deemed to have been of sound mind when she made out the directives and appointed her daughter.

The ethical dilemma for the social worker is whether to support the patient's freedom to end her life or persuade her to continue to live and improve the quality of that life. The dilemma is based on conflicting social work values and ethical principles. A fundamental social work value is client self-determination, which is circumscribed when it can harm others and oneself and when the capacity to make decisions may be limited. Depression may be one of the conditions that diminishes capacity and limits the free exercise of self-determination. Another fundamental social work value is the preservation of life. This, too, is not an absolute value, for a prolonged life accompanied by suffering and pain may contribute to debilitation and depression. The challenging moral dilemma of long-term care is highlighted by this case: to support patient self-determination or persuade the patient to continue to live.

Three ethical principles are in conflict: respect for autonomy, the duty to prevent harm, and beneficence. The issue at stake here is determining the effects of the patient's autonomous action. Does the action of starving herself to death fall in the category of causing harm, or is it a liberation from pain? Is her depression influencing her decision to die? If the depression were lifted, would she reaffirm her desire to live? At 89, is she simply tired of living and ready to let go? Does she really want to die, or is her ceasing to eat her way of maintaining control and getting attention? Despite her disclaimers, is her action harming her family too? How clear is her thinking that would determine whether her decision is autonomous and reflects capacity?

The questions about her autonomy evoke an essential ambiguity in applying the principle of nonmaleficence. The duty to prevent harm—the first principle in ethics—is unclear in connection with the social worker's responsibilities in this case. What constitutes harm—supporting the patient's wish to die or persuading her to continue to live? The patient deems it harmful to continue to live under the conditions of the nursing home. The social worker empathizes with her but also deems it harmful to all involved were the patient to commit suicide. With regard to the principle of beneficence, is supporting the patient's wishes a contribution to her welfare, or does beneficence require the prolongation of life, not its premature cessation? Does overriding the patient's wishes constitute a beneficent act or a paternalistic act?

If the social worker disagrees with the patient's values because the social worker is personally opposed to suicide, overriding the patient's autonomy is paternalistic and not justified. However, the social worker's action could stem from professional concerns—that the patient's action causes harm to herself and her family and violates the moral principle of preservation of life.

Lynn and Childress (1983), discussing the moral issues in feeding the dying, differentiate between competent and incompetent patients. They support competent patients' wishes to have feeding tubes discontinued. "Patients who are competent to determine the course of their therapy may refuse any and all interventions proposed by others, as long as their refusals do not seriously harm or impose unfair burdens upon others" (p. 17). In *Bouvia* v. *Superior Court* (1986), the court decided that competent patients have a right to refuse all medical treatment even if doing so will hasten death. Hydration and nutrition, though, are not in the category of medical treatment. A patient refusing hydration and nutrition may not be in the category of patients covered by the court's decision. The patient also claims that when she dies, no harm will come to her family, who are grown and independent of her. The dilemma is seemingly resolved. Yet the psychiatrist has diagnosed depression as a possible cause of these wishes. He opines that if the depression were lifted, the desire to live might be reawakened; thus he raises the possibility of causing harm were the patient to proceed with her wishes.

Callahan (1983) adds a moral dimension to the issue. The feeding of the hungry is the perfect symbol of the fact that human life is inescapably social and communal. The giving of nourishment is the first and most basic manifestation of the duty of parents to children. Surely, when the dependency needs are reversed, when parents are the ones who need nourishment, the children have a duty to provide it despite parental objections.

CONCLUSION

The fine line contributing to the ambiguity in this case is that the patient could still swallow, albeit with some difficulty. Her refusal to eat when she can take in food is viewed as a conscious, deliberate effort to harm herself and, if carried to the end, to commit suicide.

Although this case had a "happy" ending—the patient did not die from her starvation regimen—the issues that it poses remain. The case takes place against a backdrop of the judicial system's increasing support for individual autonomy over beneficence. It becomes very difficult for religious caregivers, social workers, and other health care providers to dissuade individuals from committing even a slow suicide, especially when they have already signed a living will, appointed a proxy, and seek to exercise their autonomy.

The religious caregiver does not accept the patient's decision at face value because other values such as preservation of life may supersede it.

While not imposing personal values, the religious caregiver holds out the benefits of continued life as a precious gift to be embraced and transmitted to future generations.

The social worker engages the patient with her knowledge and skill of individual counseling, family dynamics, grief and bereavement, feelings about loss and aging, dependency, and issues of control and autonomy to assist the patient to make an informed decision. The social worker wants to be certain that the patient knows the consequences of her decision, is comfortable with them, and is in sync with her own values. The social worker must be prepared to accept the patient's decision at the end of this process.

EPILOGUE

Social Work Ethics in Practice

In the earlier chapters, a way of thinking about values and ethics in social work practice was presented. This final chapter represents a summation and closure of thoughts about values and ethics. It discusses values in conflict, ethical decision making, ethics in practice, and the ethics of ambiguity. It concludes with the character traits necessary for ethical practice.

VALUES IN CONFLICT

Numerous cases in a variety of practice areas demonstrate that many conflict situations can be attributed to clashes in professional values. Though not all conflicts are based in values (some can be attributed to psychological or emotional factors), value conflicts are difficult to unravel and resolve unless their underlying attributes have been exposed.

Disagreements over agency policies, programs, and services, conflicts between clients and practitioners, and conflicts among colleagues may become heated as each person presents his or her point of view. Beneath their respective positions lie values, both personal and professional, that are deeply ingrained and not readily amenable to change. Positions may become fixed because of the weight of personal values. When personal values intrude into professional social work functions, the boundaries of ethical practice are usurped. Personal values can be called on to contribute to the client's options, but they may not be insisted on as a preference for the client (Levy, 1976b).

Values must be distinguished from each other and not grouped into one unit. Social work values have been classified into three groups: preferred conceptions—how social workers view people; preferred outcomes—what social workers want for people; and preferred instrumentalities—how social workers work with people (Levy, 1973). The most important of these is preferred conceptions, because the way we prefer to view people determines the outcomes we desire for them and how we work with them. In many instances, incongruities between staff and agency and between social policy and social work practice reflect the different ways in which the conflicting parties prefer to view the clients served. Because preferred views of people are so deeply imbedded—whether through prejudice, stereotyping, education, or direct interaction—they do not change easily. The influence of such values on public policy and program services is profound. Social action by social workers to change policies affecting clients must challenge negative preferred conceptions of the target group.

Conflicts between social workers and other parties such as politicians in the welfare reform debate are likely to originate in different preferred conceptions of clients. But among themselves, social workers would hardly disagree in their preferred conceptions of clients. We believe that people have worth and dignity, are basically decent and inherently good, and can change. Inevitably, as Perlman (1976) suggests, values will most likely clash on the level of instrumentalities because each morally uncertain situation is likely to evoke different-preferences in different practitioners.

Value conflicts require criteria by which to prioritize. How does one go about deciding which value should take precedence in a given situation? Loewenberg and Dolgoff (1992) created an "Ethical Principles Screen" that establishes priorities among principles (see Table 12.3). By inference, one could possibly discern priorities in values from that screen, since principles are based on values. For example, the first ethical principle is the preservation of life. The underlying value is the human being's sanctity and the worth of life. The third ethical principle is autonomy and freedom. The value underlying that principle is self-determination. Thus, the preservation of life should take precedence over self-determination, but this is not always so. The "Ethical Principles Screen" is only suggestive, not authoritative, for decision making. Practitioners are not absolutely bound by its priorities, although it represents a valuable addition to the literature on ethical decision making.

ETHICAL DECISION MAKING

In addition to the values classification model (Levy, 1973) for understanding conflict, we have presented a model that considers rules, principles, and theories as vital components in ethical decision making (Beauchamp & Childress, 1994). Ethical decision making is a process that requires thought and cannot be accelerated through instinct or practice wisdom, because each ethical dilemma is different and is idiosyncratic to the particular situation and the parties involved. Nevertheless, rules, principles, and theories enable ethical dilemmas to be generalized from their particularity in order to create "case laws" and classifications. The application of rules, principles, and theories to cases does not impose uniformity on decisions but, to the contrary, encourages creative thinking and diversity in decision making. The model is merely an analytical tool, not a prescriptive resolution.

Because ethical dilemmas exist at the interface of ethical reasoning and clinical practice, Murphy (1997) cautions against using a "rule book" for resolving ethical dilemmas. Although guidelines are needed for ethical practice, she contends that not all ethical issues in practice can be reconciled or satisfactorily concluded. Nevertheless, they must be dealt with to fulfill ethical responsibility. Addressing such issues requires the application of logical reasoning to both sides and to the context of the ethical dilemma. Mindless adherence to rules has no place in ethical decision making, but rules do serve positive functions when viewed in the context of principles and theory.

ETHICS IN PRACTICE

With regard to ethics, the question practitioners must ask themselves is: "What is the right thing to do?" With regard to practice, the question is: "What is most efficient?" What is right may not always be what is efficient. In a clash between these two choices, the preference is for what is right—the ethical choice. According to Reamer (1982a), competent practice is efficient, and ethical practice is obligatory: one must act ethically even though the result may not be efficient. Practice wisdom may direct the social worker to act in a way that is designed to be helpful to the client, but he or she may refrain from acting on ethical grounds. For example, the social worker may "know" on the basis of diagnosis and experience that the client's marriage is destined to be destructive but would avoid intruding on the client's responsibility to make his or her own choice and on the client's right to err. Informing the client of the prognosis for the marriage would be a practice judgment; not intruding on the client's responsibility to make the decision, an ethical one. The first is based on knowledge; the second, on values (Levy, 1976a).

The practice judgment of informing or not informing is based on the social worker's knowledge of the dysfunctions in the relationship. If the social worker decides to warn the client of the possibly dire consequences of remaining in the marriage, the action is based on knowledge derived from assessment. If the social worker refrains from sharing this knowledge and instead encourages the client to make his or her own decision, the decision constitutes ethical practice: the social worker has settled for an ethical choice that proves to be an impractical one—that is, an "ineffective" one from the perspective of social work practice. The client may opt to continue in a destructive marriage and suffer the consequences. "The choice amounts to unused competence in the interest of applied ethics" (Levy, 1976a, p. 24), and the values of ethics triumph over the knowledge of practice.

Another option for the social worker is to combine both the knowledge and the ethical components in the service of the client. The social worker could share the prognosis with the client and still allow the client self-determination. By sharing the prognosis, the social worker does not lead the client into a specific action but merely informs the client of diagnostic impressions. The obligatory ethical action is to give the client an unbiased choice about whether to proceed with the marriage.

Values connote behavioral expectations. Ethics, as the action component of values, in addition to guiding the social worker's actions, also serves as a basis of expectations and predictions (Levy, 1973). Internally, ethics compels actions, what the social worker ought or ought not do. Externally, ethics is a source of evaluation of conduct to help determine whether the social worker has met expectations in the social work service situation.

THE ETHICS OF AMBIGUITY

Discussing ethical dilemmas in treating infants born with spina bifida and other severe medical problems, Arras (1984) asks whether severely ill infants should be treated or permitted to die. Treatment will inevitably lead to a life of suffering for the child and for the parents. Death brings the end of suffering. What is the right thing to do? "When it comes to matters of life and death, our society prefers procedure to substance. Instead of asking, 'What is the right thing to do?' we ask, 'Who should decide'" (p. 25)?

The beginning of wisdom is to come to grips with complexity, not to sweep it under the rug. Confronting complexity means acknowledging the pull of equally fundamental but contradictory moral imperatives—to sustain life and to ameliorate suffering by ending life. It also means acknowledging the vast spectrum of conditions and possible interventions. Public policy must be grounded on respect for this complex reality, not on one or two sensational cases (Arras, 1984).

The issue is pervaded by ethical ambiguity. How shall we deal with children who are seriously deformed and have little chance to live? What is understood by the "best interests of the child" in those situations? From the child's point of view, the best-interest standard would mandate treatment even in the worst cases. Others might contend that such children should not be kept alive and that the best-interest standard has been pushed too far.

> We can either attempt to sustain the lives of such patients in spite of their empty prognoses or we can engage in the risky business of designating a threshold of meaningful human life. The latter alternative might well be dangerous but the former position is pointless and burdensome to parents and society. (Arras, 1984, p. 32)

Decisions concerning treatment of both young and old require criteria that define serious impairment and are fraught with ambiguity. "Although this pervasive ambiguity is difficult to live with, we can be sure that attempts to ignore it, to reduce the problem to a simple formula, will lead to an illusory and counterproductive quest for moral certainty" (Arras, 1984, p. 33).

Gelman (1986) echoes many of Arras's sentiments about the search for certainty in ethical decision making. Simple responses to life-or-death situations that pose ethical dilemmas are inappropriate. In circumstances pervaded by ethical ambiguity, the key is to acknowledge the complexity of the issues and the pull of contradictory moral imperatives. An understanding of complexity that is the result of a deliberate and reflective process can provide guidance but not clear-cut, decisive rules or principles for practitioners to follow. Although most practitioners would prefer clear directions in the course of their deliberations over ethical dilemmas, ethical certainty cannot be obtained and should be avoided. When certainty exists, decision making becomes routine and practitioners lose sight of the individuality of their clients.

The danger for practitioners is to know with a high degree of certainty that the course of action chosen is absolutely correct. It is dangerous because it brooks no doubt in situations that are fraught with uncertainty. Doubt is essential for ethical practice. In certain situations, ambiguity can have the salutary effect of preventing rash actions or irreversible easy solutions. When the decision-making process becomes too easy, practitioners not only disregard dependent clients but also lose the capacity to function as responsible professionals (Gelman, 1986).

Caplan (1986) suggests that moral uncertainty is one of the factors that contributes to the need for professional ethics. Society has apparently decided to transfer moral ambiguities to professionals rather than laypersons because professionals are better equipped to make difficult decisions. The moral ambiguities in social work are legion. Should children neglected by their parents be removed from their home? Should confidentiality be broken when there is suspicion of a threat to others? Should elderly patients who want to starve to death be permitted to do so? Should the power of laypeople be able to influence professionals to circumvent the waiting list at a nursing home? Should the closed records of an adult adoptee be unsealed at his or her request? Is it possible to maintain the confidentiality of client records in an age of information technology and managed care? What is the social worker's ethical responsibility when the managed-care company limits the number of sessions and the client requires more? What are the social worker's moral and ethical responsibilities to the welfare system and to welfare recipients during a period of radical systems change, when the client with HIV does not want to tell his partner, when the client with AIDS wants to commit suicide, when elderly clients who require home care refuse it, when the batterer threatens to kill his wife whether she leaves him or stays?

The moral and ethical dilemmas in social work defy easy resolution. There are no simple answers to any of the situations mentioned above. People's motives, feelings, and lives are complex; the facts are not always available, and complete knowledge is lacking. Sometimes decisions are influenced by the personal values of the social worker, which prevent objectivity and clear thinking, especially in emotionally charged situations. The social worker may not always be aware of the intrusion of personal values. Awareness may come when the outcome becomes dysfunctional, as when personal values are substituted for professional knowledge (Gordon, 1965).

In the process of ethical decision making, the practitioner should obtain as much knowledge of the situation as possible before proceeding with the necessary steps. Every bit of knowledge may affect the outcome (Lewis, 1984). In the case of the elderly couple who insisted on remaining in their own home rather than being placed in an institution, the social worker's knowledge of their changing physical condition was indispensable to the process of ethical decision making. They may have had a relapse and could no longer function in their home. They may have shown significant physical improvement so that placement was unnecessary. It is necessary to monitor the client's situation carefully for any changes that might clarify the ethically ambiguous situation.

The AIDS patient may have become too ill and disoriented to take his or her own life. The elderly woman's resistance to home care may have waned as the Alzheimer's disease progressed. The birth mother may feel secure in her marriage and would not oppose the release of the sealed records to the adult adoptee. The professional may feel secure in his or her job and would not hesitate to take a strong stand in opposition to the influential layperson's pressure to circumvent the waiting list. If the parents enroll in parenting classes, the father gets a decent paying job, and the mother enters a detoxification program, the decision to remove the child may be reversed in the face of the positive changes in the parents' lives. In any one of the cases cited, the ethical decision could incline in either direction, depending on the facts and the changing circumstances. The social worker may feel less immobilized and more empowered to make an ethical decision when the most up-to-date information is available and inclines in one direction more than in the other. Thus, ethical dilemmas are specific to the context of the situation *now,* and the nature of the dilemma may alter significantly as the context changes.

ETHICS AND CHARACTER

Models of value classification and ethical decision making have been presented that require delineation of values, rules, principles, and theory. These tools represent the "technical" part of the analytical enterprise. Students and practitioners need to have techniques available for use when ethical dilemmas present themselves. But techniques are only one part, though an indispensable part, of the study of applied ethics. The other necessary part is character.

Often what counts the most in moral life is not consistent adherence to rules, principles, and theory but reliable character, good sense, and emotional responsiveness. Principles and rules are objective guidelines that cannot fully encompass what occurs when parents lovingly play with their children or social workers provide comfort to a dying patient or to an abused woman. Feelings toward others lead us to actions that cannot be reduced to principles and rules but that derive from our character, emotions, and ideals.

In professional life, the character traits that deserve to be encouraged often derive from roles. Roles of social workers encompass social expectations as well as professional standards, but their virtues derive from their professional relationships. If we penetrate deeply into the social work service situation, we will discover the virtues and character traits that social workers ought to have to practice the profession ably. Four of the virtues are compassion, discernment, trustworthiness, and integrity (Beauchamp & Childress, 1994).

Compassion combines an active regard for another person's welfare with an emotional response of deep sympathy, tenderness, and discomfort at the other person's misfortune or suffering. It presupposes sympathy, is connected with mercy, and is expressed in acts of beneficence that attempt to alleviate the suffering of the other person. Compassion is focused on others (Beauchamp & Childress, 1994).

Compassion must be displayed. The expression of compassion makes a moral difference, as others feel reassured and cared for by a person with compassion. Social workers who express no emotion in their behavior, though highly skilled, often fail to provide the compassion that clients need most. The downside of compassion is that it may also cloud judgment and rational responses. Constant contact with suffering, such as work with AIDS clients, can overwhelm a compassionate social worker and cause burnout. A social worker who is emotionally overinvolved with a client will not be able to discern the meaning of the client's communication and behavior. For this reason, compassionate detachment or compassionate restraint is the goal in the client–social worker relationship.

Discernment is the ability to make judgments and decisions without being unduly influenced by extraneous considerations, personal attachments, or fears. It is also associated with practice wisdom. Social workers who possess practice wisdom know which course of action to choose and how to bring about desired ends while keeping emotions in proper bounds. When a rule guides behavior, *how* to follow the rule involves a form of discernment. Discernment requires sensitivity to the demands of a particular context, to the feelings of a client and what needs to be done in a given situation (Beauchamp & Childress, 1994).

Trust is a belief in, and reliance on, the moral character of another person. It entails confidence that the other will act morally with the right motives. Such trust is often the most important ingredient in the client's choice of one social worker over another—and in the decision to switch social workers.

Moral integrity, in its most general sense, means soundness, reliability, wholeness, and moral character; in its more specific sense, it means adherence to moral norms. Integrity represents two aspects of a person's character:

> The first is a coherent integration of aspects of the self—emotions, aspirations, knowledge, etc.—so that each complements and does not frustrate the others. The second is the character trait of being faithful to moral values and standing up in their defense when they are threatened or under attack. (Beauchamp & Childress, 1994, p. 471)

Compassion, trust, discernment, and integrity are virtues that contribute to the ethical personality of social workers. Virtues consist of those traits within the individual that predispose the person to do what is right. Moral character is learned, cultivated, and practiced throughout one's lifetime (Murphy, 1997). Although it is important that practitioners have a good grasp of values, rules, principles, and theories for ethical practice, it is more essential that their moral character not be impugned. In striving for excellence in their service to people, social workers will combine their knowledge, attitudes, and skills with their moral character, all of which together will provide the motivation and strength to do what is right and good.

REFERENCES

Aaronson, S., & Hartmann, H. (1996). Reform, not rhetoric: A critique of welfare policy and charting of new directions. *American Journal of Orthopsychiatry, 66* (4), 583–598.

Abramson, J. S., Donnelly, J., King, M. A., & Mailick, M. D. (1993). Disagreements in discharge planning: A normative phenomenon. *Health and Social Work, 18* (1), 57–64.

Abramson, M. (1981). Ethical dilemmas for social workers in discharge planning. *Social Work in Health Care, 6* (4), 33–42.

Abramson, M. (1983). A model for organizing an ethical analysis of the discharge planning process. *Social Work in Health Care, 9* (1), 45–51.

Abramson, M. (1985). The autonomy–paternalism dilemma in social work practice. *Social Casework, 66* (7), 385–393.

Abramson, M. (1989). Autonomy versus paternalistic beneficence: Practice strategies. *Social Casework, 70* (2), 101–105.

Abramson, M. (1990). Keeping secrets: Social workers and AIDS. *Social Work, 35* (2), 169–172.

Ahronheim, J. C. (1996). Nutrition and hydration in the terminal patient. *Clinic in Geriatric Medicine, 12* (2), 379–391.

AIDS: Public health and civil liberties. (1986). *The Hastings Center Report* (Suppl.), *16* (6), 1–36.

Alexander, Jr., R. (1997). Social workers and privileged communication in the federal legal system. *Social Work, 42* (4), 387–391.

Arras, J. D. (1984). Toward an ethic of ambiguity. *The Hastings Center Report, 14* (2), 25–33.

Assisted suicide: The philosophers' brief. (1997, March 27). *The New York Review of Books,* 41–47.

Autonomy, paternalism and community. (1984). *The Hastings Center Report, 14* (5), 5–44.

209

Baran, A., Pannor, R., & Sorosky, A. D. (1976). Open adoption. *Social Work, 21* (2), 97–100.

Beallor, G. (1997, December 1). *An issue paper on managed care and social work.* New York: National Association of Social Workers, New York City Chapter.

Beauchamp, T., & Childress, J. (1989). *Principles of biomedical ethics* (3rd ed.). New York: Oxford University Press.

Beauchamp, T., & Childress, J. (1994). *Principles of biomedical ethics* (4th ed.). New York: Oxford University Press.

Berger, J. (1996, March 24). Unneeded services inflate home care cost. *The New York Times,* pp. A1, A44.

Berger, P. L. (1967). *The sacred canopy.* New York: Doubleday.

Berkman, C. S., & Zinberg, G. (1997). Homophobia and heterosexism in social workers. *Social Work, 42* (4), 319–332.

Berliner, L. (1993). Is family preservation in the best interests of children? *Journal of Interpersonal Violence, 8* (4), 556–562.

Bernstein, N. (1997, September 15). On line, high-tech sleuths find private facts. *The New York Times.* pp. A1, A20.

Biestek, F. P. (1957). *The casework relationship.* Chicago: Loyola University Press.

Binkly, L. (1961). *Contemporary ethical theories.* New York: Philosophical Library.

Bleich, M. (1997). Open versus closed adoption: Social work and Jewish law perspectives. *Journal of Jewish Communal Service, 73* (4), 308–318.

Blum, S. R. (1992). Ethical issues in managed mental health. In S. Feldman (Ed.), *Managed mental health services* (pp. 245–265). Springfield, IL: Charles C. Thomas.

Bok, S. (1983). The limits of confidentiality. *The Hastings Center Report, 13* (1), 24–31.

Bopp, Jr., J., & Coleson, R. E. (1995). The constitutional case against permitting physician-assisted suicide for competent adults with "terminal conditions." *Issues in Law and Medicine, 11* (3), 239–268.

Borgman, R. (1982). The consequences of open and closed adoption for older children. *Child Welfare, 61,* (4), 217–226.

Bouvia v. Superior Court (Glenchur), 179 Cal. App. 3d 1127, 225 Cal. Rptr. 297 (Ct. App. 1986), *review denied* (Cal. June 5, 1986).

Boyle, P. J., & Callahan, D. (1995). Managed care in mental health: The ethical issues. *Health Affairs, 14* (3), 7–22.

Brackl, M. A., Thibault, J. M., Netting, F. E., & Ellor, J. W. (1990). Principles of integrating spiritual assessment into counseling with older adults. *Generations, 14* (4), 55–58.

Brandt, R. B. (1983). The real and alleged problems of utilitarianism. *The Hastings Center Report, 13* (2), 37–43.

Brophy v. New England Sinai Hospital, 398 Mass. 417, 497 N.E. 2d 626 (Massachusetts Supreme Judicial Court, 1986).

Burstein, B. (1988). Involuntary aged clients: Ethical and treatment issues. *Social Casework, 69* (8), 518–524.

Callahan, D. T. (1981). Minimalist ethics. *The Hastings Center Report, 7* (5), 19–25.

Callahan, D. T. (1983). On feeding the dying. *The Hastings Center Report, 13* (5), 22.

Callahan, D. T. (1984). Autonomy: A moral good, not a moral obsession. *The Hastings Center Report, 14* (5), 40–42.

Callahan, D. T. (1985). What do children owe elderly parents? *The Hastings Center Report, 15* (2), 32–37.

Campbell, C. S. (1991). Religious ethics and active euthanasia in a pluralistic society. *Kennedy Institute of Ethics Journal, 2* (3), 253–277.

Campi, C. W. (1998, January 5). When dying is as hard as birth. *The New York Times,* p. A19.

Canda, E. R. (1988). Conceptualizing spirituality for social work: Insights from diverse perspectives. *Social Thought, 14* (1), 30–46.

Canda, E. R. (1989). Religious content in social work education: A comparative approach. *Journal of Social Work Education, 25* (1), 36–45.

Caplan, A. L. (1986). Professional ethics: Virtue or vice. *Jewish Social Work Forum, 22,* 1–14.

Case studies. (1984). If I have AIDS, then let me die now! *The Hastings Center Report, 14* (1), 24–26.

Cassel, C. K. (1987). Decisions to forgo life-sustaining therapy: The limits of ethics. *Social Service Review, 61* (4), 552–564.

Chachkes, E. (1986). *Ethical issues in long-term care.* Unpublished manuscript, New York Academy of Medicine, New York.

Chachkes, E. (1988). Ethics in hospital care. *Jewish Social Work Forum, 24,* 30–35.

Childress, J. F. (1981). *Priorities in biomedical ethics.* Philadelphia: Westminster Press.

Client self-determination in end-of-life decisions. Policy statement (1993). Washington, DC: National Association of Social Workers Delegate Assembly, 58–61.

Collopy, B., Dubler, N., & Zuckerman, C. (1990). The ethics of home care: Autonomy and accommodation. *The Hastings Center Report, 20* (2), 1–16.

Compassion in Dying v. Washington, 79 F.3d 790 (9th Cir. 1996) (en banc) (cert. granted, No. 96–110). United States Court of Appeals, Ninth Circuit.

Congress, E. P. (1996, February/March). What's new in the proposed 1996 Code of Ethics? *Currents, L* (5), 5, 6.

Conrad, P. (1987). The noncompliant patient in search of autonomy. *The Hastings Center Report, 17* (4), 14–17.

In re Conroy, 98 N.J. 321, 486 A.2d 1209 (1985).

Corcoran, K. (1997). Managed care: Implications for social work practice. In R. L. Edwards (Ed.-in-Chief), *Encyclopedia of social work* (19th ed.), 1997 Suppl. (pp. 191–200). Washington, DC: NASW Press.

Corcoran, K., & Vandivir, V. (1996). *Maneuvering the maze of managed care.* New York: Free Press.

Corcoran, K., & Winslade, W. J. (1994). Eavesdropping on the 50-minute hour: Managed health care and confidentiality. *Behavioral Science and the Law, 12* (4), 351–365.

Corey, G. (1996). *Theory and practice of counseling and psychotherapy* (5th ed.). Pacific Grove, CA: Brooks/Cole.

Curtis, P. A. (1986). The dialectics of open versus closed adoption of infants. *Child Welfare, 65* (5), 437–445.

Cruzan v. Director, Missouri Department of Health, 497 U.S. 261 (U.S. Supreme Court 1990).

Danzig, R. A. (1986). Religious values versus professional values: Dichotomy or dialectic? *The Jewish Social Work Forum, 22,* 41–53.

David, L. (1995). The legal ramifications in criminal law of knowingly transmitting AIDS. *Law and Psychology Review, 19,* 259–266.

Davidson, J. R., & Davidson, T. (1996). Confidentiality and managed care. *Social Work, 21* (3), 208–215.

Davidson, J. R., Davidson, T., & Weinstein, D. (1997, May). Managed care and social work practice: A call for action. *Currents, 39* (7), 4, 8.

Davis, L. V. (1995). Domestic violence. In R. L. Edwards (Ed.-in-Chief), *Encyclopedia of social work* (19th ed., pp. 780–789). Washington, DC: NASW Press.

Delegate Assembly. (1996, May). *NASW News,* 16–17.

DeParle, J. (1997, December 30). Success and frustration as welfare rules change. *The New York Times,* pp. A1, A16.

Doe v. Roe, 400 N.Y.S. 2d 688 (1977).

Doe v. Sundquist (96-6197 February 11, 1997). U.S. Court of Appeals, Sixth Circuit.

Dukette, R. (1984). Value issues in present-day adoption. *Child Welfare, 63* (3), 233–243.

Dulaney, D. D., & Kelly, J. (1982). Improving services to gay and lesbian clients. *Social Work, 27* (2), 178–183.

Ellwood, D. T. (1988). *Poor support: Poverty in the American family.* New York: Basic Books.

Emanuel, E. J., & Emanuel, L. L. (1997, July 24). Assisted suicide? Not in my state. *The New York Times,* p. A21.

England, M. J., & Vaccaro, V. A. (1991). New systems to manage mental health care. *Health Affairs, 10,* 129–137.

Enos, V. P. (1996). Prosecuting battered mothers: States' laws failure to protect battered woman and abused children. *Harvard Women's Law Journal, 19,* 229–268.

Ethical currents. (1996, Summer), *40,* 1–5.

Ethical issues in managed care: Council report. (1995, January 25). *Journal of the American Medical Association, 273* (4), 330–335.

Etzioni, A. (1991, October 8). A new community of thinkers, both liberal and conservative. *The Wall Street Journal,* p. A22.

Excerpts from the Court's decision upholding bans on assisted suicide. (1997, June 27). *The New York Times,* p. A18.

Fawcett, S., Seekins, T., & Silber, L. (1988). Agency-based voter registration: How well does it work? *Social Policy, 18* (3), 16.

Feldman, S. (1992). Managed mental health services: Ideas and issues. In S. Feldman (Ed.), *Managed mental health services* (pp. 3–26). Springfield, IL: Charles C. Thomas.

Fitten, L. J., Lusky, R., & Hamann, C. (1990). Assessing treatment decision-making capacity in elderly nursing home residents. *Journal of the American Geriatrics Society, 38* (10), 1100–1199.

Freedberg, S. (1989). Self-determination: Historical perspectives and effects on current practice. *Social Work, 34* (1), 33–38.

Freedberg, S. (1993). The feminine ethic of care and the professionalization of social work. *Social Work, 38* (5), 535–540.

Gardner, D. J. (1995). Long-term care. In R. L. Edwards (Ed.-in-Chief), *Encyclopedia of social work* (19th ed., Vol. 2, pp. 1625–1633). Washington, DC: NASW Press.

Gelles, R. J. (1993). Family reunification/family preservation: Are children really being protected? *Journal of Interpersonal Violence, 8* (4), 556–562.

Gelman, S. R. (1986). Life versus death: The value of ethical uncertainty. *Health and Social Work*, 11 (2), 118–125.

Gelman, S. R., Pollack, D., & Weiner, A. (1997). *Record confidentiality in the computer age*. Unpublished manuscript, Wurzweiler School of Social Work, Yeshiva University, New York.

Germain, C. (1991). *Human behavior in the social environment: An ecological view*. New York: Columbia University Press.

Gibelman, M. (1978). *Professional social work practice in public social service bureaucracies*. Unpublished manuscript, Adelphi University School of Social Work, New York.

Gibelman, M. (1995). *What social workers do*. Washington, DC: NASW Press.

Gibelman, M., & Schervish, P. H. (1997). *Who we are*. Washington, DC: NASW Press.

Gibelman, M., & Whiting, L. (1997, December). *Negotiating and contracting in a managed care environment: Considerations for practitioners*. Unpublished paper, New York: Yeshiva University.

Gilliland-Mallo, D., & Judd, P. (1986). The effectiveness of residential care facilities for adolescent boys. *Adolescence*, 21 (82), 311–321.

Gillon, R. (1985). Autonomy and consent. In M. Lockwood (Ed.), *Moral dilemmas in modern medicine* (pp. 111–125). New York: Oxford University Press

Glasser, P. (1984). Being honest with ourselves: What happens when our values conflict with those of our clients? *Practice Digest*, 6 (4), 6–10.

Goldenberg, I., & Goldenberg, H. (1991). *Family therapy: An overview* (3rd ed.). Pacific Grove, CA: Brooks/Cole.

Goldman, A. (1980). *The moral foundations of professional ethics*. Totowa, NJ: Rowman and Littlefield.

Gordon, W. E. (1965). Knowledge and value: Their distinct relationship in clarifying social work practice. *Social Work*, 10 (3), 32–39.

Government of Western Australia. (1996). *Protecting children, family and children's services student information kit* [On-line]. Available: http://www.fcs.wa.gov.au

Green, S. L., & Hansen, J. C. (1989). Ethical dilemmas faced by family therapists. *Journal of Marital and Family Therapy*, 15 (2), 149–158.

Greenhouse, L. (1996, June 14). Justices uphold patient privacy with therapist. *The New York Times*, pp. A1, A25.

Hanrahan, M., Matorin, S., & Borland, D. (1986). Promoting competence through voter registration. *Social Work*, 31 (2), 141–143.

Hanson, L. C, Danis, M., Mutran, E., & Keenan, N. L. (1994). Impact of patient incompetence on decision to use or withhold life-sustaining treatment. *American Journal of Medicine*, 97, 235–240.

Health and Human Services. (1996, April). Press release. Washington, DC: U.S. Government Printing Office.

Health Care Policy and Practice Network. (1997, June 12). Minutes. New York: National Association of Social Workers, New York City Chapter.

Hendricks, C. O. (1997, November/December). Reaffirming the value of social work values. *Currents*, 39 (11), 2.

Hepworth, D., & Larsen, J. (1993). *Direct social work practice: Theory and skills* (4th ed.). Pacific Grove, CA: Brooks/Cole.

High, D. M. (1989). Caring for decisionally incapacitated elderly. *Theoretical Medicine*, 10, 83–96.

High, D. M. (1992). Research with Alzheimer's disease subjects: Informed consent and proxy decision-making. *Journal of the American Geriatrics Society, 40* (9), 950–957.

Higuchi, S. A. (1994). Recent managed care legislative and legal issues. In R. L. Lowman & R. J. Resnick (Eds.), *The mental health professional's guide to managed care* (pp. 83–118). Washington, DC: American Psychological Association.

Holland, T. P., & Kilpatrick, A. C. (1991). Ethical issues in social work: Toward a grounded theory of professional ethics. *Social Work, 39* (2), 138–144.

Imre, R. (1989). Moral theory for social work. *Social Thought, 15* (1), 18–27.

Jacobs, L., & Dimarsky, S. B. (1991). Jewish domestic abuse: Realities and responses. *Journal of Jewish Communal Service, 68* (2), 94–111.

Jaffe v. Redmond, 116 S. Ct. 1923, 135 L.ED. 2nd 337 (1996).

Johnson, O. A. (1965). *Ethics* (2nd ed.). New York: Holt, Rinehart & Winston.

Johnson, O. A. (1984). *Ethics* (5th ed.). New York: Holt, Rinehart & Winston.

Joseph, M. V. (1988). Religion and social work practice. *Social Casework, 69* (7), 443–452.

Kane, R. (1993). Ethical and legal issues in long-term care: Food for futuristic thought. *Journal of Long-Term Care Administration, 21* (3), 66–74.

Kapp, M. B. (1990a). Elder care. *Association of Operating Room Nurses Journal, 52* (4), 857–862.

Kapp, M. B. (1990b). Liability issues and assessment of decision-making capability in nursing home patients. *American Journal of Medicine, 89*, 639–642.

Kass, L. R. (1990). Death with dignity and the sanctity of life. *Commentary, 89* (3), 33–43.

Kelly, T. B. (1994). Paternalism and the marginally competent: An ethical dilemma, no easy answers. *Journal of Gerontological Social Work, 23* (1–2), 67–84.

Kennedy, G. J. (1993). Orientation to medical technology and procedures used to characterize the extent and irreversibility of impairment. Article 81, Mental Hygiene Law (pp. 171–177). New York State Bar Association, Albany.

Kilborn, P. T. (1997, December 28). Fitting managed care into emergency rooms. *The New York Times*, p. A12.

Kolata, G. (1997, June 28). Passive euthanasia in hospitals is the norm, doctors say. *The New York Times*, p. A10.

Kramer, C. (1990). An historical perspective on domestic violence. *The Jewish Social Work Forum, 26*, 51–56.

Kramer, C. (1995). *Domestic violence: Attitudes and values of legal and helping professionals.* Unpublished dissertation, Wurzweiler School of Social Work, Yeshiva University, New York.

Levenson, D. (1997, September). Online counseling: Opportunity and risk. *NASW News, 42* (8), 8.

Levine, R. A. (1993). *How urban social workers define and respond to elder abuse.* Unpublished dissertation, Wurzweiler School of Social Work, Yeshiva University, New York.

Levinson, S. A. (1990). Evaluating competence and decision-making capacity in impaired older patients. *The Older Patient*, (1), 11–16.

Levy, C. S. (1972). Values and planned change. *Social Casework, 53* (8), 488–493.

Levy, C. S. (1973). The value base of social work. *Journal of Education for Social Work, 9* (4), 34–42.

Levy, C. S. (1974). The relevance (or irrelevance) of consequences to social work ethics. *Journal of Jewish Communal Service, 51* (1), 73–82.

Levy, C. S. (1976a). *Social work ethics.* New York: Human Sciences Press.

Levy, C. S. (1976b). Personal versus professional values: The practitioner's dilemma. *Clinical Social Work Journal, 4* (2), 110–120.

Levy, C. S. (1979). *Values and ethics for social work practice.* Washington, DC: NASW Press.

Levy, C. S. (1982). *Guide to ethical decisions and actions for social service administrators.* New York: Haworth.

Levy, C. S. (1993). *Social work ethics on the line.* New York: Haworth.

Lewin, T. (1997, November 9). U.S. is divided on adoption, survey of attitudes asserts. *The New York Times,* p. B1.

Lewis, H. (1982). *The intellectual base of social work practice.* New York: Haworth.

Lewis, H. (1984). Ethical assessment. *Social Casework, 65* (4), 203–211.

Lewis, H. (1986). Response. *The Jewish Social Work Forum, 22,* 15–17.

Liederman, D. S. (1996). Child welfare overview. In R. L. Edwards (Ed.-in-Chief), *Encyclopedia of social work* (19th ed., pp. 424–433). Washington, DC: NASW Press.

Linzer, N. (1986a). The obligations of adult children to aged parents: A view from Jewish tradition. *Journal of Aging and Judaism, 1* (1), 34–48.

Linzer, N. (1986b). Resolving ethical dilemmas in Jewish communal service. *Journal of Jewish Communal Service, 63* (2), 105–117.

Linzer, N. (1989). Ethical decision-making: Implications for practice. *Journal of Jewish Communal Service, 65* (3), 182–189.

Linzer, N. (1996). *Ethical dilemmas in Jewish communal service.* Hoboken, NJ: KTAV.

Linzer, N., & Lowenstein, L. (1987). Autonomy and paternalism in work with the frail Jewish elderly. *Journal of Aging and Judaism, 2* (1), 19–34.

Lipkin, M. (1996). The corporatization of American medicine: The impact of managed care on the doctor–patient relationship. *American Journal of Managed Care, 2* (6), 734–737.

Loewenberg, F. M. (1988). *Religion and social work practice in contemporary American society.* New York: Columbia University Press.

Loewenberg, F. M., & Dolgoff, R. (1992). *Ethical decisions for social work practice* (4th ed.). Itasca, IL: F. E. Peacock.

Lohmann, R. A. (1997). Managed care: A review of recent research. In R. L. Edwards (Ed.-in-Chief), *Encyclopedia of Social Work* (19th ed.). 1997 Suppl. (pp. 200–213). Washington, DC: NASW Press.

Lynn, J., & Childress, J. F. (1983). Must patients always be given food and water? *The Hastings Center Report, 13* (5), 17–21.

Lynn, Jr., L. E. (1996). Welfare reform: Once more into the breach: An essay review. *Social Service Review, 70* (2), 305–317.

Mackenzie, K. R. (1989). Recent developments in brief psychotherapy. *Hospital and Community Psychiatry, 39,* 742–752.

Managed care curbs backed. (1988). *NASW News, 43* (1), pp. 1, 10.

Markoff, J. (1997, April 4). Used computer bares old user's secrets. *The New York Times,* p. A14.

Masters, R. (1996). Is the lifeboat full? Ethical dilemmas of managed care. *Forum* (New York State Society for Clinical Social Work), *7* (2), 1–9.

Matlaw, J. R., and Mayer, J. B. (1986). Elder abuse: Ethical and practical dilemmas for social work. *Health and Social Work, 11* (2), 85–94.

McArthur, J. H., & Moore, F. D. (1997). The two cultures and the health care revolution. *Journal of the American Medical Association, 277* (12), 985–989.

McCann, R. M., Hall, W. J., & Groth-Juncker, A. (1994, October 26). Comfort care for terminally ill patients. *Journal of the American Medical Association, 272* (16), 1263–1266.

McKinnon, K., Cournos, F., & Stanley, B. (1989). *Rivers* in practice: Clinicians' assessments of patients' decision-making capacity. *Hospital and Community Psychiatry, 40* (11), 1159–1162.

Medicaid managed care: Important information on program changes. (1997, September, 15). New York: New York City Office of Medicaid Managed Care.

Meilaender, G. (1984). On removing food and water: Against the stream. *The Hastings Center Report, 14* (6), 137–142.

Miller, B. L. (1981). Autonomy and the refusal of life-saving treatment. *The Hastings Center Report, 11* (4), 22–28.

Miller, I. (1996). Ethical and liability issues concerning invisible rationing. *Professional Psychology: Research and Practice, 27* (6), 583–587.

Millison, M. B. (1994). A comparison between religious and nonreligious social workers' approaches to practice. *Journal of Jewish Communal Service, 70* (4), 289–295.

Mills, F. B. (1996). The ideology of welfare reform: Deconstructing stigma. *Social Work, 41* (4), 391–395.

Moody, H. R. (1983). Ethical dilemmas in long-term care. *Journal of Gerontological Social Work, 5* (1–2), 97–111.

Moody, H. R. (1992). *Ethics in an aging society.* Baltimore: Johns Hopkins University Press.

Munson, C. E. (1996). Autonomy and managed care in clinical social work practice. In G. Shamus (Ed.), *The corporate and human faces of managed health care: The interplay between mental health policy and practice* (pp. 243–260). Northhampton, MA: Smith College Studies in Social Work.

Murdach, A. D. (1996). Beneficence re-examined: Protective intervention in mental health. *Social Work, 41* (1), 26–32.

Murphy, K. E. (1997). Is the NASW Code of Ethics an effective guide for practitioners? In E. Gambrill & R. Pruger (Eds.), *Controversial issues in social work ethics, values, and obligations* (pp. 114–119). Boston: Allyn & Bacon.

Murray, C. (1984). *Losing ground: American social policy: 1950–1980.* New York: Basic Books.

NASW News. (1998, January). Managed care curbs backed. *43* (1), pp. 1 and 10.

National Association of Social Workers. (1967). *Values in social work: A re-examination.* Washington, DC: Author.

National Association of Social Workers. (1996). *Code of Ethics.* Washington, DC: Author.

Navarro, M. (1997, July 3). Assisted suicide decision looms in Florida. *The New York Times,* p. A14.

New York State Public Health Law. (Section 2782, February 1, 1989). (McKinney 1993 and Suppl. 1997–98).

Nice, J. A., & Trubek, L. G. (1997). *Cases and materials on poverty law: Theory and practice.* St. Paul, MN: West Publishing.

Nulman, E. (1984). *The morality of social work ethics: A philosophical inquiry.* Unpublished dissertation, Wurzweiler School of Social Work, Yeshiva University, New York.

Ozawa, M. N. (1994). Women, children, and welfare reform. *Affilia, 9* (4), 338–359.

Pannor, R., & Baran, A. (1984). Open adoption as standard practice. *Child Welfare, 63* (3), 245–250.

Parry, J. K. (1981). Informed consent: For whose benefit? *Social Casework, 62* (9), 537–542.

Pear, R. (1996, March 27). U.S. issues rules for H.M.O's in an effort to protect patients. *The New York Times,* p. B8.

Pear, R. (1997a, September 10). Clinton would broaden access of the police to medical records. *The New York Times,* pp. A1, A15.

Pear, R. (1997b, September 27). Three big health plans join in call for national standards. *The New York Times,* p. A28.

Pellegrino, E. D. (1991). Informal judgments of competence and incompetence. In M. A. G. Cutter & E. E. Shelp (Eds). *Competency* (pp. 29–39). Netherlands: Kluwer Academic.

Pelligrino, E. D. (1994). Ethics. *Journal of the American Medical Association, 271* (21), 1668–1669.

Perlman, H. H. (1976). Believing and doing: Values in social work education. *Social Casework, 57* (6), 381–390.

Personal Responsibility Act of 1995. (H.R. 4). 104th Congress, 1st Session (January 4, 1995). United States Congress (104th 1st Session: 1995) Personal Responsibility and Work Opportunity Act of 1995: Conference Report to accompany H.R.4 Report/104th Congress, 1st Session H.R. 104–430.

Personal Responsibility and Work Oppportunity Act (P.L. 104–193). 110 Stat. 2105, 42 USC 1305, 1996.

Phillips, D. G. (1996). Legal and ethical issues in the era of managed care. In R. M. Alperin & D. Phillips (Eds.), *The impact of managed care on the practice of psychotherapy: Innovation, implementation, and controversy* (pp. 171–184). New York: Brunner/Mazel.

Pinderhughes, E. (1989). *Understanding race, ethnicity, and power.* New York: Free Press.

Piven, F., & Cloward, R. (1988). New prospects for voter registration reform. *Social Policy, 18* (3), 2–14.

Poole, D. L. (1996). Welfare reform: The bad, the ugly, and maybe not too awful. *Health and Social Work, 21* (4), 243–246.

Popper, K. (1965). *Conjectures and refutations: The growth of scientific knowledge.* New York: Harper & Row.

President's Commission for the Study of Ethical Problems in Medicine and Biomedical and Behavioral Research. (1982). *Making Health Care Decisions,* Washington, DC: U.S. Government Printing Office.

Pritchard, H. A. (1912). Does moral philosophy rest on a mistake? *Mind, 21.*

Proctor, E. K., Morrow-Howell, N., & Lott, C. L. (1993). Classification and correlates of ethical dilemmas in hospital social work. *Social Work, 38* (2), 166–177.

Promislo, E. (1979). Confidentiality and privileged communication. *Social Work, 24* (1), 10–13.

Proposals for welfare. (1996, July 31). *The New York Times*, p. A11.

Pumphrey, M. W. (1959). *The teaching of values and ethics in social work education.* Vol. 13 of the Curriculum Study. New York: Council on Social Work Education.

Quill v. Vacco, 80 F.3d 716 (2d Cir. 1996). (cert. granted No. 95-1858). U.S. Court of Appeals, Second Circuit.

Quinn, M. J. (1985). Elder abuse and neglect: Raise new dilemmas. *Generations, 10* (2), 22–25.

Rawls, J. (1981). *A theory of justice.* Cambridge, MA: Harvard University Press.

Reamer, F. G. (1979). Fundamental ethical issues in social work: An essay review. *Social Service Review, 53* (2), 229–243.

Reamer, F. G. (1980). Ethical content in social work. *Social Casework, 61* (9), 531–540.

Reamer, F. G. (1982a). *Ethical dilemmas in social service.* New York: Columbia University Press.

Reamer, F. G. (1982b). Conflicts of professional duty in social work. *Social Casework, 63* (10), 579–585.

Reamer, F. G. (1983a). Ethical dilemmas in social work practice. *Social Work, 28* (1), 31–35.

Reamer, F. G. (1983b). The concept of paternalism in social work. *Social Service Review, 57* (2), 254–271.

Reamer, F. G. (1988). AIDS and ethics: The agenda for social workers. *Social Work, 33* (5), 460–464.

Reamer, F. G. (1991). AIDS, social work, and the duty to protect. *Social Work, 36* (1), 56–60.

Reamer, F. G. (1993). *The philosophical foundations of social work.* New York: Columbia University Press.

Reamer, F. G. (1996). Ethics and values. In R. L. Edwards (Ed.-in-Chief), *Encyclopedia of social work* (19th ed., pp. 893–902). Washington, DC: NASW Press.

Reamer, F. G. (1997). Managing ethics under managed care. *Families in Society, 78* (1), 96–101.

Reamer, F., & Gelman, S. R. (1992). Is *Tarasoff* relevant to AIDS-related cases? In E. Gambrill & R. Pruger (Eds.), *Controversial issues in social work* (pp. 342–355). Boston: Allyn & Bacon.

Reeser, L. (1992). Professional role orientation and social activism. *Journal of Sociology and Social Welfare, 19* (2), 79–94.

Reshen, A. B. (1992). Analyzing value conflicts: Autonomy versus paternalism in long-term care. *The Jewish Social Work Forum, 28,* 24–40.

Reynolds, M. (1976). Threats to confidentiality. *Social Work, 21* (2), 108–113.

Richardson, L. (1997, August 21). Progress on AIDS brings movement for less secrecy. *The New York Times*, pp. A1, B4.

Rivers v. Katz, 67 NY 2d 485 (1986).

Roberts, C. S. (1989). Conflicting professional values in social work and medicine. *Health and Social Work, 14* (3), 211–218.

Roca, R. P. (1994). Determining decisional capacity: A medical perspective. *Fordham Law Review, 64,* 1177–1196.

Rokeach, M. (1973). *The nature of human values*. New York: Free Press.

Romirowsky, R. L. (1997). Managed care and caring: Ethical issues in service delivery. *Association of Psychiatric Outpatient Centers of the Americas* (POCA Press), *24* (3), 5–7.

Rompf, E. L. (1993). Open adoption: What does the "average person" think? *Child Welfare, 72* (3), 219–230.

Rosenbaum, D. E. (1997, June 8). Americans want a right to die. Or so they think. *The New York Times*, p. E3.

Ross, J. W. (1995). Hospital social work. In R. L. Edwards (Ed.-in-Chief), *Encyclopedia of social work* (19th ed., Vol. 2, pp. 1365–1376). Washington, DC: NASW Press.

Ross, W.D. (1930). *The right and the good*. New York: Oxford University Press.

Rothman, J., Smith, W., Nakashima, J., Paterson, M. A., & Mustin, J. (1996). Client self-determination and professional intervention: Striking a balance. *Social Work, 41* (4), 396–404.

Rothstein, M. (1996). Preventing the discovery of plaintiff genetic profiles by defendants seeking to limit damages in personal injury litigation. *Indiana Law Journal, 71*, 877–910.

Sabin, J. E. (1994). Caring about patients and caring about money: The American Psychiatric Association Code of Ethics meets managed care. *Behavioral Sciences and the Law, 12*, 317–330.

Salzberger, R. P. (1979). Casework and a client's right to self-determination. *Social Work, 24* (5), 398–400.

Saunders, D. G. (1995). Domestic violence: Legal issues. In R. L. Edwards (Ed.-in-Chief), *Encyclopedia of social work* (19th ed., pp. 789–795). Washington, DC: NASW Press.

Scannapieco, M., & Jackson, S. (1996). Kinship care: The African-American response to family preservation. *Social Work, 41* (2), 190–196.

Schoech, D. (1982). *Computer use in human services*. New York: Human Sciences Press.

Schur, E. M. (1984). *Living on the edge: The realities of welfare in America*. New York: Columbia University Press.

Schwartz, H. I., Vingiano, W., & Bezirganian, C. (1988). Autonomy and the right to refuse treatment: Patients' attitudes after involuntary medication. *Hospital and Community Psychiatry, 39* (10), 1049–1054.

Segal, E. (1997). Welfare reform and the myth of the marketplace. *Journal of Poverty, 1* (1), 5–18.

Sheridan, M. J., Bullis, R. K., Adcock, C. R., Berlin, S. D., & Miller, P. C. (1992). Practitioners' personal and professional attitudes and behaviors toward religion and spirituality: Issues for education and practice. *Journal of Social Work Education, 28* (2), 190–203.

Siegel, R. (1994). Domestic abuse and Jewish women: Opening the shutters. *The Jewish Women's Journal, 2* (3), 17–19.

Siegler, M., & Weisbard, A. J. (1985). Against the emerging stream: Should fluids and nutritional support be discontinued? *Archives of Internal Medicine, 145*, 129–131.

Siporin, M. (1975). *Introduction to social work practice.* New York: Macmillan.

Siporin, M. (1985). Current social work perspectives on clinical practice. *Clinical Social Work Journal, 13* (3), 198–217.

Siskind, A. (1997, October, 17). Letter.

Slaughter, M. E. (1996). Misuse of the psychotherapist–patient privilege in *Weisbeck v. Hess*: A step backward in the prohibition of sexual exploitation of a patient by a psychotherapist. *South Dakota Law Review, 41* (3), 575.

Spitzer, J. R. (1995). *When love is not enough: Spousal abuse in rabbinic and contemporary Judaism.* New York: Women of Reform Judaism, National Foundation of Sisterhoods.

Statement of principles. (1997, December 10). Unpublished draft manuscript, Social Work Coalition for Quality Health Care in New York State, New York.

Steinfels, P. (1997, April 5). Beliefs. *The New York Times,* p. A12.

Stern, L. (1996, June–July). Client confidentiality in a networked computer environment: Are records safe from loss and prying eyes? *Currents, xxxviii* (8), 5.

Stolberg, S. G. (1997, June 11). Considering the unthinkable: Protocol for assisted suicide. *The New York Times,* pp. A1, B10.

Stolberg, S. G. (1997, August 22). Despite new AIDS drugs, many still lose the battle. *The New York Times,* pp. A1, A20.

Strom, K. (1992). Reimbursement demands and treatment decisions: A growing dilemma for social workers. *Social Work, 37* (5), 398–403.

Strom, K. J. (1993). The effect of insurance reimbursement on services by social workers in private practice. *University microfilms international,* 6369.

Sullivan, J. F. (1994, December 6). Bill would let adoptees see birth records. *The New York Times,* p. B7.

Sullivan v. State of Florida, 352 S.2d 1212 (1977).

Swarns, R. L. (1997). Denied food stamps, many immigrants scrape for meals. *The New York Times,* pp. B1, B4.

Swigonski, M. E. (1996). Women, poverty, and welfare reform: A challenge to social workers. *Affilia, 11* (1), 95–110.

Tarasoff v. Regents of the University of California (1976, July 1). California Supreme Court, 17 California Reports, 3d series, 425.

Thomas, A. (1996). Managed care: The principles approach. *HEC Forum, 8* (2), 109–125.

Titmuss, R. (1965). *Essays on the welfare state.* London: Allyn and Litwin.

Toulmin, S. (1981). The tyranny of principles. *The Hastings Center Report, 11* (6), 31–39.

Tuckfelt, S., Fink, J., & Warren, M. P. (1997). *Managed care in the 21st century.* Northdale, NJ: Jason Aronson.

U.S. Department of Health and Human Services. (1995). *The child maltreatment reports from the states to the National Center on Child Abuse and Neglect* [On-line]. Available http://www.calib.com/nccanch/ From the menu choose "Online Publications."

Vacco v. Quill, No. 95–1888, 1997.

Van Allen, E. (1988). Reservations about advance directives. *Health and Social Work, 13* (1), 72–74.

Veatch, R. (1984). Autonomy's temporary triumph. *The Hastings Center Report, 14* (5), 38–40.

Violence Against Women Program Funding (VAWA) (n.d.) [On-line]. Available: http://lifestylesmag.com/jew-family/funds.txt

Walker, L. (1979). *The battered woman.* New York: Harper & Row.

Washington v. Glucksberg No. 96–110, 1997.

Watson, K. W. (1979). Who is the primary client? *Public Welfare, 37* (3), 11–14.

Webster's new world dictionary of the American language. College ed. (1964). New York: World Publishing.

Weinsberg, E. (1994). *A Jewish perspective on domestic violence and wife abuse.* [On-line]. Available: http//lifestylesmag.com/jewfamily/conserv.txt

Wells, S. J. (1996). Child abuse and neglect overview. In R. L. Edwards (Ed.-in-Chief), *Encyclopedia of social work* (19th ed., pp. 346–353). Washington, DC: NASW Press.

Welty, A. (1995). *Adult abuse: Hospital trainers' manual.* New York: Brookdale Center on Aging, Hunter College.

Wilson, S. (1983). Confidentiality. In A. Rosenblatt & D. Waldfogel (Eds.), *Handbook of clinical social work.* San Francisco: Jossey-Bass.

Wineburgh, M. L. (1995). The industrialization of mental health and its impact on clinical social work in private practice. *The Jewish Social Work Forum, 31,* 4–18.

Wineburgh, M. L. (1997 forthcoming). Ethics, managed care and outpatient psychotherapy. *Clinical Social Work Journal.*

Withorn, A. (1996). "Why do they hate me so much?" A history of welfare and its abandonment in the United States. *American Journal of Orthopsychiatry, 66* (4), 496–509.

Wolpe, P. R. (1996). Managed care and ethics: A Jewish perspective. *Sh'ma, 27* (524), 5–7.

Wurzburger, W. S. (1984). Obligations toward aged parents. *The Jewish woman in the middle.* New York: Hadassah.

Yaffe, R. J. (1996). The executive director confronts ethical dilemmas. *Journal of Jewish Communal Services, 72* (3), 195–202.

Zerwekh, J. V. (1997). Do dying patients really need IV fluids? *American Journal of Nursing, 97* (3), 26–30.

Zweibel, N. R., & Cassell, C. K. (1989). Treatment choices at the end of life: A comparison of decisions by older patients and their physician-selected proxies. *The Gerontologist, 29* (5), 615–621.

AUTHOR INDEX

SUBJECT INDEX